D0881136

Primitive revolutionaries
of China

Primitive revolutionaries
of China

A study of secret societies in the late nineteenth century

Fei-Ling Davis

The University Press of Hawaii
Honolulu

Contents

Illustrations

Prologue

The use of the term 'secret society' naturally raises the question: what is a secret society? To prevent conceptual confusion, I shall make a preliminary hypothesis of what a secret society is, drawing on the existing fund of ideas and insights provided by my predecessors. Only at the end of the book will a special summary of the specific features of *Chinese* secret societies be made, and briefly compared with secret societies elsewhere of the time.

First of all, *a secret society is a voluntary association*; but 'voluntary' in the sense that membership is not based on ascriptive qualifications. For membership may be acquired not only as a result of the individual's free will, but also as a consequence of social pressure.

Second, *a secret society possesses a body of knowledge not accessible to outsiders*. This may include its very existence, a language, ritual material and magical symbols, the identity of the members, and its ostensible functions. These are a protective shield against the 'outside' society and a way of differentiating morally and politically the secret society from the outside society. This secret culture permits the members as a group to behave among themselves and towards outsiders in a manner normally considered criminal, unorthodox or merely eccentric.

Third, *a secret society is distinguished from other groups with secrets in that it is organized on the basis of its secrecy*; and this secrecy can even become its *raison d'être*. For secrecy determines the type of structure and organization in two possible ways. It either creates the 'cellular' type of organization[1] in which there is a minimal identification of members with each other, as in an extreme form of the *Gesellschaft*;[2] or it can give rise to the 'communal', 'familial' or 'protective' type[3] which demands the maximal identification of members in a total involvement of common activities, as in an extreme form of the *Gemeinschaft*. This last type demands a comprehensive horizontal structure involving a number of departments or specialized agencies, which work knowingly with each other. This means that not only do agents pervade the internal organization of the society, but also the organizations outside it. Thus, only by building an 'outer' wall of protection can secret societies maintain their effective freedom of movement.

Fourth, *a secret society is a group of people who live or act together.* It may own property in common, and it may be organized according to regulations upon which the members of the association have agreed, and which all members have *consented* to obey.

Fifth, *a secret society is as dependent for its existence upon non-members as upon members; it cannot exist in a void.* Therefore, a secret society must be either conformative or alienative towards the host society, and its mode of adaptation may be either 'instrumental' or 'expressive', or both.[4] A secret society may be typologically any of these at different times and in different places.

Introduction

The officials draw their power from the law;
the people, from the secret societies.

(Chinese saying)

Surrounded by a moat, four walls, four gates bristling with armed guards, the Triad 'City of Willows'[1] was a beleaguered fortress. More than that, it was a State within a State, existing not so much in the teeth, as in the unguarded and indefensible penumbra of orthodox Chinese society. In a further sense, it was the 'plebeian' to the 'patrician' city of the bureaucratic literati. As the organized representative of the 'plebeians' the secret society was in permanent defiance of the State, constantly chipping and sometimes hacking at its agrarian, 'patrimonial' foundations.

Like all States which depend for their survival on the irrational subservience of the interests of an overwhelming majority to those of a minuscule and *self-elected* minority, Chinese traditional society suffered from a permanent conflict of interests. Briefly, this conflict led to popular unrest, organized clandestine resistance and open revolt. Succeeding for a time, repression merely stiffened, and eventually radicalized, popular resistance to the established order. A revolutionary situation developed as the old ruling class began to decompose, and a new one, based on entirely

3

different economic and social priorities, began to take its place.

Such a movement did not become visible, however, until the second half of the nineteenth century. Up until that time, the crises of Chinese society were vented in peasant rebellions, the most organized of which were led by secret societies. The problems of demography and foreign imperialism[2] in the nineteenth century finally exploded the Confucian myth of an eternal, harmonious order. The old bureaucratic, landowning class was forcibly retired by the advance of a modern 'national bourgeoisie', indispensable for national industrialization and regeneration. Secret societies became the 'left arm' of this ruling class, which had as its 'right arm' the newly constituted republican Nationalist Party, the Kuomintang.

A more specific explanation of the elements of contradiction in Chinese traditional society and their responsibility for the rise of the secret societies will be attempted in the historical introduction. Here, I shall merely sum up the main points of my thesis.

Chinese secret societies were the *organized* expression of a central contradiction in the traditional society. They embodied and identified the area of conflict between the interests of the bureaucratic and/or landowning literati ruling class and those of the other classes in society, namely, the middle and poor merchants, artisans and peasantry. As such, Chinese secret societies played a crucial role: first, in leading, articulating and organizing revolt; second, in contributing to the self-confidence and evolution of an illegal, anti-bureaucratic 'petty bourgeoisie'; and third, in elaborating an unorthodox, un-Confucian form of social organization—the non-familial, 'democratic', voluntary association. These roles tended to balance, up to 1911,[3] their propensity to parasitic, parochial, criminal and putschist activities.

Chinese State and society involuntarily developed, in the nineteenth century, the more progressive features of secret society activity. The great rebellions of the Taiping (1850–64) and the Nien (1850–68) in north and central China had reactivated secret society ambitions for national power. The combination of secret society demands for freedom from oppression of corrupt rulers,[4] Chinese rulers for the Chinese, and the republican demand for national recovery and liberation from foreign imperialism, formed, in the last resort, a revolutionary synthesis which was to topple the Manchu-dominated monarchy, and ultimately the whole structure of agrarian, mercantilist, bureaucratic Chinese society itself.

Briefly, the study of secret societies in traditional China is the study of the origins and progress of the Chinese revolution. For every movement of the secret societies in history illumines and concentrates for us every moment of this extraordinarily protracted journey: the appearance and disappearance of secret societies, the changes in their activities, organization, choice of ideology and class allies; and finally their accumulative social, economic and political role in the late nineteenth and early twentieth centuries.

This book was originally a thesis in social anthropology submitted to London University in June 1968. It was intended to be a sociological investigation of the role and organization of secret societies in the late Ch'ing, exemplified by one of the most powerful groups operating in south China at the time: the Hung League, otherwise known as the Heaven and Earth, or Triad Societies.

In writing it I benefited from the organizational assistance, if not the encouragement, of my academic supervisors at London University, and the almost total indifference of everyone else. The recognition the thesis has since received has, therefore, been all the more surprising. However, I was able to draw strength from the work of my predecessors, in particular, Georg Simmel, whose beautifully formulated insights have provided us with some kind of theoretical point of departure for the study of secret societies in general;[5] C. H. Wedgwood, whose 'Functionalist' approach helped to reduce some of the conceptual difficulties;[6] Eric J. Hobsbawm, whose survey and classification of primitive rebellious movements has not been as yet surpassed in historical depth and relevance;[7] Thomas Frost, whose two substantial volumes on secret societies of the eighteenth and nineteenth centuries in Europe have produced a wealth of comparative material;[8] and the two or three anthropologists who have explored some of the implications of Chinese secret societies *overseas*,[9] but who have not ventured beyond the threshold of secret societies *in China itself*. Jean Chesneaux's

5

survey is a step in the right direction, for it attempts, for the first time, to set the secret societies in their political, historical and, to some extent, social context.[10] I am especially indebted to him for his generous assistance in giving me access to the libraries in Paris. The rest of the material came from five principal sources,[11] four of which consist mainly of documents smuggled in from China and seized by the colonial police in Hong Kong, Malaya and the former Dutch East Indies. There are only two extensive first-hand reports available in the West, both written by republican participants in secret societies in the early twentieth century.[12] As most of these sources are restricted in number and access, I have quoted them at some length, especially when they appeared to have some documentary importance for future researchers. Ironically, there are practically no original, systematic Chinese sociological contributions to the study of secret societies,[13] owing to the scholar's habitual contempt for the activities of the unorthodox and the unprivileged. Only after 1911 (when secret societies had become necessary to the new established order) did scholars begin to take more than a passing, abusive interest in them. All this explains the fact that the term 'secret society' was coined by foreigners[14] and that most studies in Chinese draw heavily on Western sources. Traditionally, even the word for 'society', *hui*, was tabooed in official documents, and 'bandits' substituted for it.[15] This blind spot was precisely what helped secret societies to survive, and work unobtrusively for the just overthrow of those very people who most chose to ignore them.

I

The ideological background to Chinese society, 1840-1912

Ideology is the chart of power: it puts people in their places. It is the guide by which each individual negotiates the path of his freedom or servitude. It can be a justification and a rationalization of established power—or its rejection. It has its own logic, but is bound to its particular material base; and between the two is a constant dialectic. The interpretation of ideology and institution in late Ch'ing China is predicated on this assumption and should be judged according to it.

This chapter seeks to examine Confucianism as 'orthodoxy' (ideology of the ruler), and popular Buddhism and Taoism as 'heterodoxies' (ideology of the ruled). There is no attempt to discuss the philosophical merits of each case, but only to relate them to the social and political configurations within China in the period under study.

Until the victory of the British in the Opium War of 1840–1, Confucianism was the unquestioned panacea for most, if not all, of China's economic, political and moral ills. By a fortunate though not so strange coincidence, it was also the dominant ideology of the Chinese ruling class: the bureaucratic literati gentry. The lengthy success of Confucianism in China was due in principle to its suitability to the patrimonialist, agrarian State, out of which it originally sprang.

7

The *psychological* persuasiveness (whatever its political persuasiveness) of Confucianism for the individual in traditional
Chinese society was its confident paternalist humanism: the
perfectibility of man through self-cultivation because 'human
nature' is intrinsically 'good'. The highest expression of this
assumption can be seen, therefore, in the 'gentleman' (*chüntzu*),
who should embody in himself the 'five virtues' of loyalty,
justice, benevolence, wisdom and propriety. The political
expression of these virtues is seen in their transference from the
individual to the public sphere. For this reason, questions on
the canonical literature stipulating the correct behaviour between kin, friends, social and political superiors and inferiors
formed an important part of the Civil Service Examinations,
formally established in the T'ang (A.D. 618–906), though in-
formally inaugurated as early as the Han dynasties (206 B.C.–
A.D. 220). Though the object of these examinations was the
selection of the best students for imperial administration, it was
not their administrative skills which were tested, but their
ethical orthodoxy and familiarity with the Confucian texts.
These texts[1] were the basis of the rules for the division of labour,
status and power. The 'rectification of names' summed up the
universal exhortation of all ruling classes as it exhorted the
people to carry out the duties required of them by their superiors
and by their 'station in life'. 'Rectification' or *cheng*, incidentally,
also means 'orthodox' or 'correct'.

The orthodoxy of Confucianism was sanctified by its reputed
'antiquity', and antiquity was synonymous with China's 'Golden
Age'. As the reflected glory of this Age, Confucians taught that
government should be run according to the example, of course,
of the past, of the 'Sage Kings'; meaning that rulers themselves
must be prepared to set examples to posterity. For, Mencius
says, it is example and persuasion, not coercion, which should
be the guiding principles of wise government during which 'all
under heaven will be at peace'.

In return for the Emperor's benevolence, the people must
behave in a 'filial' manner to his superiors. Thus, 'filial piety'
came to be the main motor of Confucianism in action. Analogi-
cally, the Emperor was worshipped as the 'Son of Heaven', the
great mediator and representative of his people in the great
tribunals of Heaven and Hell, holding the 'Mandate of Heaven'

(*t'ien-ming*). The district magistrate, as the Emperor's most immediate ambassador to the people, was given the cosy appellation of 'the father–mother official'.[2]

However, if the Emperor abused his Mandate and became corrupt, then the people would be justified in 'cutting the Mandate' (*ke-ming*) and rising in revolt. In such circumstances, the killing of an Emperor would be an act of justice, of tyrannicide and not *lèse-majesté*. *Ke-ming* has since come to acquire the meaning of 'revolution' in modern times.

The basic assumptions of Confucianism are, first, a preference for the amateur and the gentleman to the specialist and the professional. The result was that specialization and any work which required physical labour were treated with contempt and even suspicion; while the 'pursuit of profit', in general and in particular, was regarded as definitely unethical, and sometimes quite beyond the pale. Naturally these considerations sprang from very concrete preoccupations, those of an agrarian, bureaucratic élite, bent on protecting its interests against its most dangerous rivals in society: the rich merchants and artisans, particularly the former. The ideology of frugality, of caste, of restraint[3] which is Confucianism, is hardly compatible with the ideology of prodigality, contract, and unlimited production which is capitalism.

The reason for the extraordinary durability of Confucianism as a dominant political ideology lay in the comparatively slow transformation of the material basis of Chinese society. This slowness was caused by the overall self-sufficiency of the Chinese economy, which did not have to look abroad for the development of its trade, nor raw materials for its industries. Thus Chinese traders were unlikely to develop, before the nineteenth century, the aggressive and adventurous spirit of their occidental counterparts. This kept the political and social initiative in the hands of the bureaucratic, land-owning gentry, who took maximum advantage of the bureaucratic machinery to milk the peasants for rent, and the merchants for taxes.

Nevertheless, the merchants had to be watched—their economic power could easily alchemize into political power. The Civil Service Examination System[4] ensured that the only channel for social and political 'upward mobility' was firmly under the control of its Confucian protagonists. The military examinations, a part of the same system, only became important in wartime. A knowledge of Buddhism or Taoism, while it might make a candidate literate, was not regarded as politically productive and would not help an ambitious young man to achieve office. For Taoism and Buddhism had long lost their political initiative, and were fated never to regain it. This left men with no alternative but to sink what capital they had in the 'career open to talent', by educating themselves or their children in Confucian learning.

A Confucian education could be acquired in two types of schools, only one of which was open to commoners. The first type was the 'non-government' schools (*hsüeh-hsiao*), which comprised academies (*shu-yuan*), charity schools (*yi-hsüeh*) and rural community schools (*she-hsüeh*), usually founded and financed by local gentry,[5] often with funds coming from 'school land' revenue of wealthy lineages. The 'government' schools (*kuan-hsüeh*) were limited to the children of the Imperial clan, the Eight Banners,[6] and families bearing hereditary titles.

By the fourth decade of the eighteenth century, there were already twenty-one academies in the eighteen provincial capitals, as well as others which mushroomed in the district (*hsien*) towns and villages. It was rare that a prefecture or district did not possess a school of some kind. The Emperor Yung-cheng (1723–36) attempted to control them further by subsidizing them directly from the Treasury.[7]

In addition to all this, a system of 'extra-mural' education called 'village-binding' (*hsiang-yueh*) lectures was set up. The principal lecturer was normally the village head or a prominent leader of the community. Delivered on the first and fifteenth of each month, the *hsiang-yueh* lectures reiterated the orthodox code of correct behaviour and recorded the moral deeds and misdeeds of members of the local community. The texts for these lectures came from three sources: the *Six Instructions*, compiled by the first Ch'ing or Manchu emperor Shan-chih in 1652; the *Sacred Edict*, compiled by Emperor K'ang-hsi in 1670; and the *Amplified Instructions of the Sacred Edict*, compiled by the Emperor Yung Cheng in 1724. Popularly referred to simply as the Sacred Edict, these texts were summaries of Confucian ethics, written in the vernacular to facilitate speedier assimilation by the mass of the population. Like all sermons, these were seldom an unqualified success. Their lecturers were unenthusiastic in their duties and frequently mechanical in their delivery.[8]

The message of these lectures could be summed up in the following words: 'pay your taxes and keep your peace'.[9] It is logical, then, that the *hsiang-yueh* system should be intimately connected with the *pao-chia*, or self-policing system, which I shall discuss later.[10] Indeed, it was not unusual for *pao-chia* heads to act as chief lecturers, the *yueh-cheng*.[11]

No less important was the role of the family in the education of its members, supplementing or substituting for the school. In all these ways—inculcation of the Confucian ethos, monopoly of political legitimacy, office and privileges, customary and legal restrictions on trade and manufacture, predicated upon a conveniently slow-changing agrarian base—the Confucian literati were able to maintain their domination over the consciousness of the Chinese people for about a thousand years.

This hegemony, however, was by no means uncontested; even though the contest, before the breakdown of the old social order and the arrival of European imperialism, remained largely unequal. Buddhists and Taoists were the main ideological contestants; while the former, being organized from the beginning, posed a more serious political threat. While both these heterodoxies advocated passivity as the strongest of virtues, the degree of passivity advocated in practice differed. Taoists, on the one hand, pleaded for the return to a Rousseauesque way of life: 'back to the roots' (*kuei-keng*), to the Way (*Tao*) of Nature, which is in essence effortless (*wu-wei*) and spontaneous (*tzŭ-jan*), like the erosive power of water, to the pure and uncorrupted existence which is expressed in an uncarved block of wood.

Buddhists, on the other hand, recommended abstinence both from the labours and pleasures of living, and hoped, in this way, to break the painful cycle of existence. Transcendence could only be achieved by fasting, meditation, abstinence from meat and sensual delights. As the majority of the Chinese population were *by necessity* forced to do at least two of these things (eat less or not at all; a vegetable diet; little leisure for self-indulgence), while their lives were all too often a 'painful cycle of existence', it is not difficult to understand the appeal of Buddhism to large sections of them, nor its subversive implications within the established Confucian order.

The decline of Buddhism as a major religious force in the ninth century A.D. throughout East Asia coincided, in China, with the emergence of a kind of Confucian 'Counter-Reformation' called 'Neo-Confucianism'. The fall of Buddhism from aristocratic favour pushed it further and further into the world of popular magic and shamanism and popular Taoism. Indeed, popular Buddhism and Taoism became so intimately inter-mingled that it has become difficult, if not impossible, to distinguish the elements of the one from those of the other.

The function of popular Buddhism and Taoism was, how-ever, not confined to being the 'opium of the people'. Their philosophical opposition to Confucianism, and their tendency to organize, soon involved their advocates in clandestine associa-tion and rebellious activities.[12] Frequent Government plunder of wealthy monasteries and nunneries, on various pretexts, hardened the tradition of defiance,[13] and substantiated the Government accusations of sedition and revolt. This culminated dramatically in 1368 with the overthrow of the Mongol Yüan dynasty by a Buddhist monk, Chu Yuan-chang, who made him-self the founder of the new dynasty, the Ming (1368–1644). When the Ming dynasty was in decay, there arose a powerful secret society alliance which called itself after the first character of Chu's reign-title, *Hung* (in *Hung-wu*). The Hung League (*Hung Men*) or Hung Family (*Hung Chia*),[14] known to outsiders as the Triads (*San Ho Hui*), became in the late Ch'ing dynasty the most powerful group of secret societies in central and south China. Following in the tradition of the White Lotus Societies (to which the founder of the Ming was purported to belong), whose slogan was 'Smash the Yüan and Restore the Sung',[15] the Triads coined a new slogan: 'Bring back the Ming and Smash the Ch'ing.'

The Manchus, China's war-like neighbours, came to appre-ciate the political advantages of Confucianism as orthodoxy. Indeed, they were more Confucian than the Chinese. The fervour of their conversion could be seen most conspicuously in their intensified denunciation of heterodox sects in the 'Supple-mentary Laws' of the Great Ch'ing Code.[16] These forbade the gathering of more than twenty male and able-bodied persons[17] and forty elderly persons; though the number of female persons was unrestricted. Offences against these laws were punishable by death by strangulation. Moreover, the Sacred Edict, also a Ch'ing invention, forbade holding of processions, beating of gongs and drums, chanting sutras and spells in public, and condemned such practices as inimical to peace and order in the countryside. For, the Edict argued, such flamboyant displays of unorthodox behaviour could only tempt the peasants to thoughts of idleness, frivolity and discontent.[18] Finally, it was considered criminal that able-bodied men should spend their days in unproductive, parasitic occupations (meditation and prayer), when they could be put to labour for the enrichment of society.[19]

The last argument seems to reflect the traditional suspicion of monks and nuns, condemned as the 'drones' and 'parasites' of society. This prejudice was strong enough to warrant a regulation in the Triad codes reminding secret society members not to treat monks with contempt, because, it was argued, their own founders themselves had been, after all, Buddhist monks.[20] Just as heterodoxies were traditionally associated with seditious ideas, so monasteries were traditionally associated with highly dangerous unarmed military combat. Monasteries were very often store-houses of great riches, either of their own, or of wealthy persons who deposited valuables with them for safe-keeping during travel, or in times of unrest. To defend themselves against robbers, monks learnt the art of self-defence without weapons, as they were prohibited, in principle, to carry arms. The most famous monastery in this respect was called the Shaolin, said to be somewhere in Fukien province, though its whereabouts have remained unknown.[21] According to Hung legend, the Ch'ing emperor K'ang-hsi had asked for, and obtained, the aid of the Shaolin monks in driving invaders out of the north-west in the eighteenth century; but persecuted them ruthlessly after they succeeded. This injustice was given by the Triads as a reason for their existence, as well as for their anti-Ch'ing position.[22]

For all these reasons, organized heterodoxies were condemned, *ab initio*, in the eyes of the central Government. When Christianity came to China in a militant form, it was no exception. The secret anxieties of the Government during the first decades of the dynasty turned into open hostility against

Christianity by the middle of the nineteenth century. The adoption of Christianity by the Taiping 'God Worshippers' as the credo of their rebellion was the very worst realization of the Government's nightmare: the rebellion lasted more than fourteen years, and was very nearly a revolution. It was suppressed only at great cost, and partly with the aid of foreign troops. The anti-Christian movement culminated in the Boxer uprising, originally directed by poor people against the Government's feeble efforts to stem the imperialist tide from the West; but was deflected successfully towards the foreigners by Prince Kung, the brother of the Emperor, who was supposed to have been a member of the Boxers.[23] The Boxer revolt performed the double service of assuaging the desperation of the Boxers (whose antiforeign feeling sprang from their social and economic problems) and the Government's fear of militant heterodoxies.

The success or failure of the Government in suppressing heterodox movements obviously depended as much on the power of the Government to enforce its laws, as on the relevance of Confucianism to its economic base. By the second half of the nineteenth century, it had become quite obvious that Confucianism had outlived its usefulness. The restoration movement following the suppression of the Taiping Rebellion failed because it assumed that Confucianism could be made relevant to modern industry and capitalism, and that by reforming an ideology (i.e. cleansing it of 'impurities') society could also be magically made to conform to it.

The patent impotence of the ruling class in face of internal collapse[24] and external pressures exacerbated its contradictions and weakened its morale. Widespread and deepening corruption deprived it of whatever control it might have retained at the local levels of government, while strengthening elsewhere the forces of revolt. The machinations of militant Christianity, backed by overwhelming economic and military force, deprived the Government of large areas of profit from rents, and large urban populations from its juridical control. For example, some foreign bishops, like Renaissance princes, lived on vast, rent-free ecclesiastical estates; while Chinese converts to Christianity were exempt from the jurisdiction of Chinese courts.[25]

The power and wealth of the Christian Church at first won the uncritical admiration of the Chinese heterodoxies. But when

Christian militancy began to encroach on the traditional pre-
serves of the Chinese heterodoxies—for example, in converting
the poor into 'rice christians',[26] and simultaneously seizing agricultural land for church building and subsidiary constructions
—hostility came to the surface in open attacks on Christian
churches and their favoured converts. When the Yellow River
burst its banks in the late 1890s, throwing thousands of peasants
in three provinces of the north-east (Shantung, Chihli, Honan)
off their land and into destitution, the ostentatious opulence and
power of the foreign churches could only be a bitter reminder
of the degree of degradation to which China had fallen.
Foreigners were charged with having caused the malevolent
'wind and water' (*feng-shui*)[27] disasters overtaking north-eastern
China, and revolts raged over three provinces. The Boxer rebellion was probably the last of its kind; for the uprisings which
followed 1900 began to show evidence of Western ideas, culminating in the overthrow of the Chinese monarchy as an acceptable institution in 1911. The Republic which the 1911–12
revolution established under Sun Yat-sen as President was
largely inspired by English Parliamentary Democracy.

II

The institutional background

(A) THE CENTRAL ADMINISTRATION AND THE IMPERIAL ARMIES

The Chinese State was formally organized as follows.[1] (See also Table II.1.) At the top of the political pyramid was the Emperor, flanked by his personal palace staff, eunuchs and ceremonial officials. Under the Emperor were two chief councils, the Cabinet (*Nei-k'o*), a policy-making body, responsible directly to the Emperor, and the Council of State or Grand Council (*Chün-chi ch'u*), a consultative body, which also recorded the decisions made by the Emperor and made them known to the public. The Civil Administration was divided into Six Boards (*Tu*) or Ministries, each headed by two Ministers and two deputy Ministers, one Manchu and one Chinese. These were the Ministries of Personnel (*Li*), of Revenue (*Hu*), of Rites (*Li*), of War (*Ping*), of Justice or Punishments (*Hsing*) and of Works (*Kung*). Independent of, though sometimes put in the same category with, the Civil Administration were the Nine Chief Ministries (*Ta Chiu Ching*), comprising the Imperial Censorate (*Tu Ch'a Yüan* or *Yu Shih T'ai*) which was the 'eyes and ears' of the Emperor. The duty of the Censorate was to watch out for corruption and other misdemeanours among the civil administrators of all ranks, and report the culprits to the Emperor. In some situations the Censors travelled from province to province, acting as 'judges at large', having authority to judge and punish corrupt officials before reporting them to the Emperor. The other eight Chief Ministries were the 'Colonial Office' or

TABLE II.1 *The structure of government*

1 *Civil Administration* (Six Boards divided according to function)	*Military Administration* (Five territories) 'Chief Military Commissions'	*Nine Chief Ministries* (Nine Departments, the chief of which was the *Imperial Censorate*, divided into Six Offices of Scrutiny, the functions of which corresponded to those of the Six Boards in the Civil Administration).
2 *Provincial Government* (9 Governor-Generals, 18 Governors)	*Regional Military Commissions*	*Provincial Offices of Scrutiny* (15 Circuits, lowest level of Censors)
3 *Prefectures* (183)	*Garrisons* Guards, battalions, companies	
4 *Subprefectures*		
5 *Counties* (1470)		
6 *Village and Town* pao-chia/li-chia	*Militia*	

Mongolian Superintendency (*Li Fan Yüan*), chiefly occupied by
Manchu Bannermen or hereditary princes; the Office of Trans-
mission (*T'ung Cheng Ssŭ*) in charge of transmitting memorials
to the Emperor from the provinces; the Grand Court of Revi-
sion (*Ta Li Ssŭ*), responsible for supervision and administration
of criminal law; the Han Lin Academy (*Han Lin Yüan*) engaged
in literary and scholarly production; a Directorate of Astro-
nomy, a Directorate of Parks, an Imperial Academy of Medicine and a National University.

Parallel to the Civil hierarchy was the Military Administration. This was divided into five Chief Military Commissions,
corresponding in status to the Six Ministries in the Civil Administration, but differentiated from one another according to
territorial units rather than function. Each Chief Military Commission had jurisdiction over several Regional Military
Commissions, stationed in each province and, in addition, in
each of the three vital defence areas along China's northern
frontier bordering Tibet and Mongolia. The Regional Commissions, in turn, had control over garrisons named, in descend-
ing order of rank, as guards, battalions and companies, most of
which were concentrated at the frontiers.

Under the Ch'ing, this system was incorporated into the Army
of the Green Standard (*Lü Ying*)[2] which served as auxiliaries to
the Manchu Banner Forces.

The Banner Forces were brought into China by the founder
of the Ch'ing dynasty, Nurhaci, and instituted as an army of
occupation and consolidation of the Manchu conquest of China.
Those Mongol and Chinese troops who had surrendered to the
Manchus voluntarily were also incorporated in the Banner
system.[3] Originally, the Manchu forces were divided into companies placed under Four Banners (*ch'i*), yellow, white, red and
blue, which were also the names of the units. In 1615, the Four
Banners were further divided into Eight, each bordered with
one of the four original colours. By 1643, there were Eight
Banners each of both Mongol and Chinese troops, making altogether Twenty-four Banners. Each company was composed
of approximately 300 men, located in garrisons (comprising
approximately 4,000 men) in various parts of the empire. The
men of these garrisons were set apart with their families in their
own fortified residential quarters of the garrison cities, and soon

came to form a hereditary, privileged caste drawing stipends from the imperial treasury as well as having their own land to till.

Garrisons were established in twenty-five cities in Chihli province, as a protective screen around the capital, Peking, in Manchuria and in western and north-western China to guard these traditionally threatened frontiers. In China proper, the garrisons were located in three main sectors radiating westward and southward from Peking: in the heavily populated areas such as Nanking, Chengtu, Hangchow, Foochow, Canton; the Yangtze valley, Hupei; and the Grand Canal at Chinkiang. Only Anhwei, Kiangsi, Hunan, Kwangsi, Kweichow and Yunnan provinces had no Banner Forces.

In 1644, there were 278 Manchu, 120 Mongol and 165 Chinese companies, making an army of 169,000 men.[4] In 1825, there were 293,391 minimum personnel, including craftsmen, retainers and supernumeraries.[5] The figures fluctuated according to circumstances, reflecting the warlike or peaceful mood of the country.

The Shan-chih Emperor (1644–61) made another change in the organization of the Banner Forces by regrouping these forces under Imperial control. Originally, in Manchuria, each Banner was controlled by a prince, and the Emperor had direct command of only one Banner. Now the Emperor deprived the princes of three Banners, giving them the title of the 'Three Superior Banners' and placed them directly under his own command. The Emperor Yung-cheng (1723–35) completed the process of centralization by appointing his own officers over the remaining 'Five Inferior Banners', thus depriving the princes of their direct command over them.

The remainder of the Ming military system, some of the Chinese troops who had fought for the Manchus, volunteers and local corps, were incorporated into the Army of the Green Standard, formed for the purpose of keeping internal order. The officers of this force could be both Chinese or Manchu, though the enlisted men were Chinese, and recruited on a 'volunteer' basis. The Lü Ying was divided into a Land Force (*Lu-lu*) and a Marine Force (*Shui-shih*); the troops consisting of cavalry, infantry and garrison soldiers, scattered throughout China in small units. The majority of the troops were under the nominal command of the provincial commander-in-chief (*t'i-tu*), but each governor-general and governor was also allotted a detachment. The provincial command troops were divided into brigades (*chen-piao*), territorial regiments (*hsieh-piao*), and battalions (*ying*). The battalions were further divided into smaller units like Right and Left Patrols (*tso, yu shao*), then into posts (*ssŭ*). The Director-General of the Yellow River had his own command (*Ts'ao-Ho p'iao*) which was in charge of delivering grain tribute to the Capital and of garrisoning posts along the river.[6]

In the early nineteenth century there was a total, according to statute, of about 640,000 men divided into 1,202 battalions,[7] but the Tao-kuang Emperor (1821–51) reduced the number of the troops to roughly 585,000 men by 1851.[8] The Green Standard of *Lü Ying* was under the ultimate control of the Board of War, and its finances under that of the Board of Revenue, both in the Civil Administration. The spreading out of responsibilities between both civil and military sections of the administration and between the capital and the provinces, provided, theoretically, a system of checks and balances to the growth of personal command. The practice of transferring officers from one area to another (parallel to the circulation of magistrates from one *hsien* to another) was also instituted for the same reason.

The sharing out of the top command between Manchus and Chinese was designed to meet the problem of giving high office to the latter without giving them supreme control, thus keeping the favourable balance of power in the hands of the conquerors.

By the nineteenth century, both the Banner Forces and the Army of the Green Standard had long declined as combat forces, and for the following reasons. On the one hand, once the power of the Manchu dynasty had been established, the role of the Banner Forces as an army of occupation no longer had any meaning. As a result of this and easy living, the Bannermen lost the incentive to fight, or even to keep in training. When the British attacked in 1840, they were taken completely by surprise. On the other hand, the decentralized and un-coordinated organization of the Green Standard prevented effective mobilization in any one region at short notice. It had become, in fact, nothing more than a vast constabulary engaged in the activities of crime prevention or detection, transportation of bullion, grain, prisoners, postal material and of guard duties at the frontiers.[9]

The other reasons for decline were common to both armies. The hostility of the political climate, as well as the effects of years of garrison duty, debilitated the troops and weakened their morale. Corruption among officers (as among the bureaucrats) was rife, and enlisted men were irregularly and inadequately paid and fed. Training and weapons were antiquated, discipline lax or brutal. The Bannermen became privileged parasites, the Green Standard men bandits or worse. Their depredations in the countryside were more feared than those of the ordinary bandits.[10] The decay evident in the military structure was by no means an isolated phenomenon. Chinese society in the second half of the nineteenth century was undergoing a profound crisis, as will be seen in the discussion of the other aspects of traditional organization which follows. But the demoralization of the central armies contributed more directly to the upsurge of secret society activity than the collapse of traditional institutions in the second half of the nineteenth century in that it propelled whole contingents of the underemployed, disaffected and ambitious men into the welcoming ranks of the secret societies.[11]

(B) PROVINCIAL AND LOCAL GOVERNMENT[12]

The Ch'ing Government divided the fifteen Ming provinces, for administrative purposes, into eighteen. Shensi was broken up into Shensi and Kansu, Hukwang into Hunan and Hupei, and Nan Chihli (Nanking Province) into Kiangsu and Anhwei. A single governor, the *hsün-fu*, was placed over each province except Chihli and Szechwan. A governor-general (*tsung-tu*) or 'viceroy' was assigned to every two provinces with few exceptions. In provinces where both the governor and governor-general held office, important matters for the attention of the Emperor had to come from them jointly. Two-thirds of the governor-generals were Manchus; governors, however, were mostly Chinese. Each had, as we have already seen, his own small force of men; but the chief provincial military force was normally composed of Bannermen commanded by a Manchu general.

Provincial government was composed of the Treasurer, and Head of the Provincial Service, the Provincial Judicial Commissioner, the Salt Controller and the Grain Intendant.[13] The first two officers were appointed by, and were directly responsible to, the Emperor, whom they must visit at the end of three years, the period of the duration of their office. They served thus in the capacity of checks on the ambitions of the provincial governor. Another provincial official was the Literary Chancellor (*hsüeh-cheng*) whose duties consisted of supervising provincial examinations, and the punishment of titled scholars living in the province. Scholars could only be physically punished after the Chancellor had deprived them of their rank.

Below provincial government was the Circuit or *tao*, grouping two or more Prefectures (*fu*) according to purpose, such as supervising tax or military movements. The Prefecture was then divided into a number of Districts (*hsien*), the smallest unit in the administrative hierarchy. The larger Districts were sometimes called *chou*, while the smaller Prefectures were sometimes called *t'ing*. A smaller unit could be dependent on a larger one for decisions concerning both, whenever geographically feasible.

The District Magistrate was the lowest official in the central Government, and his office was both onerous and underpaid. He was never permitted to hold office in his home district, and was required to move every three years. The reason for this was the prevention of nepotism and the political entrenchment of a magistrate in any one area. As far as the Government was concerned, the magistrate's function was to collect taxes, act as arbitrator, local constable and Justice of the Peace, postmaster, and invigilator at district Civil Service examinations. The magistrate was not permitted to use official taxes for defraying local administrative expenses, and only he and his *yamen* (office) runners and clerks were paid from official funds.[14] Consequently, an unofficial form of levy called 'customary fees' (*lou-kuei*, literally, base custom) came into being. These 'customary fees' were extracted from the local inhabitants ostensibly for the purpose of meeting the cost of local administration, payment of the magistrate's secretaries (the *mu-yu*, 'friend of the host'), his domestic servants, the collection and delivery of taxes to the central Government. Since no control could be exercised over the collection of 'customary fees', they soon degenerated into an 'accepted' form of extortion.

The pao-chia *system*

Below the level of the *hsien*, there was no formal village or town administration. Instead, government of these units was taken over by the local non-official gentry,[15] except where a magistrate or prefect or provincial governor happened to be resident.

However, there did exist, in theory, a system of mutual sur-veillance inherited from the Ming called the *pao-chia*. This was originally instituted for the registration of persons within a given area (village or town) through a systematic grouping of house-holds into larger units. The smallest unit of these was the *p'ai* composed of ten households, and ten *p'ai* were further grouped into one *chia*, and ten *chia* into one *pao*. Each of these units had a head. An official compilation of the Ch'ing, the *Ch'ing T'ung-K'ao* (19/5024), set out the organization in 1644 as follows:[16]

> In the city and rural areas of the *chou* and *hsien*, every ten households institute a *p'ai-t'ou* (headman of the *p'ai*), every ten *p'ai* a *chia-t'ou*, and every ten *chia* a *pao-chang* (headman of the *pao*). A *yin-p'ai* (seal placard) is given each house-hold, on which are to be written the names of the adult males and other persons (that belong to it). If any one of these inhabitants goes away, his destination is recorded; if a person comes into the household, the place from which he comes is ascertained (and recorded).

Families of the gentry were not exempt from the *pao-chia* system, though they were expected, of course, to help the *ti-pao*, or head of the *pao-chia*, in keeping the records straight. Large gentry lineages were sometimes organized into a *pao-chia* unit according to their size, with the head of the lineage acting as the unit head. The idea was to restrict the power of the gentry; so that heads of the commoner *pao-chia* were carefully appointed from among commoners with some qualification in literacy and landownership.[17] In the middle of the eighteenth century the *li-chia* or grain and land tax system was incorporated into the *pao-chia*.[18] The office of the *ti-pao* or *ti-fang* came into existence as a result of this merger.[19]

> The service performed by the *ti-fang* is most important. Each of the *chou* or *hsien* is divided into a number of *ti-fang* (agent) who is in charge of a number of villages. He shares the responsibility for tax payments, disputes over land and homesteads, cases of litigation, occurrences of robbery and theft, and investigation of murder cases. Whenever there is any (government) service or undertaking, he is responsible for promoting the supply of the necessary implements and materials, and for supervising the drafted corvée labourers. If he makes any slight mistake or is slightly tardy in his action, flogging will be promptly administered to him.

In the nineteenth century, the *pao-chia* system was also responsible for local self-defence, and some successful attempts were made to link it with the *t'uan-lien* or local militia bands[20] recruited from among the peasants. On the whole, however, the *pao-chia* was more or less a dead letter by the second half of the nineteenth century, and the only real function it retained was the classification of households for tax collection. For one thing, the divisions of *pao-chia* units were completely arbitrary, and did not coincide with the boundaries of town and village. For another, the atmosphere of mutual suspicion fostered by such a system violated the deep-rooted loyalties of neighbourhood, family and village, as well as militated against the privileged interests, especially in the matter of tax registration, of the gentry. For all these reasons, the *ti-fang* was less than enthusiastic in the performance of his duties; any kind of action risked the hostility either of the officials, his fellow villagers, or townsmen. His position was wholly untenable, and the only action open to him was inaction.

The T'ung-chih Restoration (Restoration of the Union for Order) in the 1870s was an attempt to put the clock back, and the Government did its best to re-activate the *pao-chia*, but without any success. The increasing social disorder of the period and the foreign pressure on the Government to build up a modern police force ultimately caused the whole project to be abandoned as both unworkable and irrelevant.

Gentry government

In those villages and towns where there were no magistrates or any other central Government representatives, the non-official gentry normally took up the responsibilities of administration.

The term 'gentry' (*shih*)[21] in the Chinese context has a different meaning from the term applied to the rural landowning group in English society. In nineteenth-century China, the gentry were defined, first of all, by their title, and only second by their ownership of land. Unlike the English gentry, their titles were in principle not hereditary, but academic, acquired through examinations. The lowest degree which admitted an individual to gentry status was the *sheng-yüan* degree, meaning 'Government student' (the popular name was usually *hsiu-ts'ai*, meaning 'budding talent'), which did not permit the holder to take up Government service. The highest degree was the *chin-shih*, 'metropolitan graduate', on attainment of which an individual could be more or less sure of at least the lowest Government post—that of the District Magistrate—or the highest, that of an Imperial Minister. These office-holding literati were called *shen-shih* and were thus distinguished from the ordinary *shih*, meaning literally 'scholar'. Landowning was thus a usual, though not an inevitable, adjunct of gentry status. If a gentry member belonged to a wealthy lineage with office-holding members, he obviously had a greater opportunity of influencing local affairs than if he was a non-office holder belonging to a poor lineage. The rewards of office were many and rich, though if one looked for them in a statute book they would be hard to find. The officials and frequently wealthy gentry benefited from a variety of invisible advantages; they were able to evade tax registration and hence taxation, raise funds ostensibly for some public works project, speculate on monopolized goods, raise local militia for their protection against both the excessive 'demands' of the local magistrate and those of the local population. The list is too lengthy for repetition.[22]

Once a man acquired gentry status, he could at once, if he wished, enter a world of privilege and influence. Even the officials were accessible to him; they were his social equals. Personal acquaintance with the local officials and their own intimate and long-standing knowledge of the area gave the gentry a powerful leverage both *vis-à-vis* the Government and the ordinary people in the area. Their role as intermediaries between the magistrate and the local community rested, in theory, on their knowledge of the Confucian canons, and, in practice, on their social and kinship connections and their wealth. In return for assisting the Government in keeping peace in their local areas, the gentry were awarded the privileges of exemption from corvée labour, physical punishment and, in practice though not in theory, exemption from land and other forms of taxation.[23] Non-cooperation with the Government could result in the gentry member being deprived of his rank by the Literary Chancellor, and shorn of all his privileges.

If they were so inclined, the gentry could (and did) participate in all spheres of local government. In this way they, too, became 'mother-and-father' officials, though in an unofficial, unpaid capacity. They took charge of general welfare, education, arbitration of disputes, the repair of temples, irrigation works, roads, dams and other public works, conducted fund-raising campaigns for local projects, and commanded the forces of local defence, the militia. In peace time, the gentry were the loyal supporters of the Government, in times of disorder, they became a dangerous centrifugal force. As leaders of the *hsiang-t'uan* or *t'uan-lien* (local militia) they were potentially as disruptive of central power as secret societies.

The militia

T'uan-lien (regiment and drill corps), *hsiang-tu'an* (village militia) or *hsiang-yung* (village braves) were formed traditionally among the local inhabitants of a village, or a cluster of villages, or town, for common defence against banditry, or for the suppression of rebellion.[24] The militia was not, however, a permanently organized institution, but its members, like those of the secret societies, were locally recruited and disbanded according to need. The militia rank-and-file were usually peasants, trained, organized and financed by the local gentry or contributions from all those whose interests were in some way threatened. The central Government, also, had, on a number of occasions, used the local militia for defence against invaders. For example, militia were deployed in Canton against the British in the 1840s[25] and against the Taiping and Nien rebels between 1850 and 1867.[26] However, a militia is known to be effective only when defending its own territory. This is understandable in view of the fact that the militia men were predominantly peasants, with their deep-rooted and sometimes fierce attachment to their land, which, after all, provided them with a livelihood and a sense of dignity—the 'dignity of honest toil'. However, in areas where tenantry was high, for example, the southern provinces of China, the situation was bound to be somewhat different. It is hardly to be expected that peasants would risk their lives to defend land which they did not own, and for which they had to pay so dearly with labour. If they joined the militia, they often did so under pressure, or as simple mercenaries, as 'braves' (*yung*). Others fled from the danger areas and hid until the storm blew over.[27]

The principle of militia organization seems to have been relatively simple compared to the Government forces, and moreover, varied from region to region, both in practice and in nomenclature. Smaller units (those of dependent villages, or sections of a village) were commanded by *t'uan-chang* or *lien-chang* (regiment heads and drill chiefs, respectively) or *t'uan-lien-chang* (regiment drill chiefs). Larger units were commanded by *t'uan-tsung* (regiment generals) or *lien-tsung* (drill generals). (The Nien rebels had no hesitation in adopting the same titles for their generals.) The size of militia units was very elastic—comprising ten, twenty-five, to a hundred men per company, presumably according to the size of the village, cluster of villages or town. *T'uan-lien chü* (regiment-drill bureaus) were set up in the localities by the *chü-chang* (bureau chiefs) or by the *shen-tung* (gentry directors) to deal with finance, supplies, drill and other important matters relating to defence.[28] Sometimes, these bureaus even undertook to settle disputes among villagers, especially during and after the Taiping rebellion when the administrative and judicial system was out of action.

The chief feature of militia defence was the construction of wooden, mud or stone stockades around villages most threatened by bandits and external attack. These were called *pao* or *yü*, and were used to great effect by the Nien rebels in the northeast against Imperial troops.[29]

If we are to judge from the evidence available, the militia was not in practice wholly beneficial to its home community. As has already been mentioned earlier, the militia came to be no more than the private armies of powerful lineages. Already, by the end of the eighteenth century, at the time of the White Lotus rebellion, the distinction between militia bands and rebel bands was dangerously blurred. A memorial submitted to the Emperor in the second half of the nineteenth century (1863) by a government official describes the *t'uan-lien* as follows:[30]

> The original purpose of setting up *t'uan-lien* and building walls or barricades in the various provinces to help local defence against robbers and bandits. . . . But the *t'uan*, emboldened by the possession of these strongholds, frequently set their officials and superiors at naught, and arrogate to themselves the right to decide law-suits. Some of these gathered around themselves large numbers of persons and refused to pay the grain taxes. Others among them perpetrated armed conflicts to give vent to personal spite. The worst of them even harboured rebellious designs, occupying cities and murdering officials, such as Liu Te-pei of Shantung, Li Chan of Honan, and Miao P'ei-lin of Anhwei, who started insurrections one after the other.

Pao Shih-ch'en, a well-known observer of the nineteenth century, gave a caustic explanation of the 'differences' between bandits, soldiers and militiamen in a letter to the famous reformer Wei Yüan:[31]

> The *chiao-fei* [religious bandits] kill and plunder but do not violate women; soldiers kill, plunder and violate women, but do not commit arson. Village braves indulge in all these things. Therefore, along with the White Lotus Sect, the people call government troops the 'Green Lotus Sect', thus giving rise to the joking term . . . 'Three sects with one source'.

A further difference between bandits and militiamen (other than the fact that the latter were commanded by the gentry and the former not) was that the militia operated openly, while the bandits could not. Bandits, if defeated, were exterminated *en masse*; but militiamen, if they had the support of the gentry, were permitted, *faute de mieux*, to continue their depredations. It would hardly have been politic for the Government to alienate the fierce opposition of a powerful group of local gentry.

Thus, at the level of local organization, the traditional State left much to be desired. The abrupt lacunae here made room for the organization of heterodoxy and rebellion. These lacunae were paralleled in the other sub-structures of Chinese society: namely, in the class structure and the kinship system.

(c) CLASS STRUCTURE

Since traditional Chinese society was based on a self-sufficient, agrarian–mercantilist economy, and organized under a central bureaucracy, the class structure reflected its priorities. Politically and socially, people were classified into four main occupations. First, intellectual work (as bureaucratic duties) was considered superior to physical work, 'therefore', it was argued, scholars were 'superior' to farmers.[32] Second, 'productive' work (agriculture) was thought to be more important than 'unproductive' work (commerce), therefore, farmers were superior to merchants.[33] Manufacture came within the category of 'productive' work, but because it is dependent upon agricultural production for much of its raw materials, craftsmen were placed immediately below the farmers, in the third place, but over the merchants, in the social order. The lowest social category of persons was excluded from the orthodox schema, and was composed of professionals or those in service occupations (including entertainment). These were the musicians, actors, prostitutes, domestic servants, slaves, *yamen* runners, beggars, doctors, other types of entertainers, and so on,[34] sometimes regionally as well as occupationally defined. A more precise, non-official classification split the above hierarchy into six categories: bureaucratic scholars (*shen-shih*), non-bureaucratic scholars (*shih*), farmers (*nung*), artisans (*kung*), merchants (*shang*) and finally, the 'low people' (*chien-min*) or outcasts. (Though never mentioned in the Confucian classics, this class is nevertheless minutely registered in the laws.)

Traditional laws formalized these divisions in meticulously defined categories covering every aspect of an individual's life. There were regulations specifying the type of food, clothing, ornament, houses, carriages, marriages, marriage ceremonies, funerals and ancestor worship which should be adopted by each category of social person.[35] These laws were amended from time to time. For example, artisans and merchants were forbidden to take the Civil Service Examinations during the Han, Sui, T'ang, Sung and Liao dynasties, but were permitted to do so in other periods.[36] By the 1720s, even the outcasts were allowed to take part in the Imperial examinations, provided they had been in the commoner class for more than four generations. Exclusions from the examinations naturally meant automatic exclusion from political office and gentry status.

The *de facto* hierarchy was, however, less clear-cut. The lowliness of the merchants' position reflects not so much any intrinsic and corresponding measure of contribution to society, but much more the literati fear of the economic power of merchants. However, literati suspicions could be lulled and partially overcome by generous financial gifts and cooperation; and it seemed that wealthy merchants frequently hobnobbed with the literati and officials,[37] which merely engendered more misgivings in literati hearts. To take themselves out of this vicious circle, merchants bought peace and respectability through educating themselves or their offspring in Confucian schools, or simply by purchasing academic degrees, by marriages of convenience or both. On the other hand, it was not unusual for the small store-keeper and street hawker to be lumped indiscriminately together with the 'low' or 'mean' people. Similarly, both wealth and academic qualification determined the degree of influence of the scholars within the literati–gentry class; the lowest of whom, like the clerks in the magistrate's *yamen*, had no prestige whatever. The only kind of influence which the lower gentry were able to achieve was in their capacity as advisors to the magistrate on local affairs, of which they had the superior and more intimate knowledge. In the second half of the nineteenth century, the lower gentry were able to distinguish themselves in the organization of the militia in the bandit-suppression campaigns. Powell[38] draws our attention to the fact that over half the new governors of provinces in the years following the suppression of the Taiping and Nien rebellions were originally militia leaders.

Moreover, the peasants at the higher economic level could, with a little effort, also buy a Confucian education for their

sons. But those at the lower economic level and the rural artisans were not able to do so. Their plight was particularly
unhappy during the second half of the nineteenth century, when
the economy had reached an unprecedentedly severe period of
recession, especially in the countryside. The reasons for this may
be found in both an internal and external situation: the disas-
trous suppression of the mid-century rebellions which laid waste
vast tracts of cultivable land in the Yangtze valley, parts of the
North China Plain, Kweichow and Yunnan, and the economic
competition from the Western Powers at the height of their
imperialist expansion. A contemporary foreign eye-witness,
T. W. Kingsmill,[39] wrote the following account of the physical
devastation after the suppression of the Taiping rebellion, which

> even altered the face of the country; destroyed its com-
> munications; deflected its rivers; broke down its sea
> defences. During its continuance smiling fields were turned
> into desolate wildernesses; 'fenced cities into ruinous
> heaps'. The plains of Kiang-nan, Kiang-si and Cheh-
> kiang, were strewn with human skeletons; their rivers
> polluted with floating carcasses . . . no hands were left to
> till the soil, and noxious weeds covered the ground once
> tilled with patient industry.

Despite all this, population growth continued to exert its
pressure on the land; floods, famine, drought, epidemics and
bureaucratic exploitation continued to undermine the security
of the peasant, already hard put to it by the powerful economic
penetration of the West.

It was possible, in some cases, for bright boys to be noted by
a benevolent local gentry, adopted by them and given an education; but such cases were rare, and do not appear to have any
statistical weight.[40] Poor peasants were thus seldom able to rise
above their poverty except through luck. The impoverishment
of the peasantry was expressed in the dramatic increase of
banditry, the great swell of secret society membership and
activity, and the progressive depopulation of the countryside
in massive emigration to the towns and cities. Since land no
longer symbolized security, the peasant saw no further reason
for clinging to his meagre plot, too often mortgaged for a life-
time, and sought his fortune in cities which were, after all, the

traditional embodiment of wealth, leisure and social advancement.[41] No one, not even the gentry, could hope to better his economic position, let alone maintain it, by remaining in the countryside.[42] Once in the cities, the great majority of the immigrants took up the occupations of the slum proletariat: porterage (coolie work), petty trading, entertainment and other semi-legal and illegal activities.

The possession of wealth, then, was as important as the possession of academic qualifications in the struggle for upward mobility. And, as wealth was more swiftly gathered in the cities, the urban populations continued to increase (pushing the boundaries of the towns and cities deeper into the rural hinterland). Hence, the countryside became more and more dependent upon the town for its economic survival and could no longer maintain any semblance of its traditional self-sufficiency. Westernization and an intensification of urbanization in nineteenth-century China could only make commerce an increasingly desirable and even 'productive' activity. The fact that the Western Powers, and especially Britain, were prepared to go to war for trading rights (during the Opium War of 1840–1) was enough to impress and persuade the defeated Chinese that commerce could not be kept down much longer by bureaucratic prejudice if China was to 'modernize' herself.

Thus wealth was becoming in the late nineteenth century the single most important criterion for the determination of status and power in Chinese society. This breakdown of the traditional delicate balance between a gentlemanly education and wealth as determinants of individual value was accentuated by the rise to public attention of the importance of professionals.[43] The development of a new intelligentsia in response to the need for industrialization gradually pushed aside the old Confucian literati, whose 'amateur gentleman's' ideals of education came to be regarded as increasingly irrelevant to modern times.

This new intelligentsia class was composed of, first, the entrepreneurs who served as intermediaries between foreign and Chinese firms[44] and who succeeded in acquiring for themselves and for their children some foreign education; second, the sons of the reformist literati who were sent abroad (to the United States, Great Britain, the European Continent and Japan) to learn what there was to learn of Western technology; and third, the growing body of Christian converts educated in the mission schools within the treaty ports and their hinterlands.

The new commercial class of treaty-port entrepreneurs developed side by side, of course, with the new intelligentsia. These 'compradors',[45] as they were later called, had their roots in an older occupation of commercial undertaking, and the nickname for them in traditional society was *ya-tzu* or *wu-tzu*, meaning 'go-between'. As a class they exploited both the peasantry and the merchants in the cities and were extremely unpopular with both. They were traditionally the only guild organization which had a Government charter.[46] Their obviously disruptive potential within the traditional agrarian society won them the full fury of the virulent nationalism which broke out during the Opium War, in which thousands of compradors were massacred by furious peasants for being 'traitors to the Han' (*Han-chien*).[47] Apart from the orthodox entrepreneurs and the foreign-employed compradors, the 'new' commercial class contained yet another, equally powerful element: the formerly illegal, anti-bureaucratic, anti-monopolist 'petty bourgeoisie' which traded on secret society aid. This 'petty bourgeoisie' was descended from the very first opponents of bureaucratic mercantilism, and boasted a long rebellious history of tax-defiance, contraband commerce and secret society complicity. It would be logical that their members supported the overthrow of the bureaucratic 'bourgeoisie' (involved in *kuan-tu shang-fan* (official control, merchant management) enterprises) and the ascendancy of a free-wheeling, aggressive, adventurous commercial class more akin to the European model. Not surprisingly, large numbers of merchants supported the boycott of Japanese goods after Japan presented its imperialist demands in 1915, and contributed to the rise of the Nationalist Party as a party of national independence, 'free enterprise' and land reform. The presence of large numbers of secret society members in this new political party was not accidental: they shared the same political and economic aspirations.[48]

A new urban working class was created with the arrival of European manufacturing and commercial enterprises in the treaty ports. This class of wage-earning, migrant labour had no precedent in traditional society, integral as they were to a capitalist economy. Most of them continued to work in the countryside as farm-hands, returning to the cities and towns during the slack seasons to work in the factories (see p. 222, n. 37). No figures are available before 1919, by which time the number of workers (both male and female) had reached at least three-quarters of a million.[49]

All three classes were recruited from the more shadowy reservoirs of the old society: frustrated and/or ideologically alienated intellectuals, the dispossessed, the politically disenfranchised sections of the population. However, those who found employment as engineers, compradors and factory workers were the fortunate minority among the rural immigrants in the cities. The rest fell into abject poverty, beggary, or became bandits or secret society members.

Thus the disintegration of the old society became visible not only in increasingly uncontrollable rebellions and bureaucratic corruption, but also in the development of new social classes, a development intensified and protected by foreign interests in China. The 'dynastic cycle'[50] was at last broken, and a new era had begun.

These changes in the class structure found their echo in the kinship system, and in the increasingly effective challenge posed by the 'voluntary association' to the ascriptive organization symbolized by the lineage and the family.

(D) KINSHIP[51]

The basic unit of the Chinese kinship system was that of the primary or nuclear family, *chia*. It was normally patrilocal or virilocal, and patrilineal in descent. Its maximal size was about three generations, composed of grandparents, parents and children. The next unit in size was the extended family, referred to as 'household' (*hu*), with a maximum generational depth of five.

The extended family or household (including concubines, married siblings, adopted children and household servants) could be part of a larger system of segmentary lineage organization, sometimes with branches (*fang*) in other villages and towns. The lineage was called the *tsu*, possessing lineage land as well as an ancestral temple, schools and a tribunal, which directed all social, economic and political activities carried out within the lineage.

As in all patrilineal societies, only men were permitted to inherit immovable property such as land and houses. But unlike many societies, all the sons had equal shares in the family land. Sometimes, however, the eldest son, who had the responsibility of caring for the ancestral temple, was allocated an extra piece of land specifically for the upkeep of the temple. The obvious danger to such a system of inheritance was the eventual extinction of the lineage as a corporate entity through fragmentation of the land. This was, in fact, a cause frequently of the impoverishment of a lineage and of its consequent political decline; which could, however, be arrested by acquisition of new land by the lineage, and by the cooperative attitude of the married sons. Women could normally only inherit moveable property, sometimes serving as trustees for male minors. (Exceptions to this were not unknown, especially if there was no suitable male heir. If the lineage council could be persuaded to accept a woman heir, then the law could do nothing about it, nor would it intervene.)

The corporate lineage was mainly a southern Chinese phenomenon, and could be maintained only when it had powerful (gentry or official) and wealthy members. Poor lineages rarely owned lineage land or lived corporately, especially if the members had to find work far afield. Wealthy lineages were able to augment their property by indirect investment in commerce, and by political influence. Further, official and gentry lineages could usually evade taxation on land by alteration of the registers or failure to report new acquisitions. Squeeze and 'presents' from wealthy but socially inferior friends, and judicious marriage alliances were the other means of maintaining a standard of life worthy of the ruling class.

Lineages without land or other financial resources seldom managed to keep together except in name, which was concretely symbolized sometimes by a shrine. Their descent in the social and economic hierarchy was naturally swifter than their more fortunate counterparts, for the reasons mentioned earlier. Not only lineages, but families, used to split up on the children reaching adulthood. The only corporate unit of the poor was the primary family. Since the wealthy and the powerful formed a minuscule minority of the Chinese population,[52] it goes without saying that the most widespread type of kinship organization was that of the primary family.

In the primary family, it was the conjugal relationship which was the pivot of the household, and not, as in the extended family, the relationship of father and son. Women usually played a more important role in poor families simply because more responsibility devolved upon their shoulders: not only did they look after the home, but they also frequently helped their husbands in the fields or traded in the market towns to earn a supplementary income. Rich women, in contrast, were conspicuous for their uselessness, a condition expressed most eloquently in the little 'lily-foot', tortured into helplessness by the custom of foot-binding.[53] Youth, too, had a more responsible role in poorer households for the same reason. The importance of women and youth in secret associations was indicative of the social and economic origins of the majority of their members.[54]

The lineage, then, like the village or town militia, was just another adjunct of official and gentry power. It was, in fact, a State within a State, and, as I have already mentioned, possessed its own court of discipline, its schools, its welfare services, its temples, its organizational committees, even its own historical records, the *tsu-p'u*. Each was surrounded by a high wall, crossed by streets, lined with houses, and physically and ritually centred in the ancestral hall.[55] All cases of dispute between the lineage members, except those of murder and treason, were tried in the lineage courts, which, like the non-official gentry, served as extensions of official power.[56] It was not unknown for lineage courts to defy the judicial decisions of the magistrate with impunity, as all too often the magistrate had little desire to alienate a potential supporter in the locality, or was too far away from the scene of the crime to do anything about it. In this way, the lineage organization, as well as the militia, came to be the most powerful weapons of the gentry, and balanced all too effectively, in the second half of the nineteenth century, the power of the local magistrates and their defunct *pao-chia*.

(E) VOLUNTARY ASSOCIATIONS

Although voluntary associations of the non-ascriptive type (that is, excluding provincial associations) were not part of orthodox Chinese society, they were, nevertheless, part of the 'external order' within which the secret societies existed. Poised on the frontiers of orthodox society, voluntary associations like trade and craft guilds managed to steer, on the whole, a cautious path between Government tolerance and Government persecution.

However, as secret societies sometimes used guild organizations as 'fronts' for their activities,[57] such associations could not always escape the unwelcome attentions of the police. For this reason, guilds would sometimes be forced to resort to secret society methods of self protection. This made it impossible often for outsiders to differentiate between what might be called secret guilds and secret societies proper, though the functions of the two types of association were distinct.[58] It is all too probable that the ties developed between these two kinds of voluntary association and another, the religious association, have much in common in their respective principles of organization. A brief account of the types of voluntary associations found in nineteenth century China would, therefore, be relevant to the discussion.

According to Morse (1909), there were at least four types of voluntary association (*hui* or *kung-so*): the religious fraternity, the craft guild, the merchant guild, the provincial club. According to Wou (1931),[59] there was, besides craft and trade guilds (*corporations de métier, de commerçants*), also a corporation of brokers or middlemen (*courtiers de commerce*) called *ya-tzu*, already alluded to earlier in the section on class structure (see p. 29). This type of guild seems to have escaped the attention of the other writers on the subject, though it appears to have played an important part in the traditional economy.

Brokers' associations

Unlike all other voluntary associations, the *ya-tzu* were licensed by the Government. Known in Peking as *la-chien-ti* (literally, 'barge-haulers'), in Shanghai as *tan-hsien-ti* (literally, 'thread-carriers'), and in Tientsin as *p'ao-ho-ti* (literally, 'Yellow River runners'), they formed powerful intermediaries who knew how to exploit opportunities presented by the unwary peasant, craftsman or merchant. Nor was the bureaucracy immune from their machinations; and its decentralized character was particularly vulnerable to the brokers' interceptions.[60]

> In olden days, as now, the corporation of brokers did not practise ancestor worship, it was very democratic and good natured. It consisted of fellow brokers who looked on themselves as brothers, or as elective sons when they asked for help from an older member. They were classed according to age; they exchanged birth certificates written on red paper decorated with gilt drawings. From the day they joined, they were called brother and were given a number indicating their rank according to age: first brother (the eldest), second brother, etc.
>
> Business was made easy as independently of the corporation each broker could have for brother or elective son (*Moung-sieou-ti* and *Yi-tseu*) merchants or rich country folk.[61]

The absence of an 'ancestral' or founder shrine, the possibility of having 'elective brothers' *outside* the association itself, and the evocation of a substitute 'father–son' relationship, are the three main features distinguishing the brokers' association from both the guild and the secret society. However, the substitute 'sibling' relationship between members, and the 'democratic' choice of leaders or organization (Wou does not specify what form this took) appear to have been two features which were common to all voluntary associations in China.

Craft and trade guilds

The craft and trade guilds appear to have developed not only out of the need for cooperation in work or trade, but also from the desire for mutual protection and friendship. According to Wou, the precursor of the craft guild was the friendship association of *pai-mong* (literally, 'to bow and take oath'), the members of which called each other 'elective brothers'.[62]

> These 'elective brothers' gave each other close support. History records quite striking examples of reciprocal devotion. They even went so far as to sacrifice their life for a friend. And to establish clearly the brotherly bond which

existed between them they exchanged birth certificates by way of contract, during important feast days. Having no blood relationship, however, there were no rights of inheritance among themselves. Of necessity, these groups were kept small, generally containing fewer than 20 members. They consisted of men belonging to the same social classes and they won over the people after having been respected only in the higher strata of society.

This type of association is reminiscent of the legend of the 'Brothers of the Peach Orchard', who swore an oath of brotherhood under the peach tree, promising to live and die together and restore unity to the chaotic China of the Later Han dynasty. This story, familiar to most Chinese from childhood,[63] was ritually evoked again and again by members of secular voluntary associations and certainly by Chinese secret societies.[64] One of the 'brothers', Kuan Yü, came to be deified as the God of War, and his portrait is to be found in all kinds of associations, both within China and overseas.[65]

Developing from this, or simultaneously with it, was the organization of artisans for a large project of work, such as building construction. This brings to mind, inevitably, the masons of mediaeval Europe, whose association brought into being the Freemasons. Wou reconstructs the organization of the craft association by putting together clues from the ancient *Rites of Chou* (1122 B.C.) and from her own observations of traditional builders at work:[66]

> Only a trace of it remains in the local customs which characterize the grouping of workmen. They are equal among themselves and autonomous in relation to the central authority.
>
> Let us suppose that someone has a house to build. In former times, the owner of the land, supplied the stone . . . the lime, the soil, the timber, etc. . . ., and gave the work over to a master mason (*Wa-ts'ian-to*) who acted as architect and directed the work, like the 'master builder' in the construction of European cathedrals in the middle ages. Under his orders, a veritable association of workmen was organized. A foreman, *Kong-to*, was in charge of the work entrusted to his trade group and he himself selected the

specialized craftsmen, the apprentices, and the labourers. There was an exact division of work; all those engaged in the construction of the building worked in collaboration, and in certain regions of China they still do so at the present time. Masons were also entrusted with the management of the most important building operations; we saw it with our own eyes during the building of the University of Lio-ning (Moukden) in 1909.

The masonry undertaking which belonged to the master mason Tchao-Lao-Ki brought together several thousand workmen. Some of them were apprentices or former associates of Tchao-Lao-Ki, the others being hired in the tea houses (*keou-tseu*).

Other writers, such as H. B. Morse, P. B. Maybon, J. S. Burgess and Père Leboucq, all support Wou's thesis that craft guilds (unlike Provincial Associations) were characterized by a spirit of egalitarianism and democratic government.

While there is relatively little systematized information about Chinese guilds, it is possible, nevertheless, to extract certain common features of guild organization from the available material on late nineteenth-century and early twentieth-century associations. The main features may be summed up in note-form as follows:

Recruitment Membership open to all members of the same craft or trade, irrespective of birth or other ascribed status. Managers and workers in craft guilds were equal in status.

Election of officers By unanimous informal consent of all members. Functions of officers limited to administrative and book-keeping duties; individual ambition discouraged.

Management Democratic participation of all members, often compulsory *rotation of offices* to members—each tenure lasting one day, one week, one month, one year. Minimal hierarchization of officers, if any. Great variation in size of council and heads of guilds, and a tendency to have more than one head. Some societies had no heads at all, with one or more paid, literate secretaries responsible for the book-keeping and other paper work.

Sanctions By group ostracism and economic boycott. Formerly corporal punishment was also used, the offender having been brought before the whole guild and punished. Other penalties included (a) a fine of candles for the temple (where festival services and meetings were often held); (b) a dinner for ten or more people; (c) a theatrical representation in guild hall or temple; (d) cash fines. Sanctions also ensured that the primary loyalty of each member was to the guild, and not to the central government.

Purposes May be summed up by Morse as follows:[67]

> The Chinese trade guilds . . . fix prices and enforce cohesion; they settle or modify trade customs and obtain instant acquiescence; they impose their will on traders in and out of the guilds, and may even, through the measure known as the 'cessation of all business', cause the government to modify or withdraw its orders; and their end, that of having the absolute control of their craft, is obtained by methods of which some are indicated above.

Some elaboration of the above summary is necessary here. Writing about the structure of the trade and craft guilds in Peking on which he did field work, Burgess reports:[68]

> The organization of the Peking guilds varies greatly in form. There are the guilds with practically no formal organization and controlled for the most part by an informal meeting of the older heads of a few shops. The majority of the guilds, however, are controlled by boards of directors, standing committees, or other designated groups of a fixed number. In a few cases it is specifically stated that there is 'no board of directors'. The executive matters are handled by the president of the guild or by the president and vice-president.
>
> The usual organization . . . has some sort of group designated as 'the elders', 'the group of officers', 'the board of directors', or 'the yearly committee'. These committees vary greatly in size. The Carpenters' yearly committee numbers twenty; the Cloth Pasters are controlled by sixteen elders; the Cloisonné Designers have a council of ten;

the Shoe Stores have eight directors; the Mutton Shops are controlled by ten directors.

Morse confirms this picture in an earlier study (1909):[69]

> Guild government is . . . democratic. The Tea guild at Shanghai has at its head an annually elected committee of twelve, each committee-man acting in rotation for one month as chairman, or manager; *no guild member may refuse to serve on this committee* . . . The Millers' guild at Wenchow is composed of sixteen mill proprietors, who select annually from their number a committee of four, in such a way as to bring each guild member in his turn, on the committee; but the ruling price of flour for each month is settled by the entire craft in conference.

A Swatow guild is cited in illustration of the system of rotation of office in practice:[70]

> It is divided, territorially, into two divisions, each of which elects annually twenty-four firms as representatives, making a committee of management of forty-eight members. The routine business of the guild is managed by four clerks, nominated by four members of the committee, two from each division in rotation, the four serving as accountants and treasurers for one month. In important affairs the committee is advised by three secretaries, one to represent each of the divisions, and the third being the salaried literate secretary, whose qualifications and duties have been described in connexion with the provincial clubs. While the government is thus democratic, in practice a question affecting any branch of trade is first discussed among the principal firms whose interests are touched; having come to an agreement, the smaller firms concerned are taken into their council; and when all are agreed, then the matter is brought before the guild.

The rotation system, it appears, was particularly in evidence in *large* groups[71]

> where different districts in rotation supply the committee in charge for the year. . . . In another group, this principle is applied by the month, the different members of the

executive committee or board taking charge during different months. . . . As the work of the officers and the committeemen is purely voluntary, this scheme serves to lighten the burden on any one person or group of persons.

Thus the rotation system dispensed with the need and expense of a separate and large administrative staff, and, moreover, permitted a more direct and therefore more efficient system of cooperation in guild activities; not only did it avoid the divisiveness of electioneering, it also served as a system of sanctions or control over the members. The rotation system, moreover, provided checks against embezzlement of public funds and other forms of corruption endemic in Chinese bureaucracies; while it gave the members of the guild a positive sense of participation and reponsibility in guild decisions which could only strengthen the solidarity of the group. This was an advantage not missed in secret societies where the participation of all members in tribunals was made compulsory.[72]

The most effective form of sanction used against reprobates was group ostracism, boycott or the permanent expulsion of a member from the guild: 'the craftsman who is not a guild member is as one exposed to the wintry blast without a cloak . . . The result is that membership is open . . . on terms laid down by the guild, and these terms are readily accepted.'[73] Moreover, 'Their [the guilds'] jurisdiction over their members is absolute, not by reason of any charter or delegated power, but by virtue of the faculty of combination by the community and of coercion on the individual which is so characteristic of the Chinese race.'[74]

Morse cites a specific illustration of this method of group control and the power it can exercise in the wider society:[75]

When the guild wishes to enforce its decrees, there are no inflammatory placards and no riots; it would seem almost as if an aura pervaded the minds of members of the guild, leading them without preconcert, to do the same thing at the same time in the same way. A steamship company, in order to close a loophole for possible fraudulent claims, inserts a clause in its bill of lading without previous consultation with the guild. A few friendly, very friendly, hints are given, but there is no formal protest; only merchants, apparently without reason, cease to ship by the steamers of that company; a sugar refinery at another port, under the management of the same firm, suddenly remarks a serious falling off in its orders; and when the loss in all directions has assumed serious proportions, the hint is probably taken and the obnoxious clause struck out of the bill of lading. . . . There are no lawsuits, not even a reference to arbitration; the company finds its freights falling off and is soon brought to view that class of claim with a more lenient eye.

The election of officers was carried out, it seems, in the same unobtrusive way. Nomination of officers and their election appears to have been made by unanimous 'gentlemen's agreement'. The competition for office was reduced by the prospect of heavy responsibility and little personal power. The criteria for election to office appear to correlate closely with the particular needs of each type of association. When Burgess did a survey of Peking guilds, he asked the question 'What type of men are elected to office?', and the replies are set out in his Table ix[76] which I have simplified for convenience in Table ii.2.

TABLE II.2

Guilds	Age	Economic standing	Moral character	Capability	Fame
Craft (11)	4	3	4	8	2
Commercial (13)	3	8	1	7	3
Professional (7)	3	0	5	6	1
Total	10	11	10	21	6

Explanation: the numbers in brackets are those of guilds to whom the question 'What type of men are elected to office?' was put; the arabic numerals indicate the number of times each type or group of guilds chose the qualities set down in the questionnaire.

In general, we can see that 'capability' ranked the highest of the five qualifications; next comes 'economic standing', then 'age' and 'moral character'; and finally 'fame'. But the typical emphases of each group of guilds are somewhat different: the craft guilds held capability the highest qualification; the merchant guilds, economic standing with capability a close second; while the professionals rated, like the craftsmen, capability the highest. It is also interesting to note that craft guilds appear to have cared little for fame, merchant guilds little for moral character, and professional guilds 'nothing' for economic standing!

Professional guilds

These are composed of guilds of actors, barbers, cooks, kitchen coolies, porters, waiters, storytellers, domestic servants, even the blind. Professional guilds appear to have possessed the most elaborate organization and the most detailed division of labour of all.[77] They were also the largest group of guilds (both in terms of guild units and in overall numbers) in traditional China. Certainly, a large membership implied that the division of labour, and hence, organization, had to be more complex, especially if the work had to be rotated among the members.

Burgess's study again provides us with the details of how the more elaborate guilds in Peking worked:[78]

> There is the 'annual head of the guild', the 'monthly head', and the 'daily head'. The annual head is the chief director. The monthly head manages the monthly affairs, and the daily, one day's affairs. If the daily head does not finish his day's work, what is left undone is taken charge of by the head for the next day. In similar manner business may be carried over from one month to the next. If the monthly head has matters of great importance which he cannot transact, he refers them to the annual head. *There are more than 100 heads.*

Tenure of office could also be permanent, especially in commercial guilds, for 'It is evident that the commercial guilds generally tend to have greater definiteness with regard to official tenure and a more clear-cut organization than the craft and professional guilds.'[79] This of course is always true of all activities relating to economics, the very nature of which requires greater precision of organization.

Provincial associations

This type of association was based on ascriptive qualifications for membership, and cannot therefore be termed voluntary, and will thus not concern us directly here.

Religious associations

While there are many studies of Chinese philosophy and religion, very few scholars have turned their attention to religious, and especially heterodox, institutions. One general reason may be the relative youthfulness of Chinese sociological research as compared to studies of the language, literature and history. A more specific reason may be the total absence of interest among official Chinese historians for thought and institutions not directly encompassed by the orthodoxy; and since Confucianism cannot be strictly termed a 'religion' (in the Indo-European sense of the word), nor indeed did the Chinese have a proper *neutral* term for it.[80] For a Chinese to study 'religion' would have been tantamount to studying 'superstition' or 'false doctrines'. Few self-respecting Chinese literati would have dreamt of polluting their intellectual purity with such lowly concerns.[81]

Despite the scorn with which the orthodox historians always regarded heterodoxy and its organizations, the bureaucrats were all too conscious of the power which organized heterodoxy could wield in fomenting and organizing political opposition.[82] In order to awaken the people to the dangers of such associations, the Government applied the most unflattering terms to heterodox sects. For example, *hsieh-chiao* (depraved sects) (*chiao* also means institutionalized belief), *yin-chiao* (obscene sects), *wei-chiao* (pseudo-religious sects), and *yao-chiao* (perverse sects). Logically, members of such sects were nothing better than *chiao-fei* or 'sectarian bandits', not so very different from members of secret societies who were called *hui-fei* or 'society bandits'.[83]

Of course, the bureaucratic literati were right, as the following quotation (among many others) testifies:[84]

Societies originally political became also religious with the addition of fresh blood or in new conditions, and vice versa; some died out or were persecuted into silence, to be revived perhaps under a new name and in another place, with or without modifications in doctrine and organization; large societies divided and the parts developed differently; while the literature was mostly in manuscript, and often had to

be hurriedly destroyed ... It is impossible to say how many
of the sects still exist, but in 1896, they were said to average
anything from 20,000 to 2,000,000 members per province.

This continual transformation of religious sect (*chiao-men*) into
political association (*hui-tang*) was a phenomenon more common, probably, to the north than to the south of China. In the
north, the White Lotus Sect, the Eight Trigrams Sects, the
Nien, the Boxers, etc., were known to be both secret and religious societies; indeed, the captured members of these sects
confessed as much.[85] In the south, however, secret societies
tended to be relatively secular, taking their origins as much
from the Brothers of the Peach Garden (see p. 39 and Ch. III)
as from the association of the five monks of Shaolin temple.[86]
The religious elements in the southern secret societies were
confined to the ritual and prayers, and only the form, rather
than the content, of heterodox mysticism were retained.
For example, the 'clairvoyant' or *ming-yen*, who had a crucial
role in the northern sects,[87] was omitted from the officer hierarchy in the southern societies, and similarly, the 'nine palaces'
(*chiu-kung*) of the Buddhist Nirvana were forgotten, and nine
grades of office took their place.[88]

Thus, it could be argued that northern secret societies derived
their origin directly from the religious tradition of association,
while the southern societies (represented by the Hung League
or Triad Societies) derived theirs from the secular *pai-meng* or
mutual-aid or friendship association. Nevertheless, both types
of secret society, as indeed all types of voluntary association in
China, had a religious focus; some founder or 'ancestor' or
heterodox deity was usually invoked in the assembly of members.[89] These were the patron gods or guardians of the particular associations. Burgess's survey of twenty-eight Peking guilds
in 1928 reveals that only four had no patron saint of any kind.
Even now, in socialist Cuba, displayed in halls next to others
showing portraits of revolutionary leaders (see Appendix D),
are portraits of Kwan Kung, or of the latter plus his two
famous brothers, certainly the most popular gods of Chinese
associations anywhere. The more specialized associations had
more professionally qualified saints, for example, Lu-pan, a
deified craftsman, for the construction trade; Hua-t'o, a famed

surgeon of the third century A.D. for the medical profession; and T'ien-hou (a chaste virgin and miracle-worker of the tenth century who appeared at sea to help sailors in distress) for the associations of sailors, and so on.

Religious associations came into being with the advent of Buddhism into China in the first century A.D. Until that time, Taoism barely had an institutional existence, though there was a brief moment of glory at the end of the Han dynasty, when the Taoist spiritualist leader Chang Chüeh founded the first 'church state' evolved from a secret society and made up of followers of the *T'ai-p'ing Tao* (The Way of Great Peace).[90] They launched a widespread rebellion in east China, known as the 'Yellow Turban Rebellion', which was eventually suppressed (though not very successfully) in the second century after Christ. But it is generally believed that Buddhism was the first organizer of religion in China, and inspired the Taoists to do the same.[91] Although the Taoist 'church' was eventually destroyed as a centralized organization, the local 'parishes' remained, each presided over by a local priest known as the *Tao-shih* (Teacher of the Way), who was supported by gifts called 'banquets' and traditional tithes of 'five pecks of rice' from his followers.[92] Other attempts to reunite the Taoist church failed, though temporary unity was sometimes re-established during the reigns of Taoistically inclined Emperors.

A more significant development was the appearance of sects, again under the influence of sectarian Chinese Buddhism. There came to be as many as eighty-six Taoist sects, including a 'Northern' sect, founded in the twelfth century and subsequently centered at Peking, and two 'Southern' sects. The second of the 'Southern' sects was controlled by a hereditary line of Taoist priests who claimed descent from Chang Ling. (Founder of Five Pecks of Rice cult around middle of the second century.) In 1019 a Chinese emperor gave a priest of this line a great tract of land in Kiangsi in South China and invested him with the traditional title of *T'ien Shih* (Heavenly Master). In the late thirteenth century the Chang family was accorded official recognition as the leader of the Taoist church and during the next century was given a certain degree of official control over the Taoist priests of the whole land. The so-called Chang 'popes' maintained their rich holdings and at least the theory of their leadership until 1927, when the last *T'ien Shih*, who claimed to be the sixty-third in lineal descent from Chang Ling, was ousted, apparently by Communists, from both his property and his title.[93]

The temples which were controlled by the State had the following hierarchy: first, the director; second, the hierophant (initiating priest); third, the thaumaturgist (wonder-worker) (for drought and inundation); fourth, ordinary priests.[94]

It is interesting to compare the above with the non-government heterodox associations of the White Lotus Society, a predominantly Buddhist sect: first, king; second, president (*i-shih*); third, section chiefs (*fa-shih*); fourth, decurions (*hao-shih*).[95] All the other northern secret sects also had four grades of membership. D. H. Porter reported, in 1886, that one group of northern sects had the following officers: first, president (*chang-shih*); second, registrar (*hao-shih*); third, fiscal (*fa-shih*); fourth, clairvoyant (*ming-yen*).[96] The Boxers of Shantung province substituted the last office by another, that of the 'spirit-inviter' or *ch'ing-shen*.[97] There appear to be few significant variations from this pattern and size of hierarchy, though terminology varied from one society to another,[98] as did the degree of Buddhist or Taoist emphasis—though, most of the time, the distinction between the two heterodoxies was not at all clear.

Most of the northern sects were organized according to the principle of the *Pa-kua* or 'Eight Trigrams', that is, into eight sections, four of which were 'civil' (*wen*) and four 'military' (*wu*).[99] Among the Boxers, the military sections were controlled by the *t'uan-shou* or military chiefs, and the civil sections by the *kuan-shih-che* or administrators.[100] The *t'uan* meant simply 'band' (or in the modern army 'regiment'), the same term as that applied to the village militia. It is also a term for the basic unit of the Boxers, called *t'an* (literally, 'altar') in the cities, and could comprise anything from twenty-five to a hundred men. Under the military chiefs were the 'masters' in three grades: 'Great', 'Second' and 'Third'. The 'teachers' in the civil sections were graded similarly. (The Chinese terms are *hsien-sheng* and *shih-hsiung*, respectively.) Sometimes, the sects were also divided in sections according to the 'Five Directions' (*wu-fang*), the 'Five Elements' (*wu-hsing*) or the 'Four Sides' (*ssu-mian*).[101]

The key functionary in the northern heterodox sects (whether open or secret) appears to have been the 'clairvoyant' (*ming-yen*) who discharged both sacred and profane duties. Not only was he or she a medium but was also given the right of veto on recruitment and promotion.[102] Apart from this, the recruitment and election of officers appear to have been determined by ability and merit: when a leader failed to fulfil the expectations of his electors (the rank-and-file members), such as bringing his troops to victory, then they had the liberty to 'substitute another leader of supposedly greater magic powers to try again'.[103] This was particularly true of the Boxers.

From this we can see that spiritual or magical power was sometimes regarded as synonymous with military prowess; this was probably the attitude adopted during rebellion. In peace-time, purely spiritual worth would do as well; as Père Leboucq reported in his *Lettres*, election of White Lotus officers was done by competition in fasting, the members who fasted longest had the 'greatest' spiritual powers. The frauds practised in such rivalries (such as hiding food in ingenious pockets) were no less a test of the more profane abilities required in leadership.[104]

The above sects, with their principal emphases on heterodoxy and political opposition, could be distinguished from another type of religious association or 'club' which stressed the aspect of economic mutual-aid. These were probably more open in character, resembling the funeral associations of other cultures. In his article 'Buddhist Monasteries and Money-raising Institutions' Lien-sheng Yang wrote:[105]

Religious clubs known as *i-i* or *i-hui* existed as early as the Northern and Southern dynasties, when lay adherents organized themselves to finance religious activities in Buddhist monasteries, notably for the erection of stone monuments bearing images of Buddhas and Boddhisattvas. Monks and nuns might become officers or members of these religious clubs, or at least they were glad to work through patron groups. Inscriptions on the numerous steles which are preserved indicate how active these religious clubs were from the Northern Wei to the early T'ang.

According to references derived from late T'ang manu-
scripts found in Tun-huang, similar clubs known as *she-i* or
she financed activities like vegetable dinner parties given to
monks and nuns, recitation and copying of sutras, popular
sermons known as *su-chiang* and printing of images of
Buddhas and Bodhisattvas. NABA estimates that in the
ninth and tenth centuries there were usually ten to fifteen
such clubs attached to one monastery and the membership of each club numbered about twenty-five to forty
people.

Many of these religious clubs performed also social and
economic functions. Contributions were made jointly to a
fellow member to help him pay for a funeral or for travel.
The practice was known as *chui-hsiung chu-chi*, 'to follow up
when there is a happy or unhappy event'. In such mutual
financing associations, hereditary membership was naturally encouraged. Many circulars from club officers, known
as *she-ssü chuan-t'ieh*, to call meetings or to ask for contributions have been preserved. NABA notices that many of
these clubs had no clerical members and were no longer
religious in nature. This he interprets as a sign of the rise
of secular interests in the ninth and tenth centuries. This is
certainly significant, but the facts that in some cases monks
were also members of these mutual financing associations
and that in most cases their meeting places were at monasteries nevertheless indicate a close connection between
them. It is probably not far fetched to suggest that these
mutual financing associations were offspring of the purely
religious clubs.

Maybon also mentions religious clubs which aided members on
pilgrimages:[106]

China has many shrines, which are visited at fixed periods
of the year by thousands of pilgrims. The most famous are
'The pilgrimages of the four points of the compass', to the
mountains Han-Chou, Hou-Chan and especially Tai-chan
in the Chan-Tong. The provinces also often have their
Buddhist, Taoist, or other shrines.

As this movement of people, often over some tens of
miles, involves considerable expense, mutual associations

called 'Mountain Societies' are created among the common people. Each member pays a certain sum every month which the treasurer invests at a good rate of interest and at the end of one, two or more years, if the society's funds, with the addition of income to the capital, contain enough money, those who are to take part in the pilgrimage are chosen by lot and form the travel group.

Each town, village and hamlet, even of two or three families, has its religious association, which makes pilgrimages every year to the most famous pagodas in the vicinity. These associations bear the generic title of association of Aromatics, from the sort of incense made from powdered bark of the elm tree, soaked in oil and dried in the sun, which is burned in small sticks, in honour of the gods, in all the temples.

These associations are composed mainly of women, their treasurers, and their zealots. Even the poorest possess a drum and cymbals with which to accompany the chanting on feast days. Their members visit and care for the sick, carry out the weekly services, and anniversary services for the dead, and help to settle family disputes.

The recurrence of certain words like 'mountains' (being the foci of pilgrimages), 'incense associations', etc., in the above passage is interesting because these words also occur frequently in southern secret society parlance, especially in the Elder Brothers Society (*Kelao Hui*). For example, lodges were called 'mountain halls' (*shan-t'ang*), and the initiation rite 'open mountain rite' (*k'ai-shan shih*), while members of all southern secret societies were known as 'incense', translated also as 'fragrance' (*hsiang*) among other things.

Chinese religious associations had, however, very limited welfare functions, as Morse[107] points out. Apart from helping members to carry out pilgrimages, build temples,[108] and bury their dead with a degree of respect which members could not afford individually, religious associations did not, apparently, dispense charity to *outsiders* at all. Such functions were sometimes taken over by specifically benevolent societies called *t'ang*[109] or *kung-so*, meaning 'hall' or 'public place' (the last also a generic name for guilds), which existed for the provision of 'free coffins, for maintaining soup kitchens, for the rescue of stray dogs . . .'[110] and appear not to have had strong religious connections.

A strong characteristic of the heterodox religious society is the prominence of women members. Widows, repudiated wives, spinsters, virgins and even prostitutes[111] found consolation in heterodox cults to the extent proportionate to their lack of political, ritual and economic honour in the orthodox society. As Chinese women were traditionally disqualified from participation in politics both within the State and the lineage,[112] and poor women disqualified from every kind of public activity outside the home, their preponderance and role in the heterodox organizations were therefore commensurately greater. Their free admission into secret societies and the importance of their role there are reflections of the general trend of the absorption of the underprivileged groups of orthodox society into organized heterodoxy.

CONCLUSIONS

The foregoing discussion of traditional Chinese society discloses a recurring theme, and that is that the degree of an individual's influence depended, directly, on his social origins, and indirectly, upon his wealth. This can be seen at every level of orthodox social organization: in the bureaucracy, in the informal government, in the class system, in the kinship structure of authority. During the nineteenth century, wealth increasingly became the direct determinant of status and power. The trend became visible in the *unprecedented* increase in the sale of offices, ranks and academic titles, and in the simultaneous decay of the Examination System.[113] It became concretized in the rise of the merchant and entrepreneurial classes to political prominence in the confrontation of China with European imperialism, which taught that trade was *productive*, not only of wealth, but of power, both military and political.

This upsetting of the delicate equilibrium between wealth and status in determining the influence which an individual could exert in society, damaged the hegemony of the bureaucratic ruling class beyond repair. Suddenly, as it were, the vulnerable areas of the State structure were exposed to the critical attention of its enemies.

Increasingly, people, in particular the new merchants and the foreign-educated intelligentsia, came to realize how the Chinese State had been little more than an instrument for the continued dominance of a small ruling minority over the majority, and the much vaunted Confucian paternalism[114] no more than another device for perfecting this dominance. The greater part of the population, handicapped by a high rate of illiteracy and poverty, had always become politically impotent under strong rulers. It was only during periods of dynastic decline (with all their accompanying features of factionalism at court, bureaucratic inflation and corruption at every level of Government, and chaos in the countryside) that peasants could organize themselves, under the leadership of secret societies, for revolt. In less critical periods, and 'lost in the swarming mass of Chinese crowds, the man of small means, who forms the great majority in China, would quickly fall prey to hunger, sickness and misery if he did not join with others equally as unfortunate as himself'.[115]

The associations of mutual aid (craft and trade guilds, heterodox religious sects and secret societies) gave a degree of security to their members which the orthodox legal institutions were unable or unwilling to provide.[116] As non-official organizations, they were periodically subjected to Government persecution. It was the custom, therefore, for heterodox and popular organizations to keep themselves more or less within the limits of official tolerance, and by confining their activities to economic, religious and criminal spheres, to avoid any *wider political contest* with their rulers. In periods of crisis, however, it was no longer in their interest to continue pursuing this policy. When the centripetal forces were out of Government control, the centrifugal forces naturally came into their own. It was at such moments that the underprivileged, sensing their freedom, surged through the breaches in the political structure, and forcibly seized power.

Up until the second half of the nineteenth century, however, only the *organizational*[117] flaws of the Government were apparent. No matter how great the dissatisfaction, these flaws were always successfully papered over once the guilty Emperor (considered morally responsible) had been dethroned, and his corrupt officials dismissed; the aims of all rebellions (as opposed to revolution) rarely go beyond reform. That is, the structural and ideological assumptions remain intact. The causes underlying this traditional pattern of rebellion and reform lay in the traditional balance of land to population ratio.

Up until the eighteenth century the peasant was able, on the average, to eke out a tolerable existence because the population was not critically disproportionate to the available cultivable land. The impact of the centuries-old migration from the war-devastated areas of the north to the south had not yet made itself too painfully felt. Between 1651 and 1850, however, the population, having enjoyed two hundred years of relative peace and prosperity under the Ming, increased 200 per cent, from about 60 million to 430 million.[118] During a similar period, the land under cultivation had increased from 67 million acres to only 130 million acres.[119] This hopeless imbalance started a desperate scramble for land, with the result that wealthy landlords and rich merchants were able to appropriate the best lands to themselves, leaving the less fertile and fragmented holdings to the rest of the peasantry, who could barely subsist on their tiny plots. The average holding per capita in 1750 was 3·86 *mou* (1 *mou* = 1·37 acres), in 1833, 1·86 *mou*[120] so that large numbers of peasants became tenant farmers, agricultural labourers or paupers. It became quite clear that the comparatively slow expansion of the cultivable area through reclamation of unused land in the south-west and elsewhere could not, to any useful degree, keep up with the dramatic rates of increase in population. The spectacular upsurge of banditry and rebellion in the late eighteenth and the whole of the nineteenth centuries testified to the unprecedented misery in the countryside.[121]

Close upon economic chaos came the defeats of the Chinese armies by foreign troops, which resulted in the signing away of large slices of Chinese territory to foreign economic and juridical domination. These 'unequal treaties', as they came to be called, opened Chinese ports[122] not only to Western trade but also to the influence of Western religious and political thoughts. This formidable alliance of internal decay, external economic assault and ideological subversion, could no longer be resisted by the traditional armoury of bureaucratic reform and 'mandarin' superiority; the tap-root of Chinese society was afflicted with a fatal atrophy, and revolution was only a matter of course.

III

Origins and formation of Chinese secret societies

Secret societies came into existence in China as a response to needs arising out of bureaucratic inadequacy or repression. As we have seen earlier, there were two main traditions of secret association: the heterodox secret sect (*chiao*), and the *secular* mutual-aid protective association (*hui*). However, it was easy for a religious sect to change into a political association and vice versa, depending on the circumstances. As a captured member of the White Lotus Society put it: '[In peacetime we preached that] by reciting sutras and phrases, one can escape the dangers of swords and arms, water and fire. . . . In time of confusion and rebellion, [we] planned for greater enterprises.'[1] By the nineteenth century, the distinctions between the two types of association had become considerably blurred, since they had both become political in aim and action. The differences were mainly ritual. For example, the northern sects continued to practise shamanism, spirit and medium worship and chanting *sutras*; while southern secret societies appear to have confined their magical or religious practices to initiation ceremonies, and then only to the extent of 'paying respects' (*pai*) to, or invoking the witness of, Taoist and Buddhist deities to their oaths.[2] The northern societies, moreover, did appear to fulfil both a religious and a political function, but the southern societies used religious practices for profane purposes such as group solidarity and control. Triad societies[3] required their members to swear allegiance to their founders (or 'ancestors'), while it was considered sufficient to 'petition' (*ping*) the Taoist and Buddhist deities. It also appears that southern societies had, on the whole, a more elaborate structure of authority than northern ones. For example, the Triads and the Elder Brothers Societies had at least nine grades of officers,[4] whilst the northern societies appear to have had only four;[5] though even this difference is not always without exception: the number of grades depended probably on the *size* of the groups rather than on any regional characteristics.[6] Thus, the differences between north and south were those of degree, rather than of fundamental structure, as will be seen in greater detail below.[7]

TABLE III. I

Name of sect	*Province of major concentration*
Pai-lien chiao (White Lotus Sect)	Hupei, Huanpei (Anhwei), Honan
'Off-shoots' of White Lotus Sect:	
Pa-kua chiao (Eight Trigrams Sect)	Honan
Shen ch'uan chiao or *Iho ch'üan* (The Boxers, also branch of the Eight Trigrams)	Shantung, Chihli (Hopei area) up until 1900
Tsai-li chiao (Ethical Sect)	Shantung, Manchuria
Chai chiao (Vegetarian Sect)	Shantung, Anhwei
An-ching-tao-you (Blessed Way Sect)	Shantung, Anhwei

These are only some of the most famous northern sects then in existence (a list of other societies will be found in Appendix E), though some others, like the Big Knife (*Ta-tao hui*) and Small Knife (*Hsiao-tao hui*) Societies, became notorious, respectively, for attacking Roman Catholic missionaries (1898) and the German occupiers of Shantung (1897).

The shifting of the political arena from north to south in the middle of the nineteenth century[8] was reflected also in the shift to central and south China of secret society rebellions from their traditional theatre of operation in the north (see list of rebellions associated with secret sects and societies in Appendix A). The continual flow of refugees from the war-devastated North China Plain towards the rich and expanding cities of the south, especially to the boom 'treaty ports' of Shanghai, Ningpo, Foochow, Amoy and Canton,[9] must have swelled dramatically the ranks of malcontents of which the secret societies were the most organized expression. Furthermore, the anonymity of life in large cities provided excellent cover for secret society activities.

TABLE III.2

Name of society	*Province of major concentration*
Hung Men, Hung Chia (The Hung League, the Hung Family)	
T'ien-ti hui (Heaven and Earth Society)	Fukien
San-tien hui (Three-dot Society)	Kwangtung, Fukien, Kiangsi
San-ho hui (Triad Society)	Kwangtung, Kwangsi
Kelao hui (Elder Brothers Society)	Hupei, Hunan, Szechwan
Ching Pang (Society of the Blessed)	Lower Yangtze region: *hsien* (counties) in Kiangsu, Anhwei, Chekiang, Kiangsi
Chiang-hu t'uan (Rivers and Lakes Band)	Trans-Yangtze region: counties in Anhwei, Kiangsu, Chekiang

Compare this chart with that of the Triad lodge distribution in Map 1, p. 60.

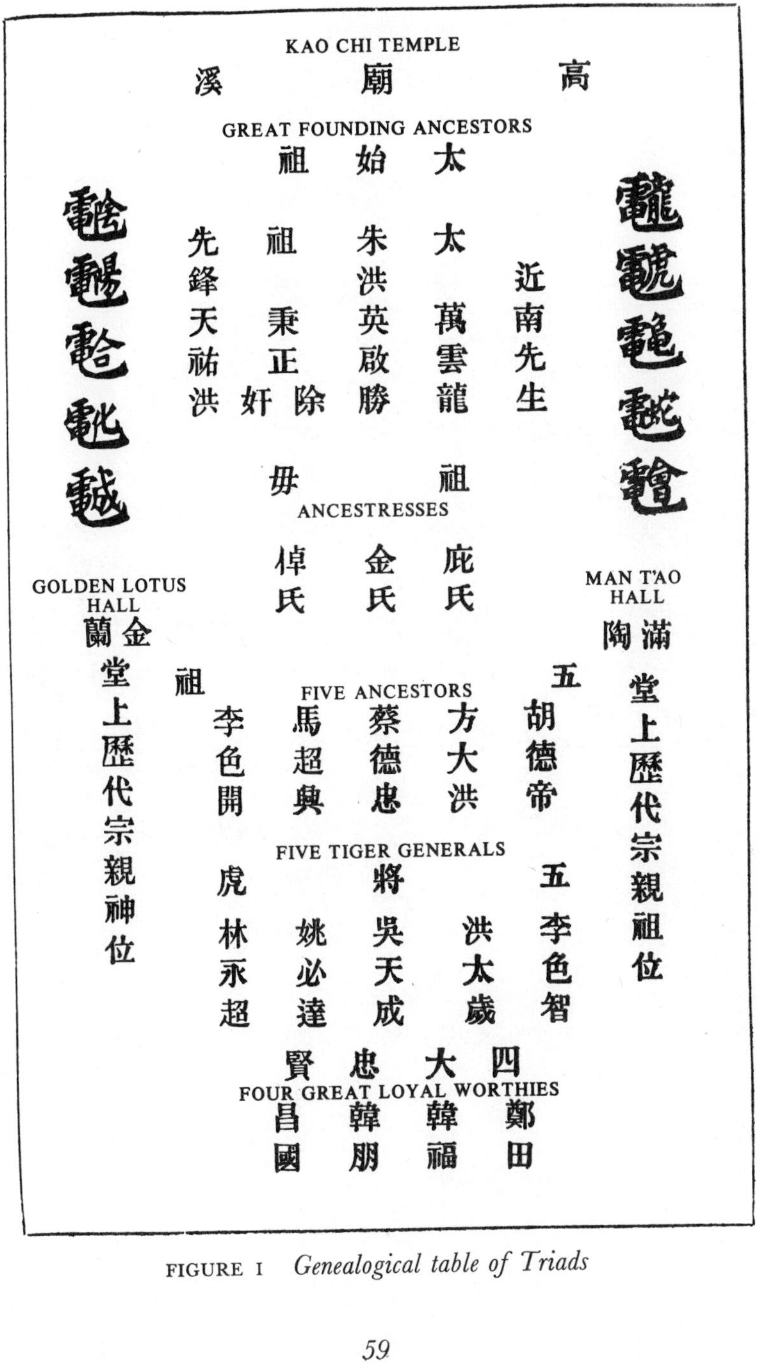

KAO CHI TEMPLE

高 廟 溪

GREAT FOUNDING ANCESTORS

太 始 祖

太 萬 雲 龍　　朱 洪 英 啟 勝　　祖 秉 正 奸 除　　先 鋒 天 祐 洪

近 南 先 生

祖　　　　母

ANCESTRESSES

庶 氏　　金 氏　　卓 氏

GOLDEN LOTUS HALL

金 蘭 堂 上 歷 代 宗 親 神 位

祖

MAN T'AO HALL

滿 陶 堂 上 歷 代 宗 親 祖 位

FIVE ANCESTORS

方 大 洪　　蔡 德 忠　　馬 超 興　　李 色 開

五 胡 德 帝

FIVE TIGER GENERALS

將

洪 太 歲　　吳 天 成　　姚 必 達　　虎 林 永 超

五 李 色 智

FOUR GREAT LOYAL WORTHIES

四 大 忠 賢

鄭 田　　韓 福　　韓 朋　　昌 國

FIGURE I　*Genealogical table of Triads*

Roman numerals = former lodges
Arabic numerals = later lodges

CHIHLI

SHANSI

SHANTUNG

KANSU
1

SHENSI

HONAN
5

KIANSU

ANH/WEI

HU\PEI
4

CHEKIANG
V

3
SZECHWAN

KIANGSI
5

IV
HUNAN

I
FUKIEN

KWEICHOW

II
KWANGTUNG

III
YUNNAN

2
KWANGSI

MAP I   *The provincial distribution of Triad lodges*

Up until 1868, when the last of the great northern rebellions was crushed, the pattern of concentration of the northern sects was that given in Table III.1.[10]

The southern secret societies, known collectively as the 'Hung League' or 'Hung Family' (see p. 12 and p. 62) (*Hung Men, Hung Chia*), are popularly supposed to have 'descended' from the White Lotus Sects during the first reign of the Ch'ing dynasty, about 1674.[11] But the first Triad rebellion did not occur until 1787, and then only in Formosa. In 1814, borrowing impetus from the White Lotus rebellion in the north, the Triads began to rebel in Kiangsi, Canton (in 1817) and Hunan (in 1832). By the end of the 1860s the southern societies had completely overtaken the northern sects as leaders of rebellion; from then onwards, the south was to be the decisive area (the 'south' including the Yangtze basin) for the enactment of the civil war which lasted into the early decades of the twentieth century.

The distribution of southern secret societies (Table III.2) may be said to apply properly only during the nineteenth century, when their existence became visible in rebellion. Figure 1 shows the genealogical table of Triads.

THE TRIADS: THE MODEL OF THE HUI

As the dearth of material precludes the possibility of a detailed study of any one secret society in any one region, it will be necessary to apply a more macroscopic method of analysis; that of making an ideal type from a synthesis of the information available on a number of societies. Indeed, it may be argued that this is the only way to approach the study of Chinese secret societies, for their mobile and decentralized organization makes a microscopic study inadequate if not misleading. The frequent changes, dictated by secrecy, of location and disguise must have created a structure which was able to adapt itself continually to new circumstances and places. But this adaptability is nevertheless modified in form by the orthodox host society, which ultimately determines the structure of its opposing institutions. The resulting basic structure of the Chinese secret society will therefore be common to all the other societies, whatever their apparent 'super-structural' variations.

As this book is concerned chiefly with Chinese secret societies in the late Ch'ing period, the focus will naturally be on the southern political secret society, the *hui*. Material from the northern secret sects, the *chiao*, will be included when and where it may be necessary. Geographical differences will be taken into account if and when the material is specific enough. But as physical mobility appears to be one of the chief features of secret societies and their members (see p. 132) these differences played a lesser part than size, for example, or purposes, in determining the structure of the societies. However, the geographical variations did, undoubtedly, affect to some extent the social composition of the membership. For example, around the Yangtze basin, members of secret societies tended to be boatmen, river transport coolies and pirates.[12] Elsewhere agricultural labourers might predominate, and so on.

The group of societies on which this book is focused is, as indicated earlier, the 'Hung League', popularly known as 'The Triads'. According to Hsiao I-shan, the name 'Hung' was used only among the members themselves.[13] This particular group of southern societies (there must have been others) is chosen because there is more information available on them than on any other group in the region. It is generally supposed that most southern secret societies were derived from the Triads, just as the Triads were supposed to be 'off-shoots' of the White Lotus Society of the north. One of the most convincing arguments in favour of this is the Triad 'myth of origin'.

THE MYTH OF ORIGIN[14]

This legend traces the cause of the formation of 'The Triad Society'[15] to the Government persecution of Buddhist monks in the late seventeenth century, in the reign of the Emperor K'ang-hsi (1664–1722). These Buddhist monks, who lived in hidden seclusion in a monastery called Shaolin, in Fukien, had long been celebrated for their skill in the military arts.[16] For this reason, the Emperor asked for, and obtained, their help in repelling the fierce tribes of Eleuths menacing China's northern frontiers. After a brilliantly successful campaign, the monks returned to their monastery loaded with Imperial honours, having refused all offers of office in the Government. Later, two

Imperial ministers became jealous of the high regard in which the Emperor held the monks; so they incited the Emperor to destroy the monks, with the argument that they had merely returned to their temple fastness to foment rebellion, having now tested their strength in battle. Consequently, and with the treacherous connivance of a monk called 'Number Seven' (in the boxing hierarchy), the Shaolin monastery was discovered and burnt to the ground by Imperial soldiery, killing most of its occupants. With the aid of a magic yellow cloud[17] sent by Buddha, five out of the 108 monks managed to escape. On the way, they found a magic censer with the legend 'Overthrow the Ch'ing and Restore the Ming' (*Fan-Ch'ing-Fu-Ming*), and the injunction 'Act According to the Will of Heaven' (*Hsun-T'ien-Hsing Tao*); grass which turned into joss-sticks when they lit them in the bowl; magic grass-sandals which carried them across a river after turning miraculously into a boat; a two-planked bridge under which were three stepping stones on each of which were the words 'Calm', 'Sea' and 'Floating' (*Ting, Hai, Fou*), by which they were able to evade the Ch'ing guards stationed on the bridge; plum and peach-wood swords which sprang out of the ground, and which were used by the wife and sister of one of the monks to kill pursuing soldiery. These two heroic women killed themselves afterwards to avoid giving away under torture the secret whereabouts of the monks. Seeking shelter in a monastery in Kwangtung province, the monks were introduced to five rebel leaders ('horse-leaders' or 'horse-traders') who were formerly officials of the Ming dynasty. These five men became the 'Five After Ancestors' (*hou-tsu*) to the 'Five Former Ancestors' (*ch'ien-tsu*) who were the five surviving Shaolin monks. The abbot of the monastery told them that a certain Chen Chin-nan of the White Stork Grotto (whereabouts unspecified) was raising troops for the overthrow of the Manchu dynasty of the Ch'ing. The monks then went to join Chen's grotto where they decided to go to Mu Yang City (City of Willows) in Fukien province to set up headquarters, and recruit patriotic citizens for rebellion against the Ch'ing. Shops were opened as covers for receiving recruits and their accommodation until the time was ripe for revolt. A powerfully built man called Wan Yun-lung, who was fleeing the law for having killed a man, joined the party, and was later killed in an abortive rebellion, which took place in Fukien province. A young boy called Chu Hung-ying claimed to be the heir of the Ming dynasty, and was so accepted by the Triads, who made him their *Dauphin*. After the failure of the rebellion (probably in 1674 or 1794; see p. 61) the monks dispersed and founded five 'major' lodges in the five major provinces of Fukien, Kwang-tung, Yunnan, Hunan and Chekiang; while the other five men (known sometimes as the Five Tiger Generals) founded five 'minor' lodges each in the adjacent provinces of Kwangsi, Szechwan, Hupei, Kiangsi-Honan and Kansu. (See Map 1, Triad lodge distribution, p. 60.) The major lodges were known as 'The Five Former Lodges' (*Ch'ien Wu Fang*); the minor lodges were known as 'The Five After Lodges' (*Hou Wu Fang*). (See Figure 2, Triad lodge symbols, p. 65, opposite.)

Although the details of the legend are susceptible of great variation,[18] and are a pot-pourri of historical facts, certain common features, if we set them in the context of the events of the early Ch'ing dynasty, may help to explain why there were renewed irruptions of secret society activity (apart from the socio-economic reasons) in connection with the religious problems of the Manchu reign. In the following discussion, the main features of the myth are considered under these headings:

(a) the restoration of the Ming dynasty,
(b) relations of the Ch'ing with other Mongol tribes (Eleuths and Tibetans),
(c) persecution of Buddhist monasteries,
(d) rebellion against the Manchus and their 'unjust' ministers.

The collapse of the Ming dynasty under Manchurian pressure from the north-east in 1662 forced its supporters to flee to the south, where they took refuge in Buddhist monasteries. The Ming was regarded by secret societies as being pro-Buddhist. This belief was founded on three features of the Ming dynasty: first, the founder of the Ming was a Buddhist monk; second, the White Lotus rebels who had led the rebellion against the Yüan, a Mongol dynasty which preceded the Ming dynasty, did not surface at all during the whole of the long reign of the Ming. This probably means that no serious persecutions of Buddhists took place under the Ming; third, the last rulers of the Ming

Former Lodge 前	Former Ancestor 前祖	After Lodge 後堂	After Ancestor 後祖	Flags and Seals	Animal	DISTINCTIONS					Bases (ti) 底
						Rank	Cosmos	Season	Elements		
First Fukien	Ts'ai Te-chung 蔡德忠	Kansu	Wu T'ien-ch'eng 美天式	Black: rhombic 'River' chiang 江 'Glorious Ornament' piao 彪	Dragon	Duke 虎公	Yin	Spring	Metal		一七 'one-seven' Green Lotus Hall Phoenices Prefecture
Second Kwangtung	Fang Ta-hung 方大洪	Kwangsi	Hung T'ai-sui 洪大威	Red triangle 'Flood hung 洪 'Long Life' shou 壽	Tiger	Marquis 虎候	Yang	Summer	Wood		十二 'ten-two' Hung Obedience Hall Golden Lotus Prefecture
Third Yunnan	Ma Chao-hsing 馬超興	Szechwan	T'ao Pi-ta 陶必達	Carnation or Vermilion square 'Flowing water' lui 'union' ho	Tortoise	Earl 虎伯	Union	Autumn	Water		九 'nine' Empress Hall Lotus Glory Prefecture
Fourth Hunan	Hu Teh-ti 胡德帝	Hupei	Li Shih-ti 李式地	White rectangle 'tributary' Ch'i' 'Harmony' ho	Serpent	Viscount 虎子	Change	Winter	Fire		两九 'double-nine' Great Assembly Hall Embroidered Gallery Prefecture
Fifth Chekiang Kiangsi	Li Shih-k'ai 李式開	Honan	Lin Yung-chao 林永超	Green circle 'Assemble' ts'ou 'Together' t'ung	Assemble	Baron 虎男	Complete	Seasons	Earth		五七 'four-seven' Metamorphosis Hall Prosperity Prefecture

FIGURE 2 *Symbolic chart of Triad lodges*

dynasty were heavily dependent on the eunuchs,[19] who, since they were largely illiterate, were strong adherents of popular Buddhism.

The pro-Buddhist tendency of the Ming naturally led the persecuted Buddhists to identify themselves with the persecuted Ming remnants under the Manchu reign. The relentless pursuit of the last Ming Emperor to Burma, where he was strangled by Manchu agents, merely heightened Chinese hostility towards the foreign dynasty, a hostility already intensified in the southern provinces by the memory of benevolent rule by the last Ming Emperor before his flight. In the treaties following the peace with the Eleuths (who were supporters of the 'yellow' sect, as opposed to the 'red' sect, of Mahayana Buddhism practised by most Chinese) K'ang-hsi was forced to give nominal preference to the Yellow Sect. This obviously brought him into conflict with the Chinese Red Sect followers. However, the official policy had a very good reason for opposing Chinese (rather than Mongol) heterodoxy. The Manchu had become convinced that Confucianism was the philosophy most conducive to successful bureaucratic despotism, and were therefore determined to allow of no other rival philosophy within the empire which might subvert its universal authority. As we have seen already in the introduction, edicts were proclaimed all over the empire against the establishment of heterodox sects, culminating in specific denunciations of Ming Tsuen and Pai Yun sects in 1761 and 1775, respectively.[20] A White Lotus chief was banished to the province of Kansu at about the same time, where he proceeded to proselytize for his society's cause. (This probably accounts for the singular location of an 'After' or 'minor' lodge so far away from the rest of the Triad lodges, see Map on p. 60.) In the Ch'ing Code of 1810, Section CLVII of the Penal Laws, the Mi-le-so and the White Lotus Sect were specifically designated as perpetrators of sedition.[21]

Thus, the persecution of the Buddhists became indissolubly linked with the overthrow of a Chinese dynasty in the popular mind. Here heterodoxy and a growing proto-nationalism came together[22] and the natural object of such an alliance had to be the eventual destruction of the Ch'ing. A third element which added force to this alliance was of course the coming of the Europeans, against whom the Ch'ing rulers were helpless. This weakness, coupled with the national humiliation of the Chinese, aggravated the burden of blame placed on the Manchus. The last factor, that of the social composition of the southern secret associations, provided a cutting edge to the forces of opposition: the element of class opposition. This aspect will be discussed in greater detail in Chapter V (Recruitment and Social Composition).

The 'sacred' origins of the Triads were ultimately not religious but ideological *in function*. The general belief that the Triads were 'descended' from the White Lotus Sect stemmed not only from the slogan of 'Overthrow the Ch'ing and Restore the Ming' which was common to both societies, but also from the inclusion of various Buddhist deities in the Triad ritual verses—such as Kuan-yin—and even Taoist deities, which abound in other northern secret sects, such as Wu-sheng-lao-mu, or 'Old Mother without Origin'.[23] Although it is probable that many of the Triad societies originated in heterodox religious sects, it is just as likely that heterodox religious deities were deliberately incorporated into the ritual of the Triads for political reasons—for disguise, for assertion of honourable aims and for distinguishing themselves from orthodox society. Unlike the northern sects, the southern societies seem to have been unaffected in their structural forms by Buddhism and Taoism; their officers, for example, were not known by religious names, and were functionally classified.[24] Moreover, they do not appear to have been organized according to Taoist cosmology; for example, according to the eight trigrams. The statutes of the Triad, too, emphasize the secular (economic and social) aspects of the association, and the fact that they even include exhortations not to 'mistreat' Buddhist monks or 'mock' them[25] shows that irreligious practices of this kind were far from isolated incidents.

Having now dealt with the mythical and historical origins of the Triad societies, it would be useful to see how a secular, mutual-aid secret society came to be *formed*. We are fortunate in having available to us an account by Commandant Favre, who had personally observed the formation of a brotherhood among the coolies gathered in Taku, near Tientsin, on the eve of their departure for France as China's contribution to the 1914–18 war effort. Although this society, the Society of the

Golden Orchid, was set up in 1916, a period falling outside the scope of this book, its organizational principles were *consciously* taken from the tradition of the secular *hui* or *pai-meng* associations already described earlier.[26] Therefore, it would not be out of place to quote the article at some length here, particularly as it is the fullest, if not the only, eye-witness account of the formation of a secular, non-guild type society extant:

> Separated abruptly from their families and friends, worried about their unknown future, five men in the same quarters exchanged names and ages and discussed the new adventure. The eldest said suddenly, 'Nobody knows what fate awaits us, or what dangers lie ahead; individually we shall go under; united we can strive together and support each other. Let us follow the example of Huien-Te [reign title of Lin Fei, who became King of one of the Three Kingdoms, the Han], Kouan-Yu and Tchang-Fei; long ago, at the time of the Three Kingdoms, in the Peach Orchard they adopted each other as brothers. They had an illustrious future. If they had not done so, they would have succumbed and China would have continued to be subject to the most terrible misfortunes.' 'That is happening everywhere,' said another. 'We have only to agree among ourselves. I know how to write and can draw up the agreement. To-night we will meet and swear the oath with due ritual.' Thus it was done. On the steamer which carried them, the five friends linked themselves with other workmen and obtained new recruits. When they landed at Marseilles, there were 50 brethren. Each one had a complete list of them by rank according to age. At Marseilles their fears began. Would they not be separated, some being sent north and some west? Their oath, however, would endure for ever. No matter where they might be sent they would remain brothers. So as to be able more easily to recognize each other, and also to be able to distinguish themselves from similar societies which had been formed around them, they chose a name for their society, a symbol of good omen: 'The Golden Orchid'.

The words 'adopted each other' are significant, in that they express succinctly the 'structural relationship'[27] (that of the 'sibling' tie) of the association. In the orthodox kinship system, the absence of a male heir meant the extinction of the line, which was regarded as a disaster because there would be no male person to offer sacrifices to the ancestors of the household or lineage; it was believed that for this reason the ancestors would be unhappy and withhold protection from their descendants. To prevent such ancestral discontent, a son was necessary, and the adoption of male children became customary.[28] Similarly, the brotherhood, deprived of real brothers, make up for this deprivation by mutually 'adopting' one another, a process always accompanied by the exchange of a written contract.[29] The fact that only the sibling relationship was taken into the association may be due to two factors: the rough generational equivalence among the coolies and their social equality. However, the initial ranking of members according to age may have been a matter of convenience rather than a belief that the oldest was necessarily the most able. Later, when leadership qualities were revealed in action, younger men might have acquired higher office or rank than older men; or conflicts among equally able contenders for power led to schisms within one society and the development of splinter groups.[30] In an association when all the old ties of origin become little more than a memory, only ability can ultimately decide the choice of leaders.

The Golden Orchid Society itself had only about 150 members (and it was not unusual to find a dozen such societies in a camp of 1,000 workers), who met once or twice every month, sometimes more, depending on the circumstances. The purposes of the meetings were: initiation, festivals, listening to the reading of *Romance of the Three Kingdoms* and other such vernacular lore, the chanting or recitation of prayers, aid to a sworn brother in trouble, and so on, usually rounded off by a fraternal banquet.[31]

Such associations were sometimes known generically as *mengs*, or 'oaths', and several *mengs* formed a *hui* or 'meeting' or 'association'. But the names could be used interchangeably, according to size. However, a *meng* did not normally have a proper name, and would only acquire such when it was big enough. All the societies observed by Favre were characterized by initiation ceremonies, other rituals (enacted during religious festivals), hierarchization and discipline. There were usually only four grades of membership: Big Sworn-brother (*Ta-meng-hsiung*), or Master (*Ta-yeh*); Second Big Sworn-brother (*Erh-meng-hsiung*) or Second Master (*Erh-yeh*); Elder Brother (*Lao-hsiung*), and Younger Brother (*Ti*?).[32]

In China itself, fraternal associations sometimes took the form of permanent associations of outlaws (*tsei*)[33] which used secret society methods for strengthening solidarity. They were usually found in mountainous, wooded (and therefore, inaccessible) areas, and were typologically distinct from the *ad hoc* bands of robbers whose membership fluctuated continually, joining in some raids and not others.[34] The outlaws came not only from the militia disbanded after the suppression of rebellion, but from the ranks of the Taiping and Nien armies.[35] As a contemporary Chinese observer remarked at the time of the Opium War:[36]

If righteous braves assemble together, then they feed themselves from the rations of the militia; but when they dissolve, they form secret societies to lurk in the mountains and valleys, waiting to rob and plunder. The homes of the gentry are thus menaced . . . the high officials have nourished a cancer.

Later, a governor of Kiangsi submitted a memorial on the same subject:[37]

After the incident of Ling-shan [in Kwangsi, where the clash with the French troops took place in 1884], when the government forces were disbanded all weapons were not returned, [the soldiers] who became 'wandering braves', depending on their weapons to rob travellers and merchants . . . some of the robber bands numbered as many as tens of thousands. These 'wandering braves' robbed travellers only; they refrained from harming the native inhabitants. As a result, the latter became friendly to the bandits. When government troops searched for the marauders, they promptly hid themselves in the dwellings of the common people . . . coming out only after the troops had left the locality. Consequently, bandits existed virtually everywhere in Kwangsi province.

Another document recounts how outlaw bands developed into secret societies in the late nineteenth century:[38]

Hui-fei (society bandits) have been most rampant in Szechwan, Hunan, Kweichow, Kwangsi and Kwangtung. At first they were lawless wandering people who burned incense and organized societies. When their organizations have waxed strong and their members become numerous, they rely on their strength to tyrannize their neighbour-hoods and victimize the good people. The humble people, being helpless, may join their societies for self-protection. Such societies assume diverse names, for example, *Ke-lao* (Elder Brother), *An-ch'in* (Contentment-affection), *T'ien-ti* (Heaven-earth), and *San-tien* (Three-dots). They operate in every *chou* and *hsien*. Each local unit numbers several dozen or several hundred men. All the units keep in touch one with another.

Thus the southern *hui* was an institutional synthesis of all the religious, economic and political needs of those whom orthodox society ignored. In the second half of the nineteenth century, however, there was an increasingly heavy emphasis by secret societies on the more 'profane' needs, while the spiritual ener-gies were channelled into the satisfaction of political honour.

Since the structure and organization are geared to the pur-poses and aims of the association, any understanding or analysis of the first aspect would be impossible without a knowledge of the second; therefore, I shall discuss in the next chapter the purposes and activities of secret societies as far as they can be known to an outsider.

IV

Purposes and activities

So far only the activities and aims of the secret societies (as shown in the origins and formation of the Chinese Triads), that is their religious and political pre-occupations, have been discussed. In this chapter, I shall discuss the other *raisons d'être* of secret societies. But before plunging into a more detailed discussion it may well be useful to begin with a survey of the purposes and activities of voluntary associations in general.

The chief purpose of any voluntary association consists in providing its members with mutual aid or protection, whether it is religious, cultural, social, recreational, physical, economic or political. However, societies which combine all of these aspects (even when they exclude the last aspect initially) in their make-up become latently political (that is, prepared to seize political power). This kind of development is illustrated in Weber's analysis of mediaeval north German fraternities:[1]

Such . . . protective associations had not been created primarily for the purpose of influencing political conditions. *Initially they were substitutes for attachment to a clan with its protective guarantees for the members, an attachment missed with special frequency in the early medieval city.* The services to the individual lost by the family were taken over by these protective societies including: help in case of personal injury or threat; aid in economic distress; the settling of disputes and exclusion of feuds between fraternity members by means of peaceful conciliation; the physical protection (banking) of moneys of the members . . .; and the provision of social occasions for fraternization by holding periodic feasts—a practice continued from pagan times. In their function as insurance associations the protective associations even took care of the individual's funeral and the participation of the fraternity in the funeral ritual guaranteed salvation of his soul through good deeds and secured for him indulgences and the benevolence of powerful saints through shared expenses. It goes without saying that such protection associations also represented joint economic interests. [My italics.]

When such associations (or voluntary substitutes for the clan) come into conflict with the central governmental authorities and are defeated by them, they will be forced to submit to these authorities, or go underground. When a society is forced into illegal opposition, it becomes a secret society.

Secret societies could disguise themselves as open associations like friendship clubs, or maintain both their existence and their functions in strict secrecy. Chinese secret societies tended to vary their ostensible aims, activities and even to some extent, organization, according to circumstances, usually in response to the strength or weakness of the central Government. While rebellion claimed the attention of secret societies from time to time, there nevertheless existed a more permanent form of activity which may be described by 'services to the individual lost by the family'.

As the political aims of the Chinese Triads have already been discussed in the previous chapter in some detail, we need only to summarize them here. The political *aims* of the secret societies were reform of government ('restore virtuous government') and the national independence of China from alien (Manchu) rule ('smash the Ch'ing and restore the Ming'); while their main political *activity* was of course armed rebellion.

In peace-time, and even simultaneously with rebellion, the purposes of the Triad societies appear to have resembled those of ordinary protective associations as described by Weber. On their role as a substitute clan, the secret societies were highly explicit: 'To-night we pledge ourselves, and vow this promise before Heaven, that the brethren in the whole universe shall be as from one womb; as if born from one father, as if nourished by one mother; as if they were of one stock and origin.'[2] When Weber pointed out—most illuminatingly—that the need for a substitute clan sprang from the separation of individuals in the cities from their kin in the countryside, he omitted to mention the economic factor as the second reason for voluntary association. For individuals poor in material resources are nearly always deprived of influence in the lineage if not of its very physical existence for him. As Maurice Freedman has observed,[3] the *size* of a corporate kin group in China depended on its wealth in land and other immovable property; that is, the larger the corporate group, the greater its wealth tended to be. Poverty not only broke up lineages and families (for example, when individuals were forced to leave their families and look for work elsewhere, or when there was no corporately owned lineage land, and the holdings were scattered in small parcels over a wide area) but could physically exterminate them, especially during periods of famine or other disaster, when the possession of material reserves became the decisive factor in survival. Finally, poverty denied the right of an individual to legal protection under most circumstances, and rendered him excessively vulnerable to corrupt official exactions. Certainly, in the Chinese case *both* urbanization and poverty are relevant to an explanation of the individual's need for membership in a surrogate kinship group.

In every way, Chinese secret societies resembled the north German fraternities in their purposes and activities; for example:

(a) help in case of personal injury or threat:
When a brother is summoned before a tribunal, or a price is set upon him, and he cannot remain longer in the place, the powerful must help him to escape, and the less powerful pay his travelling expenses. This is helping him out of danger, like taking a fish out of a dry place, and it is saving him from difficulties, like liberating a bird out of a closed net.[4]

If brethren of the Hung-league travel or sleep together, and it happens during their passage that wicked people wish to injure them, they ought to assist each other. If the one does not care for the other, and, knowing it fortuitously beforehand, escapes the danger, but suffers his brother to be injured by them, he shall be punished with 108 heavy blows.[5]

This help should also extend to the 'Brother's' family:[6]

If a brother of the Hung-league, seeing that the wife or children of a deceased brother are insulted or ill-treated by others, and, though dwelling next door, remains looking at it with his arms sleeved up, and, designedly, does not inform the brethren of it, that they may avenge them, he shall be punished with 21 blows.

(b) aid in economic distress:
If brethren in times of distress and difficulty have no money to escape, you must assist them with passage money, no matter how much.[7]

If a brother's father or mother die and he has no money to defray the funeral expenses, he must ask the brethren to subscribe and none must refuse.[8]

When a brother is dead, and there is no money to bury him, all the members ought to unite themselves and contribute money to help. In this way the charity of the Hung-league will appear.[9]

(c) the settlement of disputes, etc.:
When brethren of the Hung-league have serious or trifling dissensions, the council is there to decide upon them according to justice, but it shall not be allowed to bring the case before the magistrates.[10]

If a brother breaks the laws, let all the brethren come and settle the matter in public, without, by using cross words and crooked language in front of the Incense Master, adding fuel to the fire.[11]

If a brother of the Hung-league sees that another brother disputes or quarrels with a member of his own family, he ought to intervene and enjoin them to leave off. He who helps his own relation and, wantonly, beats his brother, shall be punished with 108 blows.[12]

If brethren of the Hung-league have gone together to a brothel, and dispute about a prostitute or 'little friend' (catamite), so that they become foes, and are railed at by others, they shall be punished each with 36 blows. He who has helped the one brother to beat the other brother, shall be punished with 72 blows.[13]

(d) the physical protection of moneys of the members: there is no recorded evidence that a bank or banks existed among the Triads, though, as we have seen earlier in the section on voluntary associations, Buddhist monasteries had long been centres of traditional banking.[14] As secret societies appear to have had close connections with monasteries, especially in the north, it would not be inconceivable for banking practices to have been incorporated into Triad activities. If the money and goods of individual members were not actually 'banked' then they were at least physically protected by severe sanctions (cutting off ears, and even death) against robbery, swindling and betrayal of the financial trust. Even though such severe punishments were not always meted out, or less painful penalties substituted, it was in the common interest (that of mutual confidence) to prevent both insiders and outsiders from getting at the common and private funds of members:

If a brother . . . is sufficiently bad and wicked to steal the money, clothes or possessions of another brother, he shall be punished . . . with the loss of one ear.[15]

If a brother . . . , knowing that another brother has been killed by strangers, secretly purloins his money and goods, instead of informing the brotherhood of it, that they may avenge him, one of his ears will be cut off.[16]

If a brother entrusts another letters to take over the seas to his family, and if this brother purloins the money or letters, or changes the goods, he will lose one ear.[17]

If a brother . . . has found out that another brother will pass, with much gold, silver or goods, along a certain place, and he conspires secretly with other people or with the police to rob him of it, he shall be put to death.[18]

If you have to keep guard or watch over a place, you must not steal, nor allow others to steal.[19]

(e) the provision of social occasions for fraternization and feasts, etc.: all initiation ceremonies and festival assemblies were occasions for fraternization, as well as their inevitable culmination in feasts, at which was served the food first offered in sacrifice to the gods or founders.[20] As not only were a large number of fowls decapitated during the act of initiation, but sometimes even horses and oxen were slaughtered as the final offering, there was no lack of reasons for feasting. Moreover, the wine drunk with the blood during the initiation would require that any intoxication of members should be contained by the partaking of solids. It would not do for members to be released to the outside world too soon after the intake of alcohol, in case it loosened their tongues. According to Morgan, the twentieth-century Triads in Hong Kong feasted whenever there was a promotion of a member or official to office or higher office, the provision of such feasts itself being the supplementary promotion fee.[21] Besides feasting at festivals and after initiations, the Triads also celebrated their 'birthday' on the 25th of the 7th month (by the lunar calendar) when, according to the myth, the first Triad general Wan Yun-lung was elected by the first assembly of recruits to the presidency.[22]

(f) The arrangement for funerals and the participation of members on these occasions.

As we have noted above, rules existed which required members to contribute towards the funeral expenses of members and their immediate families, but rules also existed which required *attendance* at the funerals of the *parents* of members: 'If a brother of the Hung-league, knowing that the father or mother of a brother has died, remains on the burial day quietly at home and, designedly, does not attend the funeral, he shall be punished with 108 heavy blows.'[23] There is, however, no mention of the necessity to attend the funeral of a *fellow member*. This may be explained by two things; first, by the fact that funerals of non-member relatives were public affairs, and a good attendance would reflect well on the 'cover' personality of the Triad member, for the prestige and hence influence of a Triad member in the outside world could depend to some extent on the number of 'relatives' he could muster up as mourners at a funeral, and particularly at his parent's funeral. Second, the attendance at a fellow member's funeral was both dangerous and unnecessary. Dangerous, because death of secret society members, if ascertainable, could not always be explained away in terms of 'natural causes'. It was hardly politic to try to provoke the authorities into action by a public display of secret society weakness. The frequent disappearance of members on active service, no matter how long, could not always be due to death. Hence, as long as the funeral expenses were paid, the Triads did not insist on the fulfilment of normal 'brotherly' duties in every letter. But no doubt if a member chose to imperil himself by attending a fellow member's funeral it was his own look-out.

(g) Representation of joint economic interests. It was unlikely that secret societies, owing to their highly mobile existence, owned much immovable property. When necessary, they hired halls for meetings, or met in the numerous houses of entertainment which they controlled, and in which they had trusted lieutenants.[24] Père Leboucq reports, however, that the northern White Lotus Societies owned land and palaces which were inhabited by 'kings'.[25] But this appears to have been an exception, as there is no record of such properties in the hands of the Triads as such. It is probable that houses or buildings were owned by individual members of the societies in trust for the league. Personal residences, as well as the back rooms of tea-houses and brothels, were used as secret meeting places by the Kelao Societies, and undoubtedly by the Triads as well. The practice of moving from one meeting place to another (temples were also favoured retreats) was followed by both republican revolutionaries and later by communist revolutionaries, and indeed, logically by any clandestine organization which could be called professional.

Besides the control of criminal establishments, Triads also disposed, of course, of a common fund consisting of membership fees, festival, funeral and other contributions, a fluctuating income from extortion, blackmail, robbery, smuggling, piracy, assassination and so on.

Describing the economic power of the Szechwan Kelao Society in the republican revolution, an eyewitness and well-known writer Li Chieh-jen wrote:[26]

The Kelao controlled the boatmen on the River [Yangtze],

the craftsmen and small shopkeepers, the manure collectors and water carriers and sedan chair carriers, but they also had adherents among the merchants, the pawnbrokers, the landlords, and now the students. The managing of public cloacas was in their hands, for the 'manure head', or headmen of those who collected the manure, was a Kelao member, and this was a source of revenue for them.

As Jean Chesneaux has pointed out, the liaison of secret societies with smugglers, 'that original and marginal breeding ground of the rising middle class in the proto-capitalist societies', probably contributed significantly to the primitive accumulative process, a point often ignored by social historians.[27]

In a sense, secret societies did 'own' land in that they disposed of 'territories' of control, for which they feuded among themselves with such violence that gang-warfare was inseparably associated with secret societies in the public mind.[28] In the same way as crops were produced on land, so were profitable 'businesses' there in the territory for the cultivation and reaping. William G. Skinner illustrates this kind of territorial control in his essay on the Chinese market town in Szechwan, during the republican period:[29]

the secret societies collectively known as the *Ko-lao-hui* wielded supreme power at all levels of rural society—and the standard marketing community was no exception. It was in fact, a most crucial unit, for lodges of the society were organized by, and limited in almost every case to, a single standard market community. There were two lodges organized within the standard marketing community centered in Kao-tien-tzu, one 'clear' and one 'muddy', both had their headquarters and held their meetings in teahouses in the town. [According to the Rev. James Hutson (*Chinese Life in the Tibetan Foothills*, Shanghai, 1921, p. 82), the 'clear-water womb-brothers' (*ch'ing-shui-pao-ko*) belonged to the Benevolence or Senior lodge, while the 'muddy-water womb-brothers' (*hun-shui-pao-ko*) belonged to the Justice lodge, made up apparently of the 'lawless elements' from the Chengtu area, whose members addressed those of the 'clear' lodge as 'uncle'.] A majority of male adults belonged to one or the other, and on almost every market day members were able to conduct business with the officers of the lodge, who could be found in a particular tea-house. In Kao-tien-tzu, as in many other market towns of the Szechwan Basin, the market itself was controlled by one of the secret society lodges. The positions of grain measurers, pig weighers, livestock middlemen, and certain other commission agents were reserved for society members, and a portion of each agent's fees was claimed for the coffers of the lodge.

It has to be remembered that at this point the phrase 'supreme power at all levels of rural society', even of Szechwan society, applies to the republican period, during which secret societies operated openly and without official hindrance. The reasons were that China was in a state of civil war throughout the period; war not only between the republicans and the communists but also between war-lords, between central and local forces and between large and powerful lineages, especially in the south. Moreover, because of their important role in making the republican revolution a 'success', the Government made no move to control the activities of the secret societies, and indeed derived great benefit from them (see p. 171).

During the period preceding the revolution, however, secret societies were still largely unequal to the forces of order, however weak they had become. One symptom of this inequality was the continued need for secrecy; the other was, of course, the still powerful presence of rural and urban lineages of the officials and gentry. Writing of a period as late as 1948, Skinner points out that many market towns were controlled by either 'several founding villages' (that is, by their representatives, the gentry lineages), or by a 'single composite lineage' or 'great branch' located in a village outside the market town.[30]

The relationship of secret societies to lineages will have to be discussed here, especially as Maurice Freedman has suggested in his study of south-eastern lineages that they might have been 'functionally connected' in some way. I quote:[31]

> In south-eastern China, therefore, there would appear to have been two alignments of conflict which cut across each other. In some contexts lineages were ranged against lineages; in other contexts lineages, or class sections of them,

were united in their common hostility to the state. It may be that the disturbances in Fukien and Kwangtung in the nineteenth century were less productive of general chaos than they might have been precisely because this twofold alignment of conflict prevented *la guerre à outrance* in either direction.

The provinces of Kwangtung and Fukien were remarkable in China for three things: large-scale lineage organization, inter-lineage fights, and secret societies of the Triad type. We may well suspect that these phenomena were not randomly associated, but that in fact they were functionally connected. *Alliances against the state formed by the secret societies counterbalanced the opposition generated between lineage communities when agnatic organization was carried to a high pitch.* To test this hypothesis we should need to look in detail at the way in which both large-scale lineages and 'lodges' of the Triad were distributed through the two provinces. If we could establish that these two types of organization flourished together we should be much nearer an understanding of the importance of the Triad in the south-east. [My italics.]

The main points of this passage appear to be:

(a) that south-eastern Chinese society in the nineteenth century was prevented from entering into a *guerre à outrance* by ties cross-cutting lineage conflict among 'class sections' of lineages which were absorbed in common opposition to the State;

(b) that these 'cross-cutting ties' were none other than the secret societies, because they united the poor in opposition to the State (and presumably gentry and official privilege);

(c) and that, *hypothetically*, where secret societies and lineages flourished together in equal strength, there would be a 'balance' of the inter-lineage and anti-state conflict, leading to a reduction or suspension of hostilities; in this way, secret societies and lineages were 'functionally connected'.

As the last point is the key to the hypothesis, I shall begin discussing it first. As we have established earlier, political associations of a voluntary kind were traditionally always 'substitute lineages'. Chinese secret societies may also be described as such because of the over-all functions performed by them for their members. The assumption underlying the need for a substitute lineage is that its members either lacked influence within their real lineage, or did not possess any lineage ties at all. There would be no advantage for an individual with influence in his lineage in joining a secret society because, besides the absence of any guarantees for relatively greater influence there, the lineage provided him with all the advantages of a protective society and more, for membership of a large lineage (which usually means that it was a wealthy one) was prestigious, while membership of a secret society was both illegal (or socially despised) and dangerous. Assuming that legality, prestige and orthodoxy were desired by the majority, it would be difficult to see how individuals with a stake in lineage organization would be drawn into secret society membership.

For secret societies to be 'functionally connected' with lineages, or to be linked by cross-cutting ties, there would have to exist conditions which made it possible for an individual to maintain both kinds of ties *equally*. This could only have been possible (the reasons will be discussed next) if the lineage was *also* a secret society, and vice versa. As we have seen in the previous chapter, there was only one such example—the exception that proves the rule—in nineteenth-century China, the Nien,[32] in the north.[33]

The reason for this may lie in the fact that both lineages (*corporate* lineages) and secret societies demanded *absolute* allegiance from their members. The appeal to any other kind of loyalty by a member—especially in the embattled secret societies—would be regarded at best as naiveté; at worst, betrayal. Indeed, the first thing a candidate for membership in a secret society had to recite was an oath disavowing all kinship loyalties.[34] It is interesting to note that the word for lineage, *tsu*, never occurs during the whole ritual of the initiation, only the word *chia* (family), and when it does occur it is expressed in a very rude term *ma t'ung*, translated by Matthews as 'commode', literally meaning 'horse tub'. This conspicuous verbal absence of one of the most important units of social organization may be some indication of the degree of hostility felt by the secret society towards the lineage. Thus, the parallel existence of powerful secret societies and powerful lineages in one and the same area within south China could not have been logically possible—where a lineage was strong, a secret society was bound to be more efficiently suppressed, for the militia (or the military arm of powerful local groupings) was bound to be better equipped and trained. Where a lineage was weak, the secret societies were bound to be stronger than their counterparts in areas controlled by powerful lineages. Thus, it may be more useful to view the lineage–secret society relationship as a 'see-saw' of two kinds of forces than as unwitting partners in the activity of preventing total, disruptive war (*guerre à outrance*).

Therefore, secret societies were only stopped (and only temporarily) from plunging central and south China into total chaos by the ultimate alliance of Government forces and local gentry organizations against them (a two-to-one political ratio), and by the inability of secret societies as such to produce an alternative ideology or theory of social organization to that of orthodox society. When this theoretical gap was filled by republicanism and Western liberal democratic ideas, the old society was overthrown. The fact that secret societies failed to unite *themselves* together was also a factor in the creation of a stalemate. But the stalemate could not be permanent and could not be used to explain the importance of the Triads in the south. The importance of secret societies in China lay, rather, in their destructive potentialities with regard to the Confucian society, and in their revolutionary affirmation of the development of the voluntary association in opposition to the ascriptive association of birth; in other words, in their opposition to class and lineage organizations. These points will be developed in the next chapter.

To return to secret society activities, about which we have already had some indication from an examination of the regulations of the Triad, the most obvious as well as most permanent type of activity was in the criminal spheres. But the type of crime controlled by secret societies depended of course on the particular area of operation. For example, those societies concentrated in the Yangtze basin tended to be involved mainly in smuggling Government monopolies such as tea, liquor, salt and silver, and in the transportation of illicit goods as well as simple piracy. Those concentrated on the coast dealt in international contraband, in extortions from wharf labourers, gambling, prostitution and female and child slavery.[35] Inland societies normally specialized in highway robbery, 'insurance', selling protection of goods (in transport) from secret society robbers, blackmail, sale of human manure, profitable bureaucratic subversion via *yamen* underlings, and so on.

Morgan's account of the twentieth-century Triads in Hong Kong may serve as a further revelation of the normal activities of Chinese secret societies in general:[36]

In circumstances such as then existed [after the war]; of uncertainty, shortages, and hardship, the Triad societies have always excelled themselves. Robbery, housebreaking, burglary, and petty larceny were among the more obvious of the evils indulged by them. They quickly obtained control of sections of the black market and engaged in blackmail of actual or alleged collaborators of the Japanese; *but most important of all were their activities in the vice and labour fields* . . . opium divans supplied and controlled by Triad members sprang up and became centres for a major portion of all criminal activity in the colony. In them the criminals met, planned, disposed of stolen property, and shared out their proceeds.

Prostitution had been openly encouraged by the Japanese and continued to flourish, catering not only to the normal population but also to members of the Allied Occupation Forces. In some districts whole streets were mainly devoted to this vice, and such were the profits involved that the various societies jealously guarded their particular territories and viciously resisted any infiltration by other societies or groups. Practically all the women engaged in this trade were protected by one or other of the societies and any interlopers were liable to be beaten and have their establishments destroyed.

On the labour front, Triad control was concentrated at the coolie level.

Hawkers, that vast band of kerb-side merchants selling at fractional profits, paid protection money or suffered personal injury and destruction of their stock.

Their importance in the labour field is as significant as their role in creating (albeit unintentionally) a nascent 'national

bourgeoisie'; for the only 'trade unions' which existed in traditional China were the guilds and the secret societies, the one
operating in the open but on a relatively small scale, the other
in secret on a much larger scale, specializing in illegal trade.
When Western-style trade unions were formed in the first
decades of the twentieth century, secret societies were employed
by the Nationalist Government to subvert them,[37] and finally
put them out of action in July 1927 by wholesale massacre of
the largest and most militant trade union of the time, in
Shanghai.[38]

V

Recruitment and social composition

In principle, membership of the Triads was open to all, irrespective of class, sex or age. A Triad verse sums up the system as follows:[1]

> Before the Hall of Loyalty and Justice, there
>   is no great or small
> It does not cheat the rich, nor the honoured
>   nor the poor.

Another verse confirms this:[2]

> Inside the Red Flower Pavilion [the initiation room]
>   there are both high and low.

These verses appear to signify that the distinctions which normally prevented people from different classes of society from mingling together in the outside world became irrelevant once a man was initiated into the Triad society. Here a brothel-keeper might keep company with a literatus, a murderer with a policeman. It also meant in principle that a murderer could be an officer of the local society, and the literatus merely an ordinary member, according to his length of 'service' to the society or merit, and not, as was usually the case, according to his social origins. This refusal to admit the old class loyalties in secret society recruitment was reinforced in the denial of the other most important loyalty held by the orthodox society, loyalty to the family:[3]

> Once having entered the Hung doors, there is
>   no kin, no history;
> The unjust may not enter here.

and the answer to the question, 'Who are you?' is met with the reply:[4] 'I am a stranger, without parents, brothers or sisters, therefore I entreat that you will henceforth be to me in their stead.' In the earlier verse, the only impediment to membership was a moral one, 'the unjust may not enter here'—a vague enough objection. Normally secret society ethics were directly opposed to those of the orthodox society, as the statutes of the Triads will show.[5]

The blotting out of social distinctions, and the denial of relationships which were so crucial to the organization of the wider society, had two major implications: loyalty to the secret society must be placed above all those of class and family; and that loyalty to the aims of the secret society was therefore to be the *supreme* merit, whether economic, social or military.

These implications are made more explicit in the rules against the harbouring of class prejudice and the betrayal of secrets to one's family:[6]

> Of the internal affairs of the Hung family a father must not inform his son nor a son his father, nor a brother his brother, nor may any inform their nearest relations of it; and they must not speak of the books, certificates or secret words, nor secretly, through greed of money, teach others; may those who do so die beneath ten thousand knives.

In contrast to this Triad absence of class prejudice, the Elder Brothers Societies (*Kelao hui*) made some stipulations against admitting 'dishonourable people' (*sheng-chia pu ch'ing-pai*) into their ranks. These were the barbers ('shaving disciple', *sao-ch'ing sheng*), porters ('weighing-scales disciple', *t'ien-p'ing sheng*), and actors ('spring-board disciple', *t'iao-pan sheng*). But this rule was broken by the beginning of the twentieth century, when musicians (classed together with actors in the despised category of entertainers) were admitted to membership.[7]

In practice, inevitably, strict adherence to the recruitment principle of the Triads was difficult. On the one hand, the illegality of secret association automatically converted a man into an outlaw on admission to the secret society. In normal times, therefore, applications for membership of secret societies tended to come from those who were already outlaws, or aspired to illegitimate power. In other words, it was mainly those deprived of the normal legal means of effectively pursuing or protecting their interests who were susceptible to the lure of the advantages of secret association. This would logically disqualify the ruling class as a major recruiting category, although some of the unsuccessful and disaffected members, that category of 'frustrated intelligentsia', sometimes joined secret societies:[8]

> That the leading members of these organizations [secret societies] have always been recruited from the unemployed literati there can be little question. In fact, without the co-operation of literati no Chinese society could reduce its motives to writing, construct its formulae, compile its rituals, and prepared the manifestos.

This passage somewhat exaggerates the role of the literati in secret societies, as we shall see below.[9] The employed and successful literati could of course afford to look down their noses at the secret societies and dismiss them as hives of vulgar superstition and sedition.[10] The Government attitude towards secret association is well known:[11]

> the officials are uniformly suspicious of the people. The last state of mind is well warranted by what is known of the multitudinous semi-political sects, with which the whole Empire is honeycombed. A District Magistrate will pounce upon the annual gatherings of a temperance society such as the well-known Tsai-li . . . and turn over their anticipated feast to the voracious 'wolves and tigers' of his yamen, not because it is proved that the Tsai-li society are treasonable, but because it has been officially assumed long since that they must be so. All secret societies are treasonable, and this among the rest. This generalized suspicion settles the whole question, and whenever occasion arises, the government interposes, seizes the leaders, banishes or exterminates them, and thus for the moment allays its suspicions.

Not only were secret societies persecuted, but also those officials who were seen by others to have neglected the punishment of secret society members. However ineffectual the laws might have been in practice, their psychological power of deterrent against 'respectable' people joining secret societies must have been felt, or Chinese secret societies would have developed more along modern Freemasonry lines.[12]

Moreover, membership of secret societies entailed a limitation on individual liberty which was extreme, even in Confucian terms: once a man joined a secret society, he joined for life.[13] Any change of decision on the part of a recruit during or after initiation could bring upon him death or mutilation.[14] Since the secret society existed within the tolerance of the State, it was logically less powerful than the State, and therefore demanded commensurately greater devotion and discipline from its members. Without strong loyalty and strict discipline among its members, a society could hardly hope to survive. The necessity for solidarity created a traditional (and probably justified) suspicion of literati or gentry candidates for membership among secret societies. The fact that members of the gentry (however disaffected) were linked to their class by ties of kinship, social and cultural, laid them, more than the members of any other class, open to the temptations of betrayal. Père Leboucq, commenting upon the recruitment bias of the White Lotus, writes:[15]

> In general, those responsible for recruiting distrust the literate, especially those who have received an inheritance and have a reputation for respectability. Moreover, as their object is to overthrow authority, honorary titles conferred by the Emperor, either in respect of academic examinations or military tournaments, are not such as to inspire them with confidence in those who possess such titles. They are not openly refused admission but they are scorned and distrusted. I know a talented and ambitious graduate ['bachelier' in original French is probably a translation of the lowest academic degree, the *hui-tsai*, which is often translated too as 'bachelor' degree] who, after having succeeded in obtaining his ordinary member's certificate, could not get any further, not even to become a decurion [leader of ten].

Sun Yat-sen, the future President of the Chinese Republic, confirmed this picture of secret society recruitment in his frequent dealings with the Hung league: 'The Hung-men societies operated in the profoundest secrecy, carefully avoiding all contact with officials and even the intellectuals whom they regarded as the eyes and ears of the Chinese government.'[16] It is thus not surprising to find that in an official list of captured Triad leaders of Canton (see Table V.1, p. 93) only one out of thirty-nine leaders had been a member of the gentry.[17]

The literati class as a whole, then, was weakly represented in secret society membership. An old proverb sums up the situation neatly:[18]

The mandarin draws his power from the law, the people from the secret societies.

What social groups or classes then dominated the membership of secret societies? And in what proportion? Obviously, the first question is easier to answer than the second, since precise statistics are almost completely unobtainable.

A recent study of the social composition of secret societies in the second half of the nineteenth century by Wang T'ien-chiang,[19] a Chinese historian, reveals, through the local gazettes and official documents of the time, that the bulk of secret society members was composed of six main types of social persons:

1 Dispossessed peasants (*p'o-ch'an nung-min*)
2 Dispossessed and unemployed artisans (*p'o-ch'an shih-yeh shou-kung-yeh che*)
3 Small traders (*hsiao-shang jen*)
4 Small owner-managers of various land and water transport vehicles (*ch'uan-yun-kung jen*)
5 Labourers, porters (*pan-yun kung-jen*)
6 Disbanded soldiers (*san-ping you-yung*) of the Taiping and Imperial forces.

According to Chesneaux, smugglers, sorcerers, geomancers, victims of floods, droughts and other disasters were also numerous in secret societies.[20]

The features common to all these categories of people were of course their relative poverty and mobility. They came to be known as 'the floating population' or *you-min* (literally, 'wandering people'), and as such were highly susceptible to official harassment; for example, 'vagabondage' was punishable by death,[21] while any attempt at organizing themselves into voluntary associations of a non-familial type was threatened with indiscriminate official persecutions of the type mentioned earlier on p. 88. Thus, while kinlessness was seen as a dangerous social quality in orthodox society, it was regarded quite differently within the secret society; indeed, if we can judge by the Triad rules at all, it was a positive advantage for a candidate to have no kin.

The easy mobility (geographically speaking) of these kinless persons was also the result of poverty arising from misfortune during wars or natural calamities. Kinlessness and poverty appear to be parts of a vicious circle in traditional society; one state usually led to the other, and vice versa. A number of popular sayings at the end of the Taiping rebellion illustrate the conditions of the *you-min* of the time: some had 'no fields to plough', or 'no skills with which to earn a living', while others such as disbanded soldiers had 'no family to go back to'; and even if they had, their families were often hundreds of miles away from where the soldiers found themselves after the civil war. Dispossessed merchants and artisans were forced to 'close doors, stop work'; unemployed 'scholars became wandering scribes'; impoverished 'farmers turn into wandering braves' (*you-yung*), and most of them became 'society bandits' (*hui-fei*).[22]

Obviously, the proportion of the different categories of the *you-min* to one another within the secret societies depended on the location of the latter; that is, the relative proximity of the headquarters of the secret society to a communications or transport centre (for example, the Yangtze basin); or a former battle ground (for example, that of the Taipings); or large industrializing, commercial or maritime cities (for example, the Treaty Ports), or their hinterlands. As an illustration of the influence of the geographical location of secret societies upon the social composition of their members, we may look at the Yangtze basin. The Elder Brothers Society appears to have dominated this area during the second half of the nineteenth century, originating as the 'Fourth' lodge of the Triad; and recruiting the majority of its members from among the disbanded soldiers of the Army of the Green Standard and the Hunan Army, which was raised specifically for the purpose of crushing the Taipings.[23] (The name 'Elder Brothers' (*Kelao*) is believed to have derived from the practice of the Triads in sending their senior officials, 'elder brothers', to infiltrate the Imperial armies and recruit members from among them, to form a new group of societies independent of the Triad group.)[24] But the Elder Brothers Society had also strong piratical origins; they were known formerly as 'Society of the Rovers of the Rivers and Lakes' (*Chiang Hu Hui*),[25] the euphemism for pirates. The lodge officials of the Elder Brothers were sometimes known as 'Helmsmen' (*to-pa-tzu*), or 'Anchorage Heads' (*ma-t'ou*); while the lodges were, as we have seen earlier, divided into two main sections, styled, respectively, 'Clear-water' and 'Muddy-water womb-brothers'; and their secret documents were labelled 'Book of the Sea-bottom' (*hai-ti shu*), collectively.

Besides disbanded soldiers, boatmen, water-carriers, coolies and other riverine people, the Elder Brothers also recruited, in the Szechwan basin (see p. 78), 'several thousand miners of the Pure True Mountains beyond Kuanhsien', charcoal-burners, wood-cutters, timbermen, a pawnbroker, a supervisor of schools, who became Dragon Head Grand Master, or President of the Szechwan association.[26]

The naming of Triad officials as 'grass-sandals', 'iron soles', 'night brothers', 'flower-wearers, 'fruit sellers', 'horse-leaders', etc., cannot be dismissed as merely regional secret society exotica. The most logical explanation, as well as the most obvious one, is that the particular functions of espionage, liaison and internal security were traditionally carried out by certain kinds of artisans and small traders, whose professions were peculiarly suitable to the successful performance of such tasks. Itinerant makers of grass-sandals, *yamen* runners (messengers of the magistrate's office), thieves, flower and fruit sellers, smugglers of horses, etc., were ideal conveyors of information from the streets, from the magistrate's office, from private houses, and from more distant places to the secret society branch (see verse on p. 134).

It is impossible to give an accurate estimate of the proportionate numerical strength of one social category to another. According to Wang T'ien-chang, there were approximately 'sixty to seventy per cent' of the Green Standard and Hunan Armies in the secret societies during the 1860s.[27] On the eve of the Taiping Rebellion (1850) there were approximately 585,000 men in the Green Standard Army, and in 1856 roughly 60,000 men in the Hunan Army.[28] There were, of course, also the local militias, and these, disbanded, must have further increased the bulk of the secret society membership. The Rev. F. H. James estimated that by 1896 there could have been anything from 20,000 to 200,000 members in each province. Li Chieh-jen, a participant in the 1911 revolution in Szechwan, estimated that there were altogether 15,000 Elder Brothers in the province at the time, and this figure does not include other secret society members operating there.[29]

According to a list of Canton Triad *leaders* captured by the Government in 1855,[30] each social category was represented as shown in Table v.1.

TABLE V.1

Salaried workers	10
Small traders	8
Farmers	6
Fishermen	5
Artisans	5
Mendicants	2
Smugglers	1
Minor Government employees	1
Gentry	1
Total	39

This list, of course, reflects the particular bias of the Canton 'branch', where those from the working class formed one quarter of the secret society leadership. Unfortunately, no figures are available for the size of the labour force in Canton at this period, but it must have been relatively large. Assuming that industrial and population growth did not fluctuate wildly from the middle of the nineteenth century to the first decades of the twentieth century, we may cite the figures of 1919 as a rough guide: the total labour force then stood at about 50,000 to 75,000, or 0·5 per cent of the population of China.[31] But this working population was concentrated mainly in the six major industrial regions of China, where they formed a significant section of people. These areas were: Shanghai and its hinterland

and the Yangtze estuary; Hong Kong, Canton and their hinterlands; the Hupei–Hunan region; central Shantung; north-
eastern Chihli; south of the North China Plain.[32] By 1926, the
working class population in Canton stood at 55,000 persons,[33]
while the city's total population at about the same period (1931)
stood at approximately 1,200,000 persons.[34] This means that,
like Shanghai in 1919, the working class population in Canton
formed 20 to 21 per cent, or one-fifth of the citizenry.[35]

In such a context, the predominance of workers, small artisans, traders and ex-peasants in the Triad leadership is hardly
surprising. The development of capitalism, the increasing
separation of big entrepreneurs and manufacturers from small
traders and artisans, the absence of modern trade-unions in the
cities (the working class was a relatively new phenomenon on
the Chinese scene)[36] all helped to drive the 'small man' towards
the all-embracing protection of the secret societies. The strong
presence of ex-peasants in the society leadership reflected the
impoverishment of the countryside, urbanization and the
growth of tenancy in the south.[37]

Of course, the list cited may only reflect the composition of
the leadership and may be no indication of that of the rank-
and-file; and Wang's more general picture is our only guide. In
addition to the above categories of traditional social persons,
there were of course the newly created 'petty bourgeoisie' and
lumpen elements of foreign imperialism: café-owners, bicycle-
repairers, employees of the Maritime Customs, servants in
European households and others.[38]

Such was the picture of the membership of secret societies
seen in class terms. But there were also two 'biological' categories: the women and youth, one discriminated against for
their sex, the other for their tenderness of age. The relatively
strong functional presence of these two categories in secret
societies (as compared to their weak juridical and political
presence in the 'host' society) was obviously a reflection of the
economic status of secret members on the whole.

As we already know, women in rich households normally
played an insignificant part in the political and economic life
of orthodox society; their function was to rear children and
serve as moral and aesthetic ornaments to their husband's
family and lineage. For the more conspicuous was the leisure

they enjoyed, the greater was the prestige of their spouses. Poor peasant women, however, were forced to take a greater part in the upkeep and economic survival of the household, and in this way earned for themselves a more 'equal' position in family decisions. The same also applied to the children and youth of poor families. The Catholic Père Leboucq has some colourful opinions on the role of women in secret societies of the north:[39]

> I do not know whether secret societies in Europe admit women to their orders, but in China it is the shrewish women of the White Lotus who hold the first rank in the society; it is they who stir up and encourage the faint-hearted. If the White Lotus Society ever appoints a Committee of Public Safety, a Commune . . . it is certain not to lack women firebrands.
>
> China has wanted to give woman, even the mother of a family, only the rank of slave, or at least a greatly inferior position to that of man, which is a reason why the masons of the White Lotus afford her consideration, which by appealing to her self respect and her vanity, binds her to the common cause.

Further, women were able to fulfil roles in the secret society never permitted them in orthodox society:[40]

> When a married woman is admitted to the White Lotus she must promise on oath never to tell her husband or her relations, unless she knows from a reliable source that they also are members; in such a case, *the married couple have the right to contend for precedence and authority within the household, as in the society of which they are both members;* if the wife's admission is prior to that of the husband, she is thenceforth mistress of the household so far as concerns domestic matters. [My italics.]

An explanation for this may also be that women, made independent from men by choice or circumstances, were frequently to be found in religious sects, some of which were made up of women entirely. Marjorie Topley's thesis of 1958 on women's religious associations in Singapore is worth consulting on the reasons for women's need to join religious associations.

However, despite the honourable treatment accorded to them by the secret societies, women[41]

> for all that, are given neither office nor posts but compensation for this apparent exclusion is made by sending them on missions and by giving them confidential assignments which largely console them for their lack of official status.

The Rev. D. H. Porter noted among the Shantung secret societies that 'Inasmuch as men and women meet together *upon equal terms* this has been a source of wide scandal.'[42] (My italics.) Moreover, 'If the candidate be a man he is received by a man, if a woman or girl, she is admitted by a female member.'[43] In the south too the Rev. Hutson reported:

> Women play a large part; leading women being called *nu-kuang-kun* or 'female polished sticks'. . . . Many are sworn members, and the mothers and wives are often able assistants of male members. They spy out the land, hide the booty and screen the guilty. It is a rare thing for a woman to be put to death for implication in robbery.[44]

Those mothers and wives who were not sworn members served as an outer wall of protection for the inner sworn group. Probably in order to avoid political conflict with male members, women often split off, and formed autonomous all-female associations like those of the Green Lanterns (*Ch'ing-teng-chao*), and the Blue Lanterns (*Lan-teng-chao*), both of which were associations of widows, and affiliated to the Boxers.[45] Their supreme leader, called the 'Yellow Lotus Holy Mother' (*Huang-lien Sheng-mu*), was originally a procuress accredited with tremendous magical powers.[46]

The youth generally acted as guards and scouts in the adult societies, but also had societies of their own. Referring to the Elder Brothers Societies, Hutson wrote: 'Youths have a juvenile society organized on the model of the adult Society and known as the *pang hui* or Cudgel Society. They exchange cards, make vows, conduct fights and organize petty persecutions of those whom they dislike.'[47]

Such juvenile gangs also existed among the Boxers and might be of interest to us here:[48]

The Boxers include not only boys of from 12 to 15 but girls of the same age, and they form separate branches. The branch in [sic] which the girls belong is known as the Hung Tang Chiu [*teng-chao*] or Red Lantern Shines; they carry about with them red lanterns . . . The boys' branch is called the I Wo Tuan [*I-ho-t'uan*]. [Transliterations in brackets are the Cantonese pronunciations for *teng-chao* and *I-ho-t'uan*, meaning, respectively, 'lanterns' and 'bands of justice and harmony'; the last is usually translated as 'the Boxers'.]

These youthful adherents to the secret society cause appeared to have proved themselves remarkably trustworthy and useful; the reason was that they 'receive such a careful White Lotus training that they become pillars of the Society and its most discreet and tireless agents and emissaries',[49] while the young girls, once they have been initiated into the secret society, 'are rarely unfaithful to it'.

It may be stated in conclusion that the southern secret society members (including the leaders) were composed mainly of those coming from the lower echelons of the social and economic hierarchy. Specifically, those without prospect of swift, legitimate, social upward mobility, without legal protection (owing to the heavy cost in time and financial outlay), without effective family or lineage support; and, finally, those who were regarded as socially inferior because of their female sex or tenderness of age. In brief, members (or potential members) of secret societies tended to come directly from those classes of society conspicuous for (or identifiable by) their poverty, their despised occupation and their inferior ascriptive status, which also implied an absence of effective kinship ties.

This picture of the social composition of secret societies largely held true for the nineteenth century. But after the Republican Revolution of 1911 orthodox society, though far from being destroyed, had nevertheless lost both its official sanction and its social justification. However, though the old ruling classes had been discredited, the new ones had not acquired enough self-confidence or official recognition. This social fluidity plunged all sections of society into a state of near anarchy. Secret societies, now basking in the honour of their considerable participation in the Republican Revolution, were able for once to operate openly without interference from the army or police. Consequently, those who had hitherto been deterred by the fear of the law and threat of social dishonour from making contact with secret societies, now joined them openly with a view to turning them to their own advantage. Rich landlords and the discredited literati gentry were now to be found at the head of many twentieth-century secret societies, some of whom undoubtedly contributed to the development of 'war-lord' armies, those twentieth-century successors of the 'Warring States' of pre-Ch'in, late Han and post-Dynastic times.[50] It must therefore be remembered that the reports concerning the *predominance* of powerful and wealthy landowners and gentry in secret society leadership are confined to a specific historical period, the mid-twenties and the late forties of the twentieth century.[51]

METHODS OF RECRUITMENT

Members were recruited to the Triads in a number of ways: by voluntary enlistment or persuasion, or, failing this, sometimes by blackmail, physical threat or kidnapping. Schlegel reports:[52]

New members for the Heaven and Earth Society (another name for the Triads or Hung societies) are got in several ways. If the initiated are not able to seduce the people to enter the league by an enumeration of the griefs against the Tartar sway and, in this way, excite them to throw off the dominion of the hated usurpers, recourse is had to threats. A person may find some day in his house a chit of paper, stamped with the seal of the society, by which he is ordered to betake himself, at a certain hour, to such and such a place; under menace that if he dares to disobey, or breathe a word of it to the authorities, he and his whole family will be murdered, and his house or possessions burned down. Sometimes, too, he is stopped on the road by an unknown who gives him a similar order.

Violence is also used. One of the affiliated insults a person on the road by giving him a slap on his face. Of course the insulted pursues the offender, who leads him, in this way, to an isolated spot or suburb. Here, at last, he stands at bay, but the scuffle has scarcely begun when, on a signal or whistle given by the initiated, several brethren appear who knock the man down. The victim is then thrown into a bag, and carried away to the place where lodge is held.

Those who have got the mysterious warning to the appointed rendez-vous are, in the meantime, trembling for their life, for already they doubt the fate which is awaiting them, and they know, too, that it would be useless to try to escape it; as the justice of the secret society is relentless and speedy.

So, on the appointed day, the warned goes to the place which is indicated to him. He does not, however, see anybody there, as the affiliated are hidden amongst trees or behind old walls to see that he is not followed by either policemen or soldiers.

Already the man begins to breathe more freely and thinks that all danger has passed, so that he prepares himself to return home, when all at once an affiliated appears and beckons him to follow.

Those most susceptible to recruitment by kidnapping were obviously children. The advantage of recruiting children lay in their malleability to training. Père Leboucq describes how the agents of the White Lotus society[53]

scour the countryside in search of these little conscripts and woe betide children who venture into the open country! The White Lotus recruiting party falls on this easy prey, takes its pick among those who are too young to remember the name of their village and escapes into the darkness of the night. The children kidnapped in Chantung are taken to Ho-nan, those from Ho-nan to Chan-si or to Tche-ly, not often farther: and as the Chinese police function in the most inept manner, the crimes are rarely detected.

In nineteenth-century Chinese secret societies in Singapore, the methods appear to have been on the whole much harsher, probably because the Chinese population was smaller, and fell more easily prey to secret society power. The Hikayat Abdullah reports: 'People unwilling to join they tortured, impaled, or locked up in confinement, and if still unwilling, they at once put them to death.'[54]

Within China itself, the methods of recruitment were more subtle. For example, aware that Government soldiers were in the habit of plundering villages, secret society policy was to do the opposite, and buy goods from the peasants at reasonable prices. This built up both active and passive peasant support in the countryside.[55] It is this 'social banditry' of secret associations in China which distinguishes them politically from their counterpart secret societies overseas.[56] (For the discussion on the ceremony of recruitment or initiation, see Chapter VII.)

VI

Structure and organization

(A) STRUCTURE[1]

Provincial lodges

The 'Hung League' or 'Triad Society' referred to an acephalous group of southern, secular, secret societies. Each of the affiliated societies often possessed their own names, which were changed from time to time to confuse the authorities, or to distinguish themselves from one another.

According to Triad legend, there was a headquarters which was situated in Fukien province, coordinating the 'ten' lodges scattered over the eleven or twelve provinces of central and south China. (See map 1 on p. 60 and Triad chart (Figure 2), p. 65.) There were five 'former' lodges, and five 'after' lodges, respectively founded by the 'first' five ancestors (monks) and the five 'after' ancestors ('tiger generals' or 'horse-leaders'). It is probable that the 'former' lodges were senior in status to the 'after' lodges in that they were older. For example, the Kelao Hui (Elder Brothers Society) had a 'clear-water' and 'muddy-water' group of lodges, and the custom was for the members of the latter to address those of the former as 'Uncle'. However, there does not appear to be a corresponding distinction of address among the Triads. It is not clear what 'former' and 'after' lodges entail for the members in practical terms, and one can only conclude that the terms were historical and ritual rather than structural, that is, that they merely indicate the relative 'age' of secret society activity in particular provinces. It is also possible that the 'map' of Triad lodge distribution

served, in times of rebellion, as a guide for making alliances of
an inter-provincial type, since 'former' and 'after' lodges tended
(with the exception of two provinces, Kansu and Honan) to be
geographically adjacent to one another.

There is no indication whatever as to the number of lodges
within each province, and the only document available, belonging to a Mr Lo Han,[2] which may throw light on the problem, is
ambiguous. Nevertheless, for the sake of documentation, I shall
make a literal translation of it here:

> Five men each province divide lodges
> Former After Five Lodges one [plus] nine cities
> Leaders [*Yang-yüan*] assemble to shake mountains
>   and rivers
> Leopard, tiger, tortoise and snake to crush the
>   great Ch'ing
> Yin and Yang [male and female?] harmonize . . .
>   the four-nine [members]
> Three two nine five [possibly the date of the first
>   meeting in cryptic style] assemble the brothers
> Fukien, Shensi open two, seven
> Kwangtung and Hupei [Ch'u] complete three, eight
> Kwangsi and eastern Kuei-chow convene four, nine
> Yunnan, Szechwan [Hsi Shu, formerly one of the
>   Three Kingdoms 221–263 A.D.] recruit five, ten
> Ho . . . Kiangsu [Tung Wu, another of the Three
>   Kingdoms 222–280 A.D.] . . .
> The Ten Principles [*shih-ti*] make up the certificate
>   of membership [literally 'waist purse']
> Five men take power, rebel, hide well
> To re-assemble later and reveal their true feelings.

The one consistency in the numbers appears to be the con-
secutive order of *2–7, 3–8, 4–9, 5–10*, and presumably the last
provinces mentioned (could one be Honan?) would follow with
1–6 to complete the sum of 10. Whatever may have been the
precise meaning of this enumeration, it is doubtful that they
could have applied to the number of lodges within each province. The general significance to be drawn is that the sequence
of numbers corresponds to the geographical neighbourhood of
the provinces (Fukien–Kwangtung, etc.), and this is all we can

hope to glean from this Triad verse. Nothing else exists or is available on the provincial structure of the lodges. In the next section, I shall discuss this problem in terms of organization in particular, mainly with reference to the Nien experience, in the hope of arriving at a reasonable explanation of the Triad schema.

Local lodges

Both the Triads and the Elder Brothers Society classified their membership in two distinct but complementary categories: by *grades*, and by *function*. There were normally only nine grades, the number having traditionally a Buddhist significance. For example, the Chinese pagoda was always built with nine storeys, which represented the nine *kung* or 'palaces' of the ascent to Nirvana (City of Willows), a method of ranking adopted wholesale by the Shantung secret societies described by Porter. Indeed, according to quite a different source, southern Shantung secret societies called their local village lodge a *kung*, which comprised not less than ten members. Smaller *kungs* affiliated themselves to a neighbouring *kung* with more than ten members.[3] Among the Triads, the nine grades were grouped, for the purpose of meting out punishments, into three larger grades (see Table VI.1).

Sometimes there was an extra category of membership, made up of people earlier prohibited from membership because they had surrendered to the Manchu conquerors voluntarily, and for this had been rewarded both rank and emolument. Such a group was occasionally included but not graded. These were called *ta-ma, hsiao-ma, ta-yao, hsiao-yao, ch'i-p'ai, pa-p'ai*, meaning literally Big-small, Small-small, Big-bit, Small-bit, Seven-card, Eight-card, respectively.[4] Like their counterparts in the Elder Brothers Society, this category of people had been prohibited from joining the secret societies (for their 'unpatriotic' behaviour), but as time went on, were gradually allowed to enter the Triads and even achieve promotion into the *wu-t'ang* (literally, 'five halls') or ordinary membership if they proved themselves suitable. Such a category of membership may be described in more familiar terms as 'associate' as opposed to 'full' membership, and undoubtedly formed, together with the uninitiated families,[5] an outer protective 'wall' to the initiated members of the secret society.

TABLE VI. I

1	*Lao-ta-ko*	Big Brother		
2	*Lao Erh*	Second Elder	I	*Lao-ta-ko*, or
3	*Lao San*	Third Elder		*Shang-san*, Top Three
4	*Lao Ssu**	Fourth Elder		
5	*Lao Wu*	Fifth Elder	II	*Erh Ko*, Second Elder
6	*Lao Liu*	Sixth Elder		Brothers or
				Chung-san, Middle Three
7	*Lao Ch'i†*	Seventh Elder		
8	*Lao Pa*	Eighth Elder	III	*San Ti*, Third Younger
9	*Ta-chiu,*	Ordinary Members		Brothers or
	Hsiao-chiu	Big Nine,		*Hsiah-san*, Lower Three
		Small Nine		

* A taboo grade, normally not filled by officers—'four' or *ssu* being the homonym for 'death'.
† Also a taboo grade, 'seven' being the rank of the treacherous monk who had betrayed the founders of the Triads to the Imperial soldiery.

This breaking up of the nine grades into three may suggest at first glance that the Triads had adopted a 'cellular' system of organization. Maurice Duverger has the hypothesis that clandestinity forces all such groups to adopt the same kind of structure:[6]

> What characterizes this type of organization is that it is broken up into basic groups that are as small as possible (three to five men, usually), and that there is rigid separation between these basic groups. At every level only the leader of each group is in contact with the level above. In this way, leakages are reduced to a minimum: if one member of the organization is arrested and tortured, he can only denounce very few people; this is true also if the police introduce spies into the movement.

However, this system does not appear to have been adopted by Chinese secret societies, and there is also evidence against such a theory. For example, the new recruits did not only have to produce a birth certificate (*keng-t'ieh*) on admission, but they also had to have their names 'given to the hearing of all the brethren'.[7] Election of officers was by 'public vote' (*kung-chü*), and the names of all the new officers were pasted up in the meeting hall (*t'ang*) of the local lodge (*fang*) for 'public' scrutiny.[8] Secret society operations, unlike those of the French Resistance movement, had as their basic unit 10 to 100 men,[9] and many larger-scale activities, such as riots and rebellions, mobilized several thousands of men.[10] Within a particular secret society at least the members knew each other; members of other lodges or societies could only identify them by their position in the hierarchy, conveyed by secret hand and body signs or cryptic phrases. It is doubtful, incidentally, that even within a particular society the members remember the names of all their comrades all of the time, particularly in groups numbering several thousand members. The Vanguard and the Incense Master (sometimes called the 'Keeper of the Books' in northern religious sects) guarded the register of names as well as the Book of the Sea-bed (*Hai-ti Shu*), which consisted of the secret literature of the Elder Brothers Society. The Triad name for this is 'Clothes' (*shan*), or the secret language of the societies. It is not known whether ordinary members had unrestricted access to society registers and other documents.

The classification of members by *function* was somewhat variable in relation to the grades. In some accounts, the President, in other accounts the Incense Master, was given Grade I; while in others yet again, the latter was given only Grade II; similarly, the Vanguard could fill grade IV or V, while the Punishments Officer or Red Cudgel, could be given either grade V or VI. However, these divergencies are relatively minor, and they may be explained by the particular orientation or interests of the particular society; whether it was, for example, more 'civilian' (*wen*) or 'military' (*wu*) in emphasis, in other words, whether the members were more criminally or rebelliously inclined.

The model for the functional hierarchy (see Table VI.2) will be that given by Gustave Schlegel, and variations on this model will be cited in the later discussion of the functions assigned to the various officers of the Triads:

TABLE VI.2

I *Ta-ko* or *Hsiang-chu*—President (literally, Big Elder Brother or Incense Master)

II *Erh-ko*—vice-Presidents (2) (Second Elder Brother)

III *Hsien-sheng*—Master (a title used for addressing a teacher, or for ordinary polite address like 'Mister')

IV *Hsien-feng*—Vanguard (2)

V *Hung-kun*—Fiscal (Red Cudgel)

VI *I-shih*—Councillors (13) including a treasurer, a receiver and his deputy (*kuei-shih, shou-kuei*)

VII *Ts'ao-hsieh, Wan-ti, T'ieh-pan, T'ou-shang-yu-hua-che*—Agents, Messengers (literally, Grass Sandals, Night Brothers, Iron Planks, Those-with-flowers-on-their-heads, respectively)

VIII *Tai-ma*—Recruitment Agents (Horse-leaders)

IX *Ssu-ta*—Summoners (The Big Four)

For convenience of exposition, I shall group the officers along the Triad divisions of three groups of three.

'The Top Three' (*Shang-san, Lao-ta-ko*) The first three grades were normally composed of the President, vice-Presidents, Incense Master, and Master (sometimes translated as Instructor). The President and his deputies had a number of other names. They were *Lao-ta-ko*, Dragon Head (*Lung-t'ou*) (normally used by the Elder Brothers Society), Great Superintendent (*Ta Tsung-li*),[11] and Commander-in-Chief (*Cheng-chui*).[12] In Canton and Hong Kong, he was sometimes known as Mountain Chief (*Shan-Chu*)[13] and even as Red Cudgel (*Hung-kun*), because the President was sometimes chosen from among the 'fighter officials', or, as Schlegel has it, 'fiscals', of whom there must have been more than one, especially when the society had several thousand members. Sometimes, the President was also the Incense Master, as Schlegel shows. It is possible that during an operation when two lodges cooperated the President of the stronger lodge became the Grand Master of both lodges, hence the title Chief Dragon Head (*Cheng Lung-t'ou*) and Deputy Dragon Head (*Fu Lung-t'ou*).[14] The functions of the President appear to have consisted of coordination of activities within the *fang* (lodge) or *t'ang* (hall or local branch), as well as presiding over all general meetings of the Council,

including trials of members and initiations, and making the final decisions on general policy. The crucial role of the President as the focal symbol of secret loyalty cannot be overestimated; the responsibility of success or failure must ultimately lie with him, as we can see in the practice among the Boxers of replacing magically dubious leaders by others thought to have greater efficacy.[15] Coulet, in his discussion of Vietnamese secret societies (modelled on the Chinese), stressed the importance of *personal* loyalty to the leader,[16] but this does not mean that the leaders did not have to be worthy of such loyalty.

The vice-Presidents appear to have acted in the capacity of advisers and deputies. In one society they were called the *Sheng-hsien*, or literally, 'Wise Worthies', and had the function of *Ts'an-chün*, or 'Military Counsellor'.[17] This counsellor normally shared Grade II with the temporary Incense Master, temporary in that he appeared only during initiations and not at any other time.[18] Such temporary Incense Masters were a particular feature of overseas Chinese secret societies, as W. L. Blythe noted of the Malayan Chinese societies.[19] The reason for this was undoubtedly the shortage of men qualified to carry out the immensely elaborate 'theatricals' (Triad cant for rituals in general) or ritual ceremonies of Triad initiations. If the Malayan practice is any indication, then there were itinerant professional Incense Masters in China too, travelling from one society to another conducting initiation ceremonies for a fee. Thus if a society could retain an Incense Master permanently, he stood a good chance of being made President, as in the case of the Triad society described by Schlegel. Indeed, in some cases, the Incense Master was nicknamed 'Mother' (*ama*), and the initiates (in the Cantonese lodges) had to crawl between the legs of this officer as a symbol of their rebirth in the initiation ceremony.[20] The ritual importance of the Incense Master made him ideally suited to the role of supreme leader of a lodge.

The Master (*Hsien-sheng*) has often been confused with the Incense Master (*Hsiang-chu*), and the reasons may be found in the fact that the latter could, in some societies, be chosen from among the former, also known as White Fan (*Pai-shan*) or White Paper Fan (*Pai-chi-shan*) in Canton. Such was indeed the case with Morgan's Triads in Hong Kong.[21] Thus, it is highly probable that Masters deputized for Incense Masters when the latter were indisposed or absent, which meant that the former were trained to some extent, if not completely, by the latter in the function of conducting initiation ceremonies. Stanton's translations of *Hsien-sheng* by 'Instructor' may be significant also, in that it was also the Master's responsibility to instruct other members in the secret culture of the society. Among the twentieth-century Triads of Hong Kong, the Master was the 'planner' and general administrator of the society, a kind of all-purpose bureaucrat.[22]

'*The Middle Three*' (*Chung-san, Erh-ko*)   These grades refer of course to the Vanguard(s)—individuals—or Introducers (*Hsien-feng*), the Red Cudgel or Fighter Official (*Hung-kun*), and the Councillors, comprising among others the Treasurer (*Kuei-shih*), Receiver (*Shou-kuei*) and Deputy Receiver (*Tai Shou-kuei*).

The *Hsien-feng*, also known as Red Flag (*Hung-ch'i*), or in Canton, *Ti-t'ou* (Local Head)[23] was the functionary who co-operated most closely with the Incense Master during the initiation ceremony; for he was normally the officer who provided, on behalf of the candidate, the appropriate ritual responses to the questions of the Incense Master. His responsibilities outside the initiation hall were investigating potential recruits, expanding the societies, and sometimes the only officer (apart from the Incense Master or President) with the right to open branch lodges without having to consult these first.[24] His duties are thus reminiscent of those of the Section Chiefs (*Fa-shih*) of the northern secret sects—namely the White Lotus Societies—who made twice-yearly tours investigating potential recruits and making propaganda for their societies.[25] Probably there were more than two Vanguards within a large lodge, especially if one Vanguard had to be absent for part of the year, and another became indisposed. In one account, it is reported that the Red Flag shared some of his more exalted duties with the New Deputy (*Hsin-fu*), described as a secret society equivalent of an Imperial Censor (see p. 16) or the Provincial Governor (*Hsün-fu*) (see p. 21), who also made circuits of inspection in the manner of his orthodox counterparts. The post of the New Deputy was given the Grade III and that of the Red Flag, Grade V, the fourth grade having become 'obsolete', indicating that it was tabooed.[26]

The Red Cudgel (*Hung-kun*), or Blue Flag (*Lan-ch'i*) was undoubtedly the 'strong-arm man' of the Triads, and explicitly concerned with physical punishments and military operations.[27] Sometimes, the responsibility for punishments was delegated to a specialist, the *Tsui-chu*, who occupied Grade VII, though Red Cudgel occupied normally Grade V. But as Grade VII was once again 'obsolete', or explicitly tabooed,[28] the responsibility for punishments was normally given to the Red Cudgel or Blue Flag alone. The number of Red Cudgels within one society again would be determined by the size of the society or its immediate objectives. The Red Cudgel's main military duties consisted in organizing fighting units—of 10, 50 or 100 men each—and in training them in the arts of warfare, such as how to fight with irons, chains, swords, clubs and bare fists.[29] A ritual verse describes the 'eighteen military arts' as follows:[30]

> I am skilled in the use of the sword and chain-bullet;
> I handle the lance as well as Tse-lung;
> My cudgelling is not different from that of Hui-ying;
> And my single club is better than [the two of]
> Wei-chi-kung.

Besides Schlegel and a nineteenth-century journalist called Frederick Boyle, no writer specifically mentions the existence of a council.[31] According to Boyle, eight of the thirteen councillors formed a quorum. The number of thirteen, like eight, was symbolic: it represented the 'thirteen' Ming provinces of China which had been expanded to eighteen under the Manchus. The number 'eight' may refer to the Eight Trigrams, according to which some northern secret societies were organized.[32]

It is obvious that these Councillors dealt with problems beyond the individual competence of the functionaries, those directly involving all members of the society.[33] They could also have acted as the tribunal before which offenders against Triad laws were tried.[34] In other accounts, it appears that all the members have to be present in cases of trials of members,[35] and not only the leadership. The Triad described by T'ao Ch'eng-chang made no mention of a council, but did refer to a Treasurer cum Store-keeper (literally, Comptroller of Finance and

Provisions), who occupied the 'obsolete' grade IV, which function was taken over by the New Deputy.[36]

'*The Lower Three*' (*Hsiah-san, San-ti*)   These grades include of course the Agents, Messengers, Recruitment Agents and Summoners to meetings. Schlegel's account does not grade ordinary members; elsewhere, they occupied the ninth grade.

The Thirty-third Oath of the Thirty-six Oaths of the Triad Societies stipulates that: 'These men are destined to go about everywhere, and they live in all places. If there are public affairs (that is, matters concerning all the members of the society), they are sent to transmit the reports.'[37] These agents, whether working for members privately for a fee, or for the society, were entitled at all times to claim travelling expenses and board and lodging.[38] In times of rebellion they worked as liaison officers between societies or lodges, making or breaking alliances. Their crucial role of a 'secret society within a secret society', as well as their subversive activities in Government agencies, could have determined the survival or extinction of their particular association (see p. 92).

The Summoners ('horse-leaders', horse = member) performed the physical function of guiding a candidate (or kidnapping him, as the case may be) to the secret place of initiation, as well as that of informing members of future meetings.

It is not clear what the role of the 'flower' officials was; it is possible that they were ritual menials, or that they were, like the 'Double Flower' officials described by Morgan, officials of the middle and lower grades honoured under the 'numerical system'[39] for special ability and/or length of service to the society.[40]

Election of officers

Before discussing the organization of the Triads, it seems appropriate to give first an account of the principles of election and promotion of officers as well as some attempt to understand how they worked in practice.

As Commandant Favre reported, election of officers was initially done on the basis of age or seniority, and this is borne out in Hirayama Amane's version of the Triad myth of origin.[41]

But as the society developed and acquired knowledge of its members, choice of officers came to be made on the basis of merit and length of membership.[42] It is stated in the Oaths that:[43]

> After entering Hung doors, on the completion of ten months, you are eligible for a minor office and after two years for the office of Vanguard. Those who are loyal in bringing in members must not accept bribes. May thunder from all points annihilate those who disobey this injunction.

The required term of membership required for qualification to office appears to vary from account to account: from ten months (Stanton) to one year (Schlegel), to three years (Morgan). Morgan adds, however, that the three-year rule was seldom put into practice, and that by 1960 it was not unknown for members to be both admitted and promoted at the same ceremony. The deviation from the rules depended, no doubt, on the conditions of the time (war or peace), type of office sought, and the type of candidate put forward. A well-known militia leader who had recently joined a secret society might be recommended for immediate promotion to a high post (say, the Vanguard or Red Cudgel), particularly if the society was in revolt. A relatively unknown member might have had to wait much longer for recognition.

According to both Schlegel and Stanton, the election of officers was done publicly (*kung-chü*); that is, thrown open to all members' votes. Figure 3 shows an election notice in Chinese and English translation. There appears to be no specific law governing the method of nomination of candidates for office; and the only attempt to do so applied to the nomination of the Vanguard only, who was usually recommended by the Incense Master.[44] From this clue and Morgan's account, we may conclude that nominations were generally made by senior officers, and then *approved* by the rest of the members. Figure 4 shows a certificate of appointment to the Office of the Grass Shoe. In order to acquire a sponsor, the candidate for office probably had to pay a high fee as well as to provide a worthy feast for all the members, a practice much favoured in the twentieth-century Hong Kong societies.[45] The 'vote' or 'public' election

天運　年義與公司欲立上長　月　日錄照

大哥

二哥

先生

先鋒

紅棍

議事　　櫃匙　　收櫃　　代收櫃

草鞋

茲本公司內眾兄弟欲立諸人為上長今

議定着理宜聲明。倘諸上人若有違法不

公平不宜立為上長祈諸會弟務必出頭

阻止。方無後患而後可以改換別人。　是為告白

TRANSLATION

List of the Chiefs whom the I-hing Society wishes to elect for the year (the year expressed by the cyclical term) of the Heavenly motions, the　　month, the　　day.

President (the member) X　Vice-presidents (the members) X X
Master (the member) X　Introducers (the members) X X
Fiscal (the member) X　Counsellors (the members) X X
Treasurer (the member) X　Receiver (the member) X
Acting receiver (the member) X　Agents (the members) X X

The brotherhood of our society having now decided upon appointing the above-mentioned men as superiors and chiefs, it is right that we make their names public.

If there are amongst those men some who offend the law or act unjustly, being unworthy of the rank conferred upon them, we pray all the brethren of the society, each in particular, to come forward and prevent later troubles. They can then be changed and other men be appointed.

FIGURE 3　*Election notice*

許　合　乙
襄　眾　巳
兄　兄　年
為　弟　九
草　公　月
鞋　舉　廿
之　　　日
職
任
理
公
司
政
事
務
要

公
行
正
直
不
得
私
心
妄
為
付
帖
存
憑

義
興
公
司

花
紅
帖

FIGURE 4　*Certificate of appointment to the Office of the Grass Shoe* was therefore probably nothing more than a 'public' confirmation of a *fait accompli*. The only influence the ordinary members could wield on such occasions would be through verbal objection supported by evidence that the candidate was ineligible. Such a situation is illustrated in *A Chinese Testament* by T'an Shih-hua:[46]

> one of those seated around the table got up. He spoke of someone who wanted to be admitted into the membership of Golao. He vouched for him as for himself. He expressed a hope that the da-ge would support his request before the assembly. But before father [of the author] had a chance to say a word, a short, fat man rose in front of the bespectacled speaker. He looked like a merchant.
>
> 'He must not be admitted! . . . Only new born babies do not know his wife fools around with actors who often come to his house to give performances while he is away on his business trips.
>
> 'Everybody warned him—get a divorce, get a divorce, send your wife to her parents. But he is so weak he goes on keeping this two-legged disgrace in the house. He is made of wax, and a member of Go-Lao should be cast in iron . . . I am against his admission.'

The northern societies' method, according to Père Leboucq, of officer election (in Ningching, Shantung) was based on competitive fasting, a ritual carried out every three years.[47] Other northern societies, like the Boxers, determined a candidate's suitability according to the degree of his faithful observance of the rules, sincerity in worship and purity in life:[48]

> this merit is known by the Ming Yen [Clairvoyant] who watches their ascent through the 'Nine Heavens' until they enter the 'Nine Palaces' of the blessed. All the Shih [Teachers] must have passed the lower and middle grades of progress before aspiring to the rank of a leader. All aspirants to the position must be known by their fellows as virtuous, and the Ming Yen must inquire of the spirit as to his fitness for office.

Those with money but without qualifications among the Elder Brothers Society were permitted to buy honorary offices called *hsien-pai*, meaning 'Leisure grade' or *mao-ting*, 'Cap-top',[49] which distinguished them from the real functionaries, and prevented the disabling affects of having incompetents in office. It is possible that the Triads also had such sinecures, but there is no record of them.

The usurpation of power was severely sanctioned; according to the Ten Prohibitions on Appointing Meetings,[50] the usurpation of the Incense Master's office would cost the culprit either one ear and 108 strokes, or his life. An Incense Master who held meetings without informing members by circular would be guilty of holding clandestine assemblies and would be punished by death.[51] (The discussion of the role of the council, where found, in the judicial processes of the secret society will be found on p. 124 and p. 149ff.)

From the above account of the hierarchies of functionaries, we have obtained some idea of the degree of variation to be found in the Triads and Kelao societies in the nineteenth century. It is clear that the differences arose out of organizational requirements of particular societies situated temporarily in a particular place at a particular time; while the basic similarities of structure were dictated by the societies' necessarily nomadic style of existence and by their essential need for secrecy and disguise.

The *mobility* of Chinese secret societies organizationally opposed them to the assumption of *permanence and immobility* which underlie orthodox social and political organization. Like Simmel's cases, they made themselves into a 'counter-image' of the official world,[52] though they were nevertheless bound by it. It was thus inevitable that certain orthodox relationships were taken over by the secret society and used as the structure of their solidarity. For example, the symbolic sibling relationship, the magical evocation of 'family' solidarity, memorialism,[53] the 'incest' taboo, and even certain types of punishment used against wrongdoers.

Another difference lay in the relatively flexible ordering of membership rank, and the equality of the members before their officials. This contrasts strikingly with the rigidly, codified, relentless hierarchization of the central Government and orthodox society. More specifically, there was no invariable precedence of the civilian over the military and economic functionaries in the secret society. Ranking here depended on the immediate 'civilian' (i.e. criminal) or 'military' (rebellious) objectives, and not on any pre-determined law of precedence.

Moreover, functionaries in the State were chosen from above, either by direct Imperial appointment or via the Examination System, over which the Imperial bureaucrats presided.[54] The people were traditionally spectators, not participants in the power game, and their only opportunity for political action came in the somewhat doubtful 'right' to rebel against tyrants.[55] In secret societies the political participation of the rank-and-file members was fundamental to their philosophy; and the final responsibility for the choice of leaders lay with the *whole* body of members, and not merely with the powerful men at the top.[56]

The drawback to a democratic method of election lay in the increased opportunities for betrayal to the police, owing to the exposure of the members' identities. But this vulnerability was reduced by three factors: first, the severe sanctions against betrayal;[57] second, the individual vulnerability of the betrayer living in constant fear of exposure with no guarantee of police protection should his treachery be discovered; third, the very many social, economic and political ties shared by members of secret societies, ties which could not be regained once they forfeited the right to common trust; nor could these bonds be replaced for the majority of the members through orthodox channels, since it was the very absence of such means which drove them to join secret societies in the first place. Even if they did find their orthodox connections, they could not go back on their oath of membership (which was for life) without risking the avenging wrath of the betrayed secret society.

The formal simplicity of southern secret society hierarchies also differentiated them from those of the State. There appears to have been only one hierarchy in each society or lodge, combining within its competence the two-and-a-half of the State— the civil, military and censorial organs. However, like the central administration, secret societies had usually nine grades. But the Government grading system applied only to the bureaucracy (which includes the military and censorial hierarchies), while secret societies included everybody in the system, and not merely the leadership. While the orthodoxy categorized and graded the rest of society according to their *ascriptive* qualities, and economic status, secret societies graded their members according to their ability and length of service to the association, and this sometimes even included the acceptance of members made unacceptable by their voluntary submission to foreign conquest.[58]

The adaptability of the leadership to the rank and file also contrasts strikingly with the rigid, immovable machinery of the State bureaucracy in its contacts, or lack of them, with the people. The constant mobility required of secret societies under Government repression ensured that no secret society leadership could entrench itself permanently in one place and grow fat on inaction.

The most dramatic contrast between State and secret society structure was the recognition by the latter of the fundamental equality of all members within it. While relationships in the State were predicated upon that of father and son, those of the secret societies were predicated upon that of brothers.

This ideal of brotherhood tended to diminish the 'naturalness' of one man's intrinsic superiority over another, making them morally, if not politically equal. In the societies the political 'seniority' of certain members was *achieved*, and not given, as it was within the kinship system, and as it was to a large extent within the State—that is, to the extent the Examination System served as an objective gauge of ability.[59] Usually, the Emperor and his officials were assumed to be morally superior just as the people were assumed to be inferior until they were proved otherwise.

The fictive bond of brotherhood did, of course, also give rise to other symbolic bonds; for example, the bond of 'sisters' (female members), or 'sisters-in-law' (wives of fellow members), 'nieces' (daughters of fellow members), 'nephews' (sons of fellow members) and 'uncles', and so on, creating a kind of surrogate 'extended family', and conforming to the incest taboos practised in the orthodox society within the prohibited degrees.[60] Although one of the Thirty-six Oaths exhorted members to 'honour' their biological parents, there was no mention of grandparents anywhere. The lineage itself was only acknowledged once in secret Triad documents and that, as we already know, only in the most disrespectful terms (see p. 82). The explicit emphasis on the 'fraternal' bond inevitably weakened the genuine kinship ties contracted outside the secret society; for the primary, absolute loyalty was to the 'brotherhood' and nothing else, and both the Oaths and the Regulations testify to this.[61]

Though the emphasis in secret society relationships was on equality, this did not rule out an intense loyalty to one's *chosen* leaders. The ideology of equality would tend, if anything, to reinforce the authority of the leadership, since it was elected by the choice of all the members, and not, as in the State, the sole and unquestioned choice of the 'Son of Heaven' and His ministers. This sharing out of political responsibility undoubtedly strengthened the ties arising out of common interest and common weaknesses. This participation in the political process, and the opportunity to exercise choice in the judicial sphere must have contrasted dramatically with his near total impotence as an individual without kinship or economic support in the 'outside' world. The stubborn resistance of secret society members to police torture[62] testified to the reality of the secret association as a powerful and incalculable force in nineteenth-century China.

(B) ORGANIZATION

So far we have only discussed the *principles* of organization (the structure) and not the organization itself. This part of the discussion has its obvious drawbacks, there being no precise figures or other detailed information available. However, it is possible to solve the more general problem by the use of comparative material in a careful relating of 'northern' organizational experience (on which we are more precisely informed) to southern structural indications.

This method would require approaching the subject from a different point of departure. Instead of assuming that secret societies started off with a formal structure as I did in the first part of this chapter, I shall now assume that there was none to begin with. In this way we may be able to follow more accurately the process of formation of a southern secret society and its development up to the point when formalization was required.

This approach was suggested to me not only by Favre's article on the coolie societies formed in Tientsin, but also by the excellently documented study of the Nien rebels by Chiang Siang-tseh, who traces the changes in organization as the Nien developed from single or federated bands into a powerful movement under the leadership of one individual. The Nien experience will serve as the basis for our discussion as to the possibilities it may have in illuminating the Triads' organizational methods shown rather elliptically in their documents and ritual.

The most comprehensive form of the organization of a secret society is obviously the military; for it mobilized all the able-bodied members of the association, and not only the specialized agencies required for criminal enterprises.

The justification for choosing the Nien experience as a basis of secret society organization in the south is that the picture presented by the Nien in its final stages of development strikingly resembled the Triad symbolic chart (Figure 2). That the Nien was divided into 'five' divisions under 'five banners' and 'five generals' is strongly reminiscent of the Triad chart, and suggests a traditional cross-fertilization of organizational ideas between northern and southern secret societies.[63] Logically, moreover, secret society organization is limited by that of the 'host' society, as well as by the fund of existing heterodox ideas of organization. This means that unless northern Chinese orthodox institutions and culture were *qualitatively* different from those in the south, there would not be any significant differences in their respective forms of heterodox organization. The homogeneity of Chinese institutions and culture is assumed here, while the differences are seen as quantitative and aesthetic rather than as qualitative and fundamental.

Initially the Nien were roving bands of robbers, smugglers and so on who had come together spontaneously for common action. Later, they adopted the 'southern' system of the *t'ang-chu* ('Chief or host of the Hall or Lodge'), who, having gathered about him a band of men, proceeded to carry out the normal criminal and officially subversive activities in his local or surrounding area.[64] These bands came to be known generically as *nien*, meaning a 'twist' or a 'knot'. Two features which were characteristic of the Nien were, first, their great mobility, and second, their elasticity of size—one *nien* might comprise anything from three to a hundred to several thousands of men.[65]

Next, the various bands would combine into a single larger unit under a 'Nien Head' (*nien shou*), after having made sacrifice to a flag or banner (*ch'i*). This was apparently a common practice in the initial stage of a rebellion.[66] 'Sacrifice to a flag implies not only that the disunited and disorganized Nien had rallied under one standard, but that they were pledged to a greater enterprise—rebellion; that is, they bade farewell to such petty offenses as drinking, gambling, smuggling, local fighting, kidnapping, and robbing.'[67]

This system, however, did not function as well as the participants had hoped as they suffered severe reverses at the hands of the local peasant militia led by the gentry. But by 1856, four years later, the Nien had begun in earnest to build up a more systematic organization called the 'banner system', imitating the practices of the other secret 'religious bandits' of Shantung province. (The Nien base was north of the Huai tributary of the Yellow River.) The system of the northern religious secret sects was (with the exception of the Eight Trigrams[68]) the division of the forces into five major sections under five banners—called the five 'larger' banners—according to the 'Five Elements' and their 'five' accessory colours, or to the 'Five Directions' (centre, north, south, east, west), or to the 'Ten Heavenly Stems', which could be correlated to the Five Elements in pairs.[69]

Each 'larger banner' was in turn divided into five 'smaller banners', each of which assembled two to four thousand men, so that one 'larger banner's' maximum size was twenty-thousand strong.[70] In line with the innovation, the *nien* units were called *ch'i* or 'banners'. The five major banners were each given a colour and a direction: yellow-centre, black-north, red-south, blue-east, white-west; the five minor banners were similarly coloured, and then bordered on the four sides of the square or rhomb with the colours of the remaining four colours. When the Nien forces were increased, new and more complicated colour flags were introduced including a new variety of shapes.[71]

The paramount chief of all the banners was given the title of 'Lord of the Sworn [Oath or] Alliance' (*meng-chu.*) The remaining four chiefs were called the 'Four Banner Lords' (*ch'i-chu*), or 'Vice-Banner Lords' (*fu-ch'i-chu*). Leaders of the minor banners were called 'Nien Heads' (*nien-t'ou*). From the chart given by Chiang[72] the five major banner chiefs were called 'Duke', 'Marquis', 'Earl', 'Viscount' and 'Baron', just as in the Triads' symbolic chart.

The concrete bases of Nien power were the village 'earth walls' (*yü* or *chai*) which served as extremely effective protection against enemy troops.[73] Several such earth-wall villages would band together, some fighting in the vanguard, some in the rear and some raiding the lines of communications and provisions of the enemy. The Boxers made a distinction between their 'town' and 'country' bases, known respectively as *t'an* and *t'uan*, the former probably representing urban wards as well as towns in large cities.[74] The Shantung religious sects called their basic units (usually representing a town or village) 'palaces' or 'mansions' (*kung*) which coalesced along Nien lines.[75]

This summary of Nien and northern methods of organization makes the Triad symbolic chart (Figure 2) more comprehensible. This chart obviously served less as a historical record of Triad organizational development, than as a guide for future action; that is, concerted action. The only difference between the northern and southern charts lay in the Triad correlation of 'former' and 'after' lodges with provinces. Although both 'former' and 'after' lodges shared one flag and the same cosmological symbols, they did not share the same provinces but those adjacent to one another, with one exception, the provinces of Fukien and Kansu. This 'provincial' consideration may be less confusing than it may first appear. We have to remember that the Nien were active within one province only, so the 'directions' in their chart were confined to that province. The Triad chart was intended to apply to the whole of central and south China, including at least eleven provinces. This grandiose view is, in practical terms, suspect simply because even at the height of Triad collaboration (during the republican revolution of 1911–12) the Triads were able to muster together only the societies in Canton and some in Hong Kong. In terms of ideology, however, this panoramic view is consistent with the Triad political aims of freeing China from its alien rulers and corruption and restoring the country to its pristine glory and virtue. In other words, the Triads entertained ambitions to take over, not just one province, but the whole of central and south

China; and wished to be prepared when the occasion arose.

The pattern of local and intra-provincial coalition undoubtedly followed that of the Nien: first, spontaneous federation, then its systematization. In this pattern may be detected two stages: initially there were weaker bands which attached themselves to a stronger band, which, grown larger and more powerful, would then gather around itself a constellation of satellites, each with their own local command, but subject to the over-all supervision of the hegemon in more ambitious enterprises. It is almost inevitable that elements of State military organization find their way into Triad organization; for example, the echo of the 'Five Chief Military Commissions' and the 'Banner'[76] system may be heard amidst the roar of 'Tigers', 'Dragons', etc., on the ritual battlefield. The basic unit, however, appears to have been influenced by that of the militia, which consisted of ten to a hundred men per unit.[77]

Coalition was followed by dispersal, especially on defeat. This is reminiscent of guerilla tactics—dispersing before a strong advancing enemy, and reassembling to attack when the enemy's strength is worn out. The direct parallel may be seen in the 'disappearance' of secret societies during periods of strong central Government, and their 'reappearance' during those of dynastic decline.

After dispersal, secret societies continued their management of crime (protection, racketeering, robbery with or without violence, prostitution, smuggling, etc.) and its organized expansion. Such activities demanded a certain division of labour, and the society, into 'departments', over each of which a functionary presided. The ritual department, for example, was presided over by the Incense Master, the educational by the Instructor, the intelligence and liaison department by the Grass Sandals and Iron Planks, the military by the Red Cudgel, and so on. Often these departments overlapped in their functions; or subordinated themselves to one depending on the priorities of the moment. For example, a large initiation ceremony (which sometimes initiated up to fifty people) would require meticulous preparation on the part of all. Not only would a small army of menials be necessary, but there must be eight trusted guards at four of the entrances,[78] many more at points leading to the initiation hall (which might be anywhere at a given time) and messengers running back and forth assembling and surveying new and old members for the meeting. Any mis-timing or mistakes regarding identities, roles, ritual speeches would have a serious psychological effect on the new members while loss of secret documents and objects of the lodge could bring on police raids and wholesale arrests and executions. Indeed, the loss of such by members was punishable by death according to Triad laws.[79]

Similarly, with the preparations for a large-scale raiding party, all the other departments would be subject to its priorities; and so on.

The 'education' department concerned itself mainly with the teaching of secret language and ritual culture as well as the moral and practical rules of the society. The importance of this department can be understood when it is realized that a mastery of the secret language and regulations could mean the difference between life and death. Hence the need for a 'wise and discerning' teacher, that is, the Master or White Fan Instructor, as exhorted in an election rule. All the literate members had a role to play here, not only in assisting the Master in the coaching of members, but also in acting as his deputies in his absence. Besides acting in a directly educational capacity, members of this department probably occupied themselves with the printing of notices, circulars, manuals, membership tickets, the drawing up of documents, as well as the invention of new cryptograms if and when necessary.

The intelligence department was responsible for internal control and external liaison. The agents for this department were sometimes called 'wind-follower' (*hsun feng*). One of the main duties in internal control was the thorough investigation of the background and character of the new recruits:[80]

> If a brother, at the times that a lodge is held, wishes to introduce a new member to be affiliated, he ought to inform himself well. If this man (the new member) has been formerly the cause that a brother . . . has lost his life, then he himself, and the person who has introduced him, will both be slain.

The sponsors of new candidates for membership would undoubtedly have gone to the agents for assistance, since they had the best facilities and experience at their disposal for such investigations. The law against the accidental or deliberate admission of the enemy (the police) into Triad meetings is very clear:[81]

> When a fair [*hsü* is Triad cant for secret meetings] is held, all persons must be carefully examined, so that no serpents mix themselves with the dragons.
>
> He who, knowing it, does not give notice of it, shall be punished with 108 blows. He who has brought clandestinely policemen within the precincts, in order to show them the secrets, shall be killed together with the spy or spies.

The other functions include the infiltration of Government departments, in particular, the local *yamen* or magistrature, by such means as bribing or recruiting the clerks and prison warders; infiltrating rival societies; and keeping systematic contact with the underworld. The success of these undertakings depended obviously on thorough training and sophisticated methods of disguise. Agents frequently travelled as doctors, hawkers, vendors of food and other itinerant professionals; they also got themselves employed as *yamen* underlings, bodyguards and servants to the local officials and gentry; the varieties of disguise are endless.[82]

There were of course departments dealing with the financial and disciplinary aspects of the secret society. The council, when it existed, appears to have mediated between these two departments, for the treasurers could be part of the council;[83] while the council also served as a tribunal of sorts in arbitrating disputes among members and in handing out sentences of punishment. In societies where the council was not formally instituted, the whole body of the members had to serve as the 'jury'.[84] Since the council does not appear in most of the reports, while the other officers do in one form or another, we may assume that its role was supplementary and not essential to the secret society, particularly in its judicial capacity, which could easily be taken over by the leaders acting as a committee, supported by the ordinary members.

If the treasurers and occasionally a council took charge of the finances of the secret society, then the Red Cudgel organized the department of punishments (which was also the military department). The responsibility of the Red Cudgel included the supervision of guard duties, training men in the fighting skills, stock-piling of weapons, and occasionally even manufacturing them.[85]

From the above discussion of secret society organization, it is clear that every aspect of it was underlined by the necessity for internal solidarity and secrecy. This was achieved, not by keeping the maximum of members in the dark—as in the 'cellular' type of clandestine organization—but by involving the member *totally* in the activities of the secret society, which takes over responsibility for every aspect of the member's life. This type of secret organization may be dubbed 'communal' (with all the implications of Tönnies' *'Gemeinschaft'*, see p. 173), for it draws its strength from reliance on communal interdependence and voluntary acceptance of the rules and demands of the secret society, and relatively free choice of one's leaders. This community was seen symbolically as a 'family', though it was nothing of the kind by orthodox standards. Nevertheless, the functions performed by the secret society were those of the family and more; and this point is continually reiterated in the regulations, initiation and other ceremonies of the Triad societies.

The obsession with possible betrayal is hardly difficult to understand. Not only were secret societies in constant danger of exposure, but they were psychologically and socially crippled by the rejection of orthodox society. One of the most effective means of combating both these things (fear of exposure, and attraction of orthodoxy) was through periodic ritual re-affirmation of secret society solidarity, during which an alternative 'respectability' or 'social honour' was physically enacted before the eyes of all the 'brethren'. The psychological effects of this ritual cannot be over-estimated, particularly among the largely illiterate, frequently superstitious and oppressed people who formed the majority of secret society membership. The sanctions of the secret society, too, played more than a purely negative role (that of punishing wrong-doers). They were also the 'honour code' of the secret society.

VII

Ritual

The most spectacular ritual of the secret society was undoubtedly the initiation ceremony, which was also the most
crucial. Promotion ceremonies, if separately performed at all,
were kept very brief.[1] The ceremonies carried out during
seasonal and religious festivals[2] were held mainly for practical
purposes such as planning raids, other criminal enterprises or
rebellion. These normally took place during fairs, or in rural
and urban market days (indeed, to open a meeting in secret
society parlance is to 'open a fair' or 'market': *k'ai-hsü*, or *k'ai-
shih*) when the crowds were such as to make secret society movements inconspicuous.[3] Records of the rites performed on such
occasions are not available, but it is probable they were fairly
perfunctory and did not differ basically from the kind of
'memorialism' which is practised in the household on cult
days. Such ceremonies may be accompanied by secret body and
hand signals and perhaps even a secret dance, which was one
of the means by which the rank and file as well as officers
identified each other.[4]

The Triad initiation ceremony, however, has been enthusias-
tically recorded, for it has exercised by far the greatest fascina-
tion on students of secret societies. This chapter will first
summarize the main stages of the ritual, then interpret them in
the light of Simmel's hypothesis and the very existence and
organization of the secret society itself.

The wealth of detailed information on the theatrical aspect of the initiation ritual is not matched, however, by a comparable wealth on the more practical aspects, such as how often the Triads met, and when, although Figure 5 shows, in translation, the form of a circular for holding lodge. The only detailed record describes the twentieth-century Hong Kong Triads. As these claim to be the 'Second Lodge' of the Canton Triads, there is no reason to doubt one element of their claim: that the customs of all Triads are fundamentally the same. According to Morgan's informant, the Hong Kong Triads normally met for *initiation* every third and eighth day of the lunar month.[5]

The official days for opening the Lodge are: 3rd, 13th, 23rd, 8th, 18th, 28th. The 5th and 10th days of the month may be used for emergency purposes. The 4th, 14th, and 9th, 19th, 29th can also be used although the dates are not quite as auspicious as those embodying the numerals 3 and 8. The 1st, 11th, 21st, 2nd, 12th, 22nd, 16th, 7th, 17th, 27th, should never be used.

Whether the Triads in fact adhered to these dates conscientiously or not is open to question. But what is clear is that number magic played a part in deciding when members should meet. This is a traditional habit which was generalized throughout Chinese society: all traditional rites such as required by marriage, birth or funeral were regulated by numerological and astrological considerations. If a child, for example, was born on an inauspicious day, something would be done to his name to ward off the evils associated with such a date.[6] As initiations were regarded as the 'birthdays' of new members, such considerations as dates become symbolically very important. A more practical side to the dates is evident in that they tended to coincide in their ten-day intervals with the typical spacing of market days.[7] Initiations were, as has already been noted earlier, referred to as 'fairs' (*hsü*) or 'markets' (*shih*).

In order to exercise the maximum influence on the in-coming candidate, initiations must be comprehensive and thematically simple, that is, complex enough to inspire awe, but simple enough to elicit understanding for the main cause. The Triad initiation ritual has both these qualities. The Triads normally waited until a reasonable number of candidates (fifty men or

年　　小　　日
　　　弟　　裡
月　　親　　紅
　　　臨　　匕
　　　來　　夜
煩　　侯　　裡
爲　　駕　　來
通　口　　　義
知　于　桃　兄
　　　園　早
　晚　結　匕
　川　義　到
　井　理　香
　　　應　檯
　洪　該
　弟

拜

TRANSLATION
In daytime all is red (light), so come at night-time;
Come, my pledged brethren, early to the incense-table:
I, your humble servant, will come myself to wait upon you;
For it is right and proper that we pledge fraternity in the peach-garden.
The year, month, night, in the 'Hall of Obedience to Hung' a market will be opened.
The Hung-brother X presents his respects. (Seal of the Society I-hing).
Please to communicate this further.

FIGURE 5 *Form of a circular for holding lodge*

so) presented themselves for initiation, before a full-scale ceremony was staged. Sometimes, by necessity or in cases of emergency, smaller ceremonies were held in members' homes, with
only one or more of the principal officers of a lodge present.[8]

Large-scale initiations were usually held in a hall rented or
secretly owned by a lodge, or in a pre-selected and secluded
temple,[9] sometimes scurrilously known as 'dumb brothels' (*ya-pa
yao-tzu*).[10] The lodge was symbolically named 'The City of
Willows' (*Mu-yang Ch'eng*), which was the Buddhist name for
Paradise (see Figure 6, p. 130); or simply 'Mountain Hall'
(*Shan-t'ang*), where the President was known as 'Mountain
Master' (*Shan chu*). This 'City of Willows' contained an inner
sanctum called 'The Red Flower Pavilion' (*Hung Hua T'ing*), in
which the essential part of the initiation took place, and where
the secrets of the society were revealed to the recruit.[11] In a
short domestic ceremony only the Red Flower Pavilion part
was enacted.

In a full-scale ceremony, the ritual appears to be divided into
three main stages. The *first* stage consisted of the recitation and
dramatization of the Myth of Origin in the main hall of the
lodge. This was called 'performing the play' (*tso-hsi*) and 'watch-
ing the play' (*k'an-hsi*) depending on whether one was an active
or passive participant; or 'releasing the horses' (*fang-ma*).
('Horses' = recruits, or new recruits; *hsin-ting*, 'new tops', was
another name for new recruits.) The *second* part of the ritual
consisted of the oath-taking ceremony in the Red Flower
Pavilion, the issuing of the certificates of membership, and the
exhibition of secret documents, furniture and objects of the
lodge to the new members. The feast and theatricals of celebration which followed after a few days formed the third and final
part of the initiation.

Before entering a lodge, it is stipulated that a candidate must
be clean or freshly washed, and wearing a white cotton coat and
trousers. His right arm, shoulder and chest must be bare. The
left leg of the trousers must be rolled up above the knee. He
must be wearing a pair of grass sandals, and a strip of red cloth
(the Chinese word for 'red' is pronounced in the same way as
the word for Hung in Hung League) tied around his head.[12]
This may symbolize the Triad connection with the Red Turbans
(White Lotus Society) rebels who brought the Ming to power.

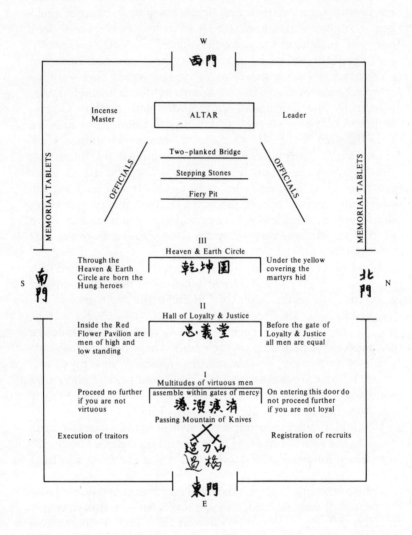

FIGURE 6 *Plan of the City of Willows*

It should be remembered that the Ming is the Chinese dynasty which the secret societies vowed to restore, after having overturned the foreign Manchu dynasty of the Ch'ing. As if to emphasize the point, the officers of the society normally dressed up in Ming costume and head-dress for the occasion.

As the initiation ceremony is too long and complicated to be reproduced in its entirety here, it may suffice us to summarize the main stages of it. The following summary is taken from Schlegel's documents which supply all the verses as well as many of the important expressions in Chinese and in translation. This version is also closest to that presented in Chinese by Hsiao I-shan who based his research on the British Museum MS. Oriental 2339, and the longest version extant.

Candidates were initiated in groups of fifty or so men together, entering the initiation room in pairs. They were instructed in certain simple responses to questions put to them by the Guards at the front gate. These questions dealt with the names and ages of the candidates, which were then registered in a book.

I.1. The Vanguard orders the Guards to form the 'bridge of swords' (*ch'iao-tao*) for the ceremony of 'passing the bridge' (*kuo-ch'iao*), during which the candidates are led by an affiliated member under an arch of swords.

I.2. The candidates each pay an entrance fee of 21 cash, which is received by the 'Fruit-seller', who was in fact a recruitment agent.

I.3. The candidates now enter the Hung Gate (*Hung Men*) an ante-room guarded by two 'generals' who demand the names of the 'new horses', and then permission from the Master for the recruits to pass.

I.4. Candidates now enter the Hall of Fidelity and Loyalty (*Chung-i t'ang*), guarded by another two 'generals' who demand their names again. Here the recruits are instructed in the political aims of the society, and the reasons for the society's opposition of the Ch'ing Government. The story of the origins of the Triad society is briefly alluded to here. Threats of death are levelled against those who refuse now to go through with the ceremony.

I.5. Candidates enter the Heaven and Earth Circle (*T'ien-ti yüan*), also guarded by two 'generals'.

I.6. Candidates cross the 'moat' or 'ditch' and reach the East Gate of the City of Willows, or the lodge proper. This gate is guarded like the others. The guard leads them to the 'Lodge of Universal Peace' (*T'ai-p'ing chuang*) where the Council sits, guarded by another two men.

I.7. The Vanguard greets and is greeted by the 'generals' (guards of the Council Room) who ask him his mission. The Vanguard asks to see the Councillors (the 'Five Founders'), and the guards request permission from the Master for the Vanguard to enter.

I.8. The Vanguard enters the Council Room and greets the Master, who proceeds to ask him to answer a number of questions[13] regarding: (a) the symbolic identity of the Vanguard, (b) the purpose of his visit, (c) the purpose of the candidates in requesting admission to lodge, (d) the historical role of the Vanguard, his knowledge of the eighteen military arts, of the educational and moral principles of the society, of the history of the founding of the society, and the various magical persons and objects encountered by the Vanguard on his voyages of recruitment. Among the persons and things he 'saw' on his voyages were:

(i) The recruits: 'They are far off at the horizon; they are near before my eyes. They roam about the world without a fixed residence.'

(ii) Three roads, of which the Vanguard took the middle one.

(iii) White herons flying past.

(iv) Eight priests, each holding eight precious objects: a fan, a pear-shaped censer, a sword, a flute, two castanets of jade, a sceptre, and a floating bridge on which stood the last monk. (These are the Eight Spirits (*Pa-hsien*) of Taoist mythology.)

(v) A woman, wearing a bamboo hat (a peasant head-gear), a white dress, on a white horse, holding a flower basket and sceptre, who entered the 'Grove of Firs and Cypresses' —another name for the secret society. The woman is evidently some kind of a deity, and is given the title of 'Princess' (*Kung-chu*).

(vi) The temple of Ling-wang (lit. Spirit King) who is the 'protecting deity' of the Hung faithful. Here the daughter of the Dragon King of the Seas was 'gathering mulberry flowers' (a password).

(vii) A mountain, called the Black Dragon Mountain, with many caves, and a cryptic legend describing different types of rain (drizzle, summer showers, hoarfrost, etc.).

(viii) The Hung Ferry Boat (*Hung-t'ou-ch'uan*) at the bottom of the mountain. The Ferry Boat was manned by three men on the top deck; the skipper (*shao-kung*) on the fore part, his wife (*shao p'o*) aft. On the lower deck or 'great ship-hold' were the Hung Brethren. There were five (sometimes, eight) compartments in the ship, each containing red wood, red rice, son of the chief (*chu-tzu*), weapons, and the members.

The verse explains:

'The true seat of the lord is in the middle of the ship
The military and civilians assist to support the sun and
    moon [these two words join to make the word Ming]
The silken sails are hoisted high and the wind is fair
We roam like clouds over the four seas to pacify the
    world.'

The ship had twenty-one holds, five sails, twenty-one deck-boards, three kinds of wood (peach on the left, plum on the right and red-wood in the middle . . .).

A number of deities, the God of Fire (the Chinese equivalent of Pluto), the 'All-hearing Ear', the 'All-seeing Eye', Kuan Yü (the God of War and voluntary associations), famous generals of the Three Kingdoms period—including the last deity—Chang-fei, Liu Pei (A.D. 168–256), the Holy Mother Queen of Heaven, the Goddess of Mercy (*Kuan-yin*), the eighteen chief disciples of Buddha (*lo-han*) (two Chinese, sixteen Hindu), etc. The ship was further described, and the symbolic numbers were re-iterated. The destination of the ship was the Market of Great Peace.

(ix) The three rivers (*san-ho*) which unite at one source (symbol of the Triad society uniting China).

(x) The Market of Great Peace, containing three markets.

(xi) Two-planked bridge (*erh-pan ch'iao*), on which stood the members, peach and plum trees, three Buddhas, a young man, a young woman, seller of Hung fruits, etc.

I.9. Recapitulation of the initiation ceremony, the *dramatis personae*, description of lodge and furniture, as streets, shops, wells, pagodas, ponds, orchards, trees, houses (only five out of the 108 were inhabited), casernes, fields, crops, the Hung lamp, the 'highest thing in the city', the volcano (or pit of fire), the Red Flower Pavilion.

End of Catechism

I.10. Recruits who refuse to join the society at this stage are now led out of the West (or traitors') Gate to be executed by decapitation; the others are handed over to the Vanguard.

II.1. *The Initiation.* The recruits enter the Red Flower Pavilion, led by the Vanguard.

II.2. The queues of the recruits are cut off, symbolizing the severance of their loyalty to the Manchu dynasty.[14]

II.3. The coiffure is then changed to the Chinese or Ming style (*kai-t'ou-fa*), with the sides shaved, and the hair combed backwards and tied up into a knot.

II.4. The recruits wash their faces (*hsi-mien*), in order 'to do away with corruptness and perversity' and to 'wash clean the dust of Ch'ing'.

II.5. The recruits are stripped of their upper garments (*kai-i*), and put on white robes of Ming style (*ch'uan pai-i*) and red kerchiefs round their heads (*pao t'ou-pu*), or a white sash for the waist (*chua-yao*). Their shoes are taken off and straw shoes (normally worn in mourning or by the poor; white is also the colour of mourning) are put on in their place.

> Our feet tread on straw-shoes, step by step
> no one would question the poor and miserable on the road.
> don't say grass-sandals are useless
> you received them in oath in the flower pavilion.

End of first part of ceremony

II.6. The recruits are now led up to the altar, where the Master again questions the Vanguard, this time about the political aims of the society summarized in the slogan 'two dragons contending for a pearl' (dragons = emperors) and 'overthrow the Ch'ing and restore the Ming'.

II.7. The recruits 'offer grass instead of incense' (*nien ts'ao wei hsiang*) in commemoration of the manner of pledging brotherhood by the 'five founding monks' of the society.

II.8. Incense is then distributed (*p'ai hsiang*) and offered to the altar gods; the formulary of the oath is placed over the incense bowl. The blades of grass are then inserted one by one into the censer (*chin hsiang*).

II.9. Two dry-wood candles are now lit (*tien ku-mu*) followed by the lighting of a red candle (*tien hung-chu*); while libations to the gods are made with three cups of wine, one for Heaven, one for Earth, and one for the Society (*hsien-chiu*).

II.10. The Lamp of the Seven Stars is lighted (*tien Ch'i Hsing teng*).

II.11. The Imperial Lamp is lighted (*tien Yü Huang teng*).

II.12. The Hung Lamp is lighted (*tien Hung teng*).

II.13. The prayer 'inviting the gods as witnesses' (*ch'ing shen piao wen*) is read out in a slow and solemn voice, reiterating the purpose of the meeting and of the brotherhood. The prayer ends as follows:

> All brethren who are brought hither are faithful and loyal: they all are iron-galled and copper-livered. From the inexhaustible metamorphoses are born millions of men, who are all of one mind and one will. All these of one affection in the two capitals and thirteen provinces have now come together to petition Father Heaven and Mother Earth; the three lights, sun, moon (and stars); all the Gods, Saints, Spirits and Buddhas, and all the Star Princes, to help all present to enlightenment. This night we pledge ourselves, and vow this before Heaven, that the brethren in the whole universe shall be as from one womb; as if born of one father, as if nourished by one mother; as if of one root and origin; that we will obey heaven and act according to its ways; that our loyal hearts shall not change, and never alter. If the august Heaven will protect and assist in the restoration of the Ming, then happiness will have a place to which to return.

II.14. The recruits rise from their knees, and fall again prostrate on the ground, during which the following verse is recited:

> First, we worship Heaven as our father
> Second, we worship Earth as our mother
> Third, we worship the Sun as our brother
> Fourth, we worship the Moon as our sister-in-law
> Fifth, we worship the Five Venerable Worthies
> Sixth, we worship Wan Yun-lung
> Seventh, we worship our brothers
> Eighth, we worship the fragrance of ten thousand years.

II.15. The Thirty-six Oaths (*Hung Chia San-shih-liu Che*) are then read out by a member to the new recruits who remain kneeling. (See Appendix C.)

II.16. The recruits now drink tea as a token that they have imbibed the aims of the association—'drunk the water of the three rivers' (*yin san-ho shui*).

II.17. The recruits prick their middle fingers (or a white cock) and let the blood drop into a large communal bowl of wine, which is then drunk by all (*yin hsieh-chiu*).

II.18. A white cock is decapitated by each new member as a warning to all potential traitors (*chan ya-ch'i pai chi*). After which, the following execration (*shuo-chou*) is solemnly pronounced:

> The white cock is the symbol that we have shed
>   blood and sworn an oath
> The disloyal and unrighteous shall perish like the cock
> The faithful and righteous shall be dukes and marquises
>   for ten thousand generations
> We have drunk the wine, confirmed the oath and
>   pledged to raise [the standard of] justice
> Traitors and traducers shall die under the sword
> Their heads severed from their bodies, and their
>   flesh and bones dispersed everywhere.

(This last threat refers to the belief that the soul will never rest, and will become a 'hungry ghost' as long as the body remains incomplete.) The recruits are now led outside the 'West Gate' where the written oaths are thrown on the fire and burned in the belief that they would reach the gods, who would then punish those who have perjured themselves.

II.19. The diplomas of membership (*Hung-tan*, *Hung-p'iao* or *Yao-p'in*) (see Figure 7) are now distributed. They are usually pieces of linen cloth, each decorated with a quatrain and the name of the recruit in cryptogram. The diploma is worn on the person (hence its name 'waist-belt', 'purse') as a protection against the rash pirates and robbers of the league who might not otherwise distinguish their colleagues from outsiders. Copies of the secret book containing oaths, laws, regulations of procedure during meetings, secret signs, vocabulary, and pairs of daggers are distributed to all the new members. The daggers can be easily concealed in the wide sleeves of the Manchu costume.

II.20. This is the time for paying the account (see Table VII.1 and Figure 8, a receipt for contributions).

TABLE VII.1

(a)	'clothes' (documents, etc.)	360 cash
(b)	'purse' (diploma)	108 cash
(c)	'Instructions' (the Oaths)	72 cash
(d)	'traitor' (the decapitated cock)	36 cash
(e)	fruit	21 cash
(f)	Hung Cash (Three Hung Cents)	3 cash
	Total	600 cash

The Hung Cash also is to be carried about on the person as a sign of mutual recognition.

End of formal ceremony

II.21. The new members are now led around the lodge and shown the furniture, objects and flags of the society; then the Hung Bushel (*Hung tou*) is raised and a verse recited, after which the Army flags are raised, and consecrated by a libation of three cups of wine and a prayer for victory is offered to the deities of Heaven, Earth, land, grain, mountains and the three rivers.

III.1. A white horse and a black ox are slaughtered and spear-heads are dipped in their blood; after which the animals

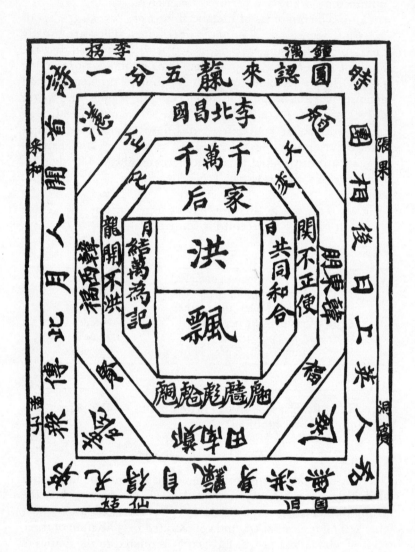

FIGURE 7 *A membership ticket*

義興館

居住　　憑單收過

底銀　　交清公司授票

爲據川大丁首关井足王

天運年月日給印

TRANSLATION
I-hing Hall
Settled at (the name of the place)— receipt; received from (the name of the member) the sum of (quantity of money expressed), paid. The society gives this ticket as a proof. Obey Heaven and act righteously! The passes are open the road is clear!

The year (expressed by the cyclical characters corresponding to that year) of the Heavenly motions, the month, day.

Given under our seal (the seal of the society) *I-hing-kwan*, 'I-hing Hall'.

FIGURE 8　*A receipt for contributions*

are taken into the kitchen and a feast is prepared for all to partake. During and after the banquet, theatricals are put on for the guests—an invariable feature of all ceremonies. This lasts till dawn when the members don again their Manchu costume and disperse to their homes.

Simmel's ideas on ritual in secret societies have particular force for the interpretation of the role of ritual in the southern Chinese Triads; for this reason, I shall reproduce them in paraphrase here:[15]

1 Secret societies are voluntary, and therefore 'artificial' associations, not pre-determined by historical precedent like families, but built up from their own bases. Therefore, the use of elaborate ritual becomes necessary as a substitute life-totality, creating external forms around the purposes of the association. Thus, the substitute life-totality is able (a) to make a *total* claim upon the individual member, both objectively and subjectively, and (b) to *protect* the purposes of the association. In this way, ritual secrecy can sometimes be emphasized at the expense of the secrecy attached to the purposes, and becomes, like the process of hierarchization, an end in itself.

2 Secret societies necessarily exist within a larger, encompassing structure, and therefore cannot but imitate the form of this structure (see p. 115). In order to distinguish itself from this encompassing structure, and reduce its subservience to it, the secret society seeks to create an alternative totality by setting up a contrasting image (in its ritual) to the official world. Only in this way can the secret society bind its members strongly to itself.

Chinese secret societies certainly reproduce these features with remarkable explicitness. The creation of a new life-totality at every stage of the Triad ritual involves both an 'external' or physical aspect, and an 'internal' or psychological dimension, expressed in the symbolic meaning of the ritual act. Stage 1, the entry of the candidate into the City of Willows and his introduction to the purposes and meaning of the secret association, gives the candidate a detailed (almost unnecessarily, repetitively so) re-creation of the society members' collective past in the form of versified history. Needless to say, the verses contribute as much to the ease of memorizing the history as to their meaning, and exercise a hypnotic effect on the listener, creating a psychological climate favourable to his further and deeper conversion. It is therefore quite logical that those who stubbornly resist this hypnotism, or the force of Triad arguments in favour of political sedition, or both, should be led out and executed beyond the traitors' gate. Besides, they already know too much for their own and the society's good. The need for roots or for a collective experience is thus satisfied in those who now proceed to the main part of the ceremony, the initiation.

The second stage is further divided into two parts: the disengagement of the candidate from orthodox and legal society (II.1–5); that is, his 'death', symbolized by his change of hairstyle and clothes and the face-washing ceremony ('washing the face' in Triad terminology means 'to kill'); and the candidate's 're-birth' ('to be born', *ch'u-shih*, means 'to enter the society') into a new life (II.7–21).

In this part of the ceremony, the collective experience is alluded to by enaction of key ideas unfolded in the first stage of the ritual. For example, the 'changing of the clothes' refers specifically to the discarding of orthodox values and adopting the new ones of the secret society—'clothes' as we know mean the documents and secret culture of the Triads. 'Cutting off the queue' has already been explained as the cutting off of the allegiance to the Manchu dynasty which had imposed this humiliating coiffure on the Chinese. (There are two explanations; see p. 231, note 14.) 'Donning the red kerchief or turban' alludes unequivocally to the connection of the Triads with the Red Turban (White Lotus) rebellions which overthrew an earlier foreign dynasty (the Yüan) and hence to the clear support of the society for future rebellion against the Ch'ing dynasty. Indeed, this particular rite is accompanied by the following verse which leaves no one in doubt as to Triad political ambitions:

> A red kerchief of brand new colour
> wound round the head to summon troops
> when we have assembled a thousand armies
>   and ten-thousand horses
> we shall exterminate the Ch'ing dynasty and protect
>   our imperial lord. [The Ming heir.]

The second half of the second stage is concerned with the actual 'metamorphosis' (*pien-hua*) of the candidate. The rite 'offering grass for incense' (II.7) symbolizes the change of the status of the candidate from that of inferiority ('grass' has the general connotation of inferiority, rusticity, coarseness, uncouthness) to one of superiority ('incense' being normally associated with refinement, superior quality—as in *hsiang p'in*—and culture). Indeed the word 'incense' or 'fragrance' (*hsiang*) has become synonymous with 'Triad member'.

This metamorphosis goes one stage further in the 'distribution of incense' (II.8) and the 'offering of incense' (II.8), accompanied by the recitation of a verse which explains that

> To-night new incense is blended with the old
> incense . . .

indicating that the older members are now willing to accept the new ones into the fold. The various candles lit after this (II.9–12) symbolize the illumination that has taken place in the dark world of the candidates now that they are being transformed. The gods are then invited to witness this transformation by prayer, which also affirms the new ties of brotherhood formed between the members. The 'drinking of the bloody wine' (II.17) is the seal of the new relationship. The decapitation of the cock, coming after so much benevolent new feeling and the imbibing of alcohol, must have a sobering effect, if not a traumatic one, depending on the psychological constitution of the members. After this, all is over, tension is released and the new members see themselves regaled in new raiment, and armed with the written confirmation of society protection as well as the concrete tokens of its trust: the distribution of the daggers. Their willingness to pay must be enhanced by the evidence of so much love. The commensality which follows is a further symbol of the benefits and mutual satisfaction to be derived from membership of the remarkable fellowship

Like the secret societies of Europe[16] the Chinese Triads too created for themselves a collective 'counter image' to that of the orthodox society; they opposed the universal kinship loyalty by the loyalty to the society, they replaced the allegiance to the state and officialdom ('lepers', *feng-tzu*, or 'enemy', *tuei-t'ou*, or 'official bandits', *kuan-fei*) by the absolute allegiance to the brotherhood; and it was 'public interest'[17] to cheat, steal, rob outsiders for profit, but 'criminal' to do so to a fellow member of the Triads. Further, the election of leaders by the members denied that the orthodox method (of appointing officials *from above*) had unique validity or any validity at all. For example, in the orthodox state, the corrupt high-ranking official was 'privileged' to commit suicide by order of the Emperor, in the secret society he was forced to do so by the general consensus of the members.[18] Finally, they replaced the Confucian and orthodox world-view by a synthesis of the different heterodox views of Buddhism, Taoism and popular magic. The peculiar character of this synthetic world-view lies in its obsessional pre-occupation with the purposes and solidarity of the secret society. This preoccupation took the explicit form of the ritual of initiation which may be analysed under two distinct but complementary heads: the 'passive' and the 'active'.

In its passive role, *ritual becomes the myth of origin, the ideological and aesthetic repository of the secret society*. In the first place, the ritual served as the explanation or justification for the political (that is, rebellious) aims of the society. The reasons given by the myth are already discussed in the chapter on the origins and formation of the Triads, but may be summed up briefly here as: (a) the tyranny of the foreign Manchu Government in persecuting Chinese Buddhism; (b) the corruption of official-dom; (c) the humiliation and misery of the victims within this political framework. Hence, it was a point of honour for the 'descendants'[19] of these victims to avenge their 'forebears' (and the Hung League was formed for this purpose) and restore a virtuous and native government to China.

Revenge for the sake of justice and honour was the moral vindication of secret society hostility towards the 'host' society; which meant that any compromise with the latter was auto-matically interpreted as capitulation to moral corruption and dishonour.

Needless to say, to those suffering from acute injustices arising from inequalities of status and wealth endemic in traditional society, such an argument had all the force of divine truth. *Thus, the myth of origin became the political manifesto of the secret society*.

In the second place, the language used in the ritual—the

'gutter' vocabulary, the eccentric phrases, the display of cryptograms on the sacred objects of the lodge, as well as the hand, body movements, cup, bowl, and other secret signals— functioned as an alternative and contrasting idiom of communication to that used in the 'outside world'.

In the third place, if the myth of origin could be called the 'point of honour', then the oaths and statutes were the 'code of honour' of the secret society, what may be called, more familiarly, 'thieves' honour'.

The combination of myth, secret language, oaths and laws of the secret society constituted an efficacious, alternative culture to that of orthodox society. In this passive form, ritual served as a *point of reference* for the individual member who could consult it when in doubt.

Ritual in the active form had a more direct psychological and perpetuative function (like all *rites de passage*). *The somewhat abstract idea of 'association' was 'realized' in ritual action.* In this, the emphasis has shifted from the necessity for association to the practical consideration of strengthening the association; that is, the necessity for internal unity in the survival of the secret society, and in the prolongation of its existence.

The myth of origin, when physically re-enacted, became the *living* manifestation of the reality and solidarity of the association. The rootlessness, the geographical separateness and mobility of individual members were compensated for by the dramatic evocation of the 'City of Willows', with its constituent streets, pagodas, temples, shops, trees, wells, and so on, creating a secret, magical and surrogate *Gemeinschaft* within the individual solitude of the *Gesellschaft*.

Like all the other features of the secret society, ritual was principally orientated towards the maintenance and strengthening of solidarity among the members. Like its organization and corporate activities, but unlike the sanctions, ritual is more an affirmation of the unity *within* the society than a negation of the outside world. Its weapon is persuasion—by logical argument, and by magic (or psychological manipulation): for the myth provides the argument, the dramatization the magic, and the whole ceremony the sense of honour which binds together and protects the physical and moral person and interests of each member.

VIII

Sanctions

Triad sanctions included not only what may be called 'penal law', 'laws of procedure', but also a moral code. But these distinctions are not recognized by the Triads themselves, just as they are not recognized in orthodox law.[1] The wide competence of such sanctions in traditional Chinese society may be summed up as follows:[2]

> The laws of the state are partly civil ordinances, partly moral requirements; so that the internal law—the knowledge on the part of the individual of the nature of his volition, as his own inmost self—even is the subject of external statutory enactment . . . moral laws are treated as legislative enactments, and law on its part has an ethical aspect.

The Triads had their own equivalent of the Great Ch'ing Code, the *Ta Ch'ing Lü-li*,[3] as well as their version of the Sacred Edict, roughly categorized as 'penal and procedural law', and 'moral code', respectively. The Triads' *lü-li* corresponded to the first type, and the *che* (oaths) corresponded, in function, to the second type.[4]

The oaths were served to 'inculcate the moral teachings of the Triad society and for the most part . . . are really a cursing formula, similar to the ceremony in the Western Church known as the Commination Service, held on Ash Wednesday.'[5]

The accuracy of this analogy is borne out repeatedly in Triad magical threats against disobedience of its moral laws: 'If any disobey this rule and forget the proper feeling (of brotherhood), they will be considered to have broken the oath, and may thunder from all points annihilate them.'[6] The threat may be varied to death 'beneath ten thousand knives', 'eating by tigers', death by drowning, etc. Such 'cursing formulae' are not normally found in the Sacred Edict.

The Triad *lü-li* tended to vary in length and complexity from society to society. Some, like the twentieth-century Hong Kong Triads, possessed no such rules at all, limiting themselves to the 'Thirty-six Oaths'; while the Elder Brothers Society in Szechwan possessed only 'Ten Commandments' of which only eight survive.[7] As usual, the society reported by Schlegel in the nineteenth century boasted the most elaborate collection of regulations. They are the 'Twenty-one Rules' (*Li Erh-shih-i t'iao*), the 'Ten Prohibitions' (*Hung-hsün-t'ang k'ai-lu shih-chin*)—regulations for the conducting of meetings—and an amplified set of laws called the 'Seventy-two Articles of the Hung Code' (*Hung-chia ch'i-shih-erh t'iao Lü-li*) which[8] probably drew some inspiration from the Great Ch'ing Code (*Ta-Ch'ing Lü-li*).

These 'laws' concerned themselves (as did their orthodox counterpart) with the setting out of different kinds of offences and their appropriate punishments—so many blows, loss of ear(s) or death, by decapitation, usually. The Triads did not go into the unpleasant refinements used by official law such as death by strangulation, by piece-meal execution, by burying alive and so on. There were also no laws punishing miscreants by exile or expulsion, though according to Morgan and Wynne these rarely were the favourite forms of punishment among Hong Kong and Malayan Triads.[9]

It is certain that the rules were not applied by the secret societies to the letter for the simple reason that if they had been applied secret society membership would have been drastically reduced if not totally destroyed. For example, twenty-two out of the seventy-two offences cited in the amplified laws were punishable by death, while the number of heavy blows stipulated could have the same effect as a death penalty. According to Hutson[10] 'a few tens of blows may be sufficient to cause death'. Again, the appearance of the ritual numbers 108, 72,

32, 21 (blows) makes it highly likely that they indicated the degree of seriousness of particular offences than provided an accurate guide for meting out punishment.

The *severity* of Triad laws, then, served some other purpose, and this purpose could only be the internal unity and ideological harmony of the secret society. In other words, the sanctions were the negative complement to ritual as the ideological 'glue' of society unity and security. Ritual affirmed the solidarity of members by dramatizing the common culture of the secret society; while sanctions ensured it by both the discouragement of intra-society conflict and the negation of the validity of the outside world.

One example of the way in which sanctions were used to discourage, if not prevent, internal conflict is shown in the rules forbidding sexual relations between spouses of members, and between the daughters of members and other members.[11] Homosexual relations, in particular pederasty, were forbidden for the same reason. It was in effect an 'incest taboo' forbidding sexual relations between 'blood brothers'. The following are some examples of the way in which these rules were worded:

> If a brother disputes with another brother about a young and fair boy, or commits unnatural sin with a younger brother, he shall, if detected, be put to death.[12,13]
> If a brother has introduced a 'little friend' into the league, and they do not amend afterwards, but go about as before, and bring in this way disgrace upon the reputation of the Hung-league, both of them shall be put to death.[14]
> If a lawless fellow seduces the wife or daughter of a brother, he shall, if detected, be punished with the loss of his life.[15]

Wife-robbery through use of force, as well as accessory to adulterous relations, was also punishable with death.

The seduction and subsequent trafficking as slaves, of children belonging to a fellow member were similarly punished:[16]

> If a brother . . . seduces with specious words and seductive language the wife and children of a brother who has gone abroad, or of a deceased brother, to go with him to another place, and if he sells them to others as slaves, he shall be slain under a shower of blows.

If a brother ravishes the male and female slaves, or the children and daughters of another brother, or carries off his oxen and horses, and sells them in another district or place, he shall be put to death.[17]

Another method of controlling internal conflict was the prohibition against economic exploitation of fellow members. Such exploitation included: betrayal of fellow member to authorities for a reward;[18] sale of society secrets to outsiders;[19] robbery of a fellow member in conspiracy with outsiders during a journey;[20] robbery with murder (by poison and hired assassins) of a fellow member;[21] embezzlement of society aid-funds;[22] living off a fellow member;[23] cheating fellow members at gambling,[24] and so on. There are, moreover, rules prohibiting the usurpation and abuse of power by the leaders of the secret societies.[25]

The purpose of the sanctions was not only to deny the validity of state laws but also to prevent exposure through carelessness and treachery. Hence the death penalty for the following offences: introduction of police spies into the initiation ceremony;[26] betrayal of the President and Master to magistrates;[27] sabotage of communications between lodges;[28] introduction of the murderer of a fellow member into the society;[29] betrayal of secret society activities leading to the arrest of fellow members;[30] betrayal of fellow member to the authorities after he had killed a man on society orders,[31] and so on.

Thus, all offences to do with 'incestuous' behaviour, with economic exploitation and political treachery were punishable by death. Others were not so severely penalized; this is clear from a close examination of all the different documents and versions of the oaths and rules available.

As for the physical punishments employed, there were three kinds: 'light' or 'heavy' blows by the bamboo (the small bamboo was called the *ch'ih*, and the larger bamboo, the *chang*) though the 'lightness' or 'heaviness' of the blows were not always stipulated; loss of one or both ears; and death by decapitation or drowning. Any of these three methods of punishment could be combined: loss of one ear and so many blows, or so many blows, followed by death.

The number of blows stipulated could vary as follows: 18, 21, 36, 72, 108, 360. As it has already been suggested earlier, these numbers were probably more a symbolic indication of the gravity of the offence than of the real number of blows applied in practice.[32] There is another symbolic significance in these numbers: their divisibility by three. This signified in Chinese semiology the union of Heaven, Earth and Man, the Triad, in fact; hence the interchangeability of the name San-ho Hui (Triad Society) with T'ien-ti Hui (Heaven and Earth Society). Chinese state laws did not, however, use these numbers, but graded their beatings by fives and tens of strokes.[33]

The types of punishment could be modified by the rank of the victim. As we have noted in the chapter on structure and organization above, the nine grades of the Triads were divided up, for purposes of measuring out punishment and for convenience, into three larger grades.[34] If the 'Upper Three' (*shang-san*) offended against the rules requiring the death penalty[35] they were required *by the whole society* to commit suicide 'voluntarily', just as high officials convicted of treason in the orthodox state were required to do so *by the Emperor*.

The 'Middle Three' (*Chung-san*) was only permitted to commit suicide by orders of the President of the society; and only the 'Lower Three' officials could be executed by orders of the Red Cudgel or Red Flag. Thus, the ultimate sanction lay with the rank-and-file in the secret society and not with the officials or Emperor alone, as in the State.

On the whole, then, Triad sanctions were instituted primarily to prevent internal conflict. They served as a warning against temptations of individuals to take their private interests (whether sexual, economic or political) too far at the expense of the other members. In the Chinese secret society, there was no room for indulgence in personal eccentricities at the expense of the collective. Life and death came too close together for a relaxed attitude to the common interest; and the message of the sanctions may be summed up in the phrase, 'United we stand, divided we fall'.

The role of the Council (*I-shih*) as a *separate* organizational element within the secret society structure does not appear to have been crucial, since we have noted earlier there were only two instances of the existence of such a council.[36] As a tribunal for arbitration of disputes it was useful, but this role could just as well be taken up by the officers of the society assisted by the ordinary members as 'jury'. It is probable that the *size* of secret societies determined whether a separate tribunal existed or not. In most cases such a council might be too unwieldy:[37]

> If a brother breaks the laws, let *all* the brethren come and settle the matter in public, without, by using cross words and crooked language in front of the Incense Master, adding fuel to the fire.

and[38]

> After entering the Hung doors, traitors and turn-coats are cudgelled, but the loyal and patriotic are not beaten. If a brother offends, let all the brethren discuss his case and punish him, and if he harbours resentment or disobeys this injunction may the gods look down and punish him.

It is absolutely clear that, whether a tribunal existed independently of the body of officers or not, it was the unique 'court of appeal' for the members:[39]

> When brethren of the Hung-league have serious or trifling dissensions, the council is there to decide upon them according to justice, but it shall not be allowed to bring the case before the magistrates. If anybody should not observe this law, the council will decide the case effectually, and, besides, will punish the plaintiff with 108 blows.

This rule obviously applied to cases of dispute *within* the secret society only, and could not have applied to cases where members were involved in litigation with outsiders or non-members. In such cases, there was no question of leaving the members to the vagaries of official justice, and it would have been normal for the society to attempt to bribe the lower official employees, or sometimes even the magistrate himself, to set the members free; if this should fail, more forceful methods of freeing the prisoners would be employed.[40]

The 'judge' of the secret council would most likely be the President or Incense Master—the supreme arbitrator, to the extent that he had also the authority to send a substitute to the authorities to be executed in place of another (presumably, more valuable) member.[41] However, the danger of such authority is recognized and leaders are warned against its abuse:[42]

The President and Master of the lodge ought to manage affairs honestly and equitably. They shall not, on account of relationship, be unjust, and neither shall they take bribes and wrong the brethren. May the offender be unhappy and unprosperous. An old adage says: 'If the emperor transgresses the law, he is a criminal as well as a man of the people.' He who disobeys this shall, therefore, be punished with death.

No account of how a Triad trial is conducted exists. However, it would be reasonable to suppose that they were fairly perfunctory, and resembled the efficient simplicity of guild practice. State-conductance trials as represented in the local magistrate's courts were notorious for their inefficiency, gratuitous length and injustice. The fact that both secret societies and guilds were voluntary associations implied many common habits of organization.[43] The following account of how a trial was conducted in a Peking guild could be instructive:[44]

The committee, the interested parties and their witnesses met in a temple. There the goods concerning which the case had arisen were set in front of the committee, and each side briefly gave its testimony. The witnesses were heard and after a short conference the committee gave its decision. This was accepted as final, both parties rose, bowed to the committee, and to each other and the matter was closed. A half hour sufficed to settle satisfactorily a case which, if taken before the official [magistrate] would have meant at least a day's travel for all the parties concerned, besides possible delays and inconveniences.

There would have been two points of difference between the secret society and guild trials, if the above could be taken as a guide, and they are (a) the decisive role of the secret society President, in comparison with the guild President, who, in principle, was little more than a chief spokesman; and (b) the absence of choice for the parties in the secret society concerned to take their case before the official magistrate.

Despite the existence of a tribunal for deciding disputes and for meting out punishment in 'public', emergency justice could be pretty rough, frequently carried out by the officers of the society without consultation with the committee or other members. T'an's account of the despatch of two traitors of the Elder Brothers Society may be characteristic (the following is a conversation overheard by the author in his father's house between two members of the Society):[45]

> 'And are there no traitors in the union?', asked our friend with the warts. 'There are two. One of them was stabbed. The other was thrown into the Yangtze with a rock round his neck. This was exactly three hours after they had reported [to the police] on the meetings in my house.'

It is fairly conclusive that Triad sanctions bear little resemblance to the State judicature. These appear to have been deliberate, explicit, and even systematic, expressions of defiance and subversion of State structure. This defiance is of course most systematically and specifically expressed in the rules of the societies. Here, not only was the validity of official justice denied, but the activities it had forbidden as 'criminal' were, for this very reason, both acceptable and desirable to the Triads. However, many elements of the morality underlying the official laws were retained by the Triads; for example, the necessity for treating one's parents respectfully, for sexual distance between people bound together by 'blood' ties, for sympathetic cooperation between members of a community, and for restraint in the exercise of power.

Metaphorically speaking, the relationship of the Triad society to its rules may be seen as that between the inhabitants and protective walls of a beleaguered city; the sanctions were the surrounding walls ornamented with spikes, and bristling with guards menacing illegal entry and exit. It is, therefore, no accident that the Triads symbolized their lodge in this way— a walled 'City of Willows' guarded by eight warriors at the four gates (corresponding to the four cardinal points), and the passwords serving as spikes on which incautious traitors and strangers could impale themselves.

IX

Conclusions

It is not always obvious to anthropologists that a useful analysis of any institution involves not only the structural (and 'super-structural') dimensions but *also* the historical one. Functionalists claim that the absence of written records in their particular field of study forces them to 'freeze' their societies in a moment of time—how long this moment should last is another problem. Structuralists now claim that structures of societies *may* be reducible to a basic universal model, and any suggestion that they may have changed fundamentally in time is naïve evolutionism. What is overlooked in both these views is the fact that societies have changed, and will continue to do so; just as history, as historians have pointed out, never repeats itself. To say that elements of structural or superstructural continuity persist is not to say the *totality* persists. For better or worse, progress continues.

Chinese secret societies illustrate this process very clearly. I shall divide this chapter into two parts. The first part will analyse the political, economic and social *raison d'être* of secret societies as the expression of a permanent structural conflict in Chinese society. The second part will discuss the role of secret societies as an instrument of revolutionary change in the late nineteenth and early twentieth centuries.

POLITICAL

The most succinct summary of secret society role has already been quoted in the Preface: 'The officials derive their power from the law, the people, from the secret societies.' It is a sentence which sums up the centuries-old conflict between rulers and ruled, rich and poor, privileged and oppressed. If it presents a view that is sometimes too simple, it is nevertheless illuminating, for it corresponds to two distinct, major ideological currents in Chinese society: the patriarchal, authoritarian and instantly classifying current normally channelled into the term 'Confucianism' on the one hand, and the anarchistic, individualistic, egalitarian and equally insistently non-classifying current understood as Taoism, and later Buddhism, on the other hand. As dynasties rose and fell, as technical advances provoked new directions of scientific and political thought, the relative position of the two currents also changed. It would not be pushing the image too far to describe them as alternating as main current and undercurrent in the general flow of social existence. But because Confucian orthodoxy was more suited to the demands of centralized Government and an agrarian economy, it retained its hold upon the upper reaches of society (from which were recruited the bureaucratic functionaries) and through them maintained an enduring influence upon the ideal patterns of traditional family organization, evaluation of the division of labour (which ranked intellectual activity, agriculture, manufacture, commerce and, finally, the service industries, in that order) and upon the traditional patrimonial bureaucracy itself.

In contrast, Taoism and Buddhism had, by the ninth century A.D., become what Max Weber has dubbed 'heterodoxies', associated not with the ruling classes, but with the retired, the aged, the female, and, ultimately, the poor. As the heterodoxies became increasingly associated with these categories of the population, so heterodox thought itself changed, becoming more and more tied to their particular psycho-social needs. Salvationist and charitable doctrines replaced the emphasis upon 'pure' withdrawal from social life; organized monasteries and nunneries replaced the solitary quest for truth; economic concerns (banking, the provision of credit, egalitarian views of land-redistribution) outweighed religious passion. Thus heterodoxy created a new political ideology, or at least the beginnings of one, which was ready to hand, so to speak, for the leaders and organizers of peasant rebellions when they arose.

Future developments were already discernible at the time of the first recorded rebellion against the State of Ch'in in 203 B.C., which had effected the first bureaucratic centralization of China. It was probably no accident that this rebellion coincided in time with the development of a new form of 'spiritualism'—later to become incorporated into both Taoism and Buddhism—summed up by the Japanese scholar Yuji Muramatsu as, first, a belief in a Spirit or spirits whose will governs social and political events; second, an associated belief in omens and portents that reflect the will of the Spirit(s) and foretell the future course of events; and third, a belief in the ability of human intermediaries (mediums) to decipher the concealed meaning of the omens.[1]

The rebellion of 203 B.C. was followed by others, the leaders of which are known to have gathered large followings by claiming successfully to possess 'spiritual' and curative powers. Such a one was Chang Chüeh, leader of the famous Yellow Turban rebellion in A.D. 184 in the area which is now Hopei. The outcome of this rebellion was the dissolution of the Later Han dynasty and the breakdown of the once unified polity into three separate states known to historians as the Three Kingdoms period (A.D. 220–80). It is significant that this is the period chosen by nearly all later secular voluntary associations in China as their 'date of origin'.

More rebellions led by the descendants of Chang followed, and though Chang Lu surrendered to the Han State (one of the Three Kingdoms) in A.D. 212 as a semi-independent ruler in the (now) Szechwan area, his turbulent state continued to be a source of anxiety to the Three Kingdoms for thirty years.[2] As time went on, these semi-political, semi-religious movements began to acquire millenarian aims, especially in the areas (now the provinces of Shantung and Hopei) where Buddhism first took root. Both Taoist and Buddhist sects adopted as their patron the Maitreya or Mi-lo, a Buddha of the Future, whose appearance after a Buddhist eon (*kalpa*) would coincide with the occurrence of an apocalyptic change. A rebellion in A.D. 515

began with the slogan: 'A new Buddha has appeared! get rid of the old devils.'

A number of other quasi-religious and spiritualist practices also became associated with rebellious groups: vegetarianism, mystical sexual cults, *sutra*-chanting, incense-burning, shamanism, and elements of Manichaeanism. The 'Five Elements' of early Chinese thought came to be seen as the cosmic principles on which the transfers of secular power were to be effected: the succession of the elements was held to reflect and to influence the successive changes of rulers, presumably the succession of dynastic houses, referred to by Chinese historians as the 'dynastic cycle'.³ Of course, heterodox priests, as distinct from heterodox thinking, were not insensible to the advantages of winning the personal favour of Emperors; and were, therefore, regarded by orthodox ruling groups with a mixture of contempt, suspicion and fear—fear arising from the prospect of priestly entrenchment in the royal household, and fear of priests in organized rebellious association should their ambitions be thwarted. The Triad myth of origin provides an excellent illustration of this situation: the Emperor K'ang-hsi employed the Buddhist priests of Shaolin monastery to fight his invaders, but his ministers advised him to persecute the monks lest they became intoxicated with Imperial favour.⁴

The heterodox priests, like unorthodox intellectuals in other societies, were thus a nagging source of anxiety for Chinese bureaucratic officials. Along with the merchants, they came to be condemned as 'unstable' elements, intervening between the Government and the people. Being also the only other social group to be literate (the ability to read the *sutras* and to transcribe them being one important means by which the largely illiterate population could be influenced) they threatened the very basis of the orthodox literati (and thence, bureaucratic) hegemony founded on a specifically *Confucian* literacy.

In the ninth century (late T'ang) two new ingredients were added to the mixture of rebel ideologies: ethnocentrism (or 'proto-nationalism') and egalitarianism, both explicit themes of the Triad manifesto. The former arose out of the background of foreign invasion, and was given impetus during the southern Sung (*c.* 1125) by the Mongols Genghis and Kublai Khan, who established the Yüan dynasty in China in 1279. Egalitarian trends in rebel thinking were simultaneously provoked by the unrestrained development of the private ownership of land, and its increasing concentration in the hands of the rich. This was formalized in the *liang-shui* or Double Tax[5] system initiating the process of the pauperization of the peasantry. This process was hastened by the evasion of taxes by the wealthy and influential families, so that the burden of the taxation fell on those (the middle and small peasants for example) who were least able to bear it. In 993 (Northern Sung dynasty), the rebels Hsiao-po and Li Shun declared that they were 'sick of the inequality which exists between the rich and the poor, and wanted to level it off for the benefit of the people'.[6] Similarly, the rebellion of Fang La in 1120–1 (which figures briefly in the episodic novel *Water Margin* or *All Men Are Brothers*) insisted that there should be no distinction in status between rich and poor, or even between male and female. A White Lotus leader who revolted against the Yüan dynasty in 1351 announced that 'Heaven has dispatched a spiritual army to wipe out inequality [*pu-p'ing*]'.[7]

During most of these centuries, the Government monopolies[8] of salt, tea and liquor created widespread smuggling, sometimes accounting for as much as 50 per cent of the total trade. This, in turn, caused prices to rise and reduced further the spending power of the poor. In such conditions, it is no surprise to find that both the rebels Hsiao and Li were bankrupt tea-traders, suffering simultaneously from the effects of Government monopoly and the crippling taxes on the monopolized goods;[9] while Fang La was a bankrupt lacquer producer suffering similarly from Government restrictions.[10] The increasing official exactions were the result of an unrestrained growth of the bureaucracy, which, in turn, increased administrative costs and inefficiency; while open corruption and intrigue used up what credit the Government had retained with the people. Thus, dispossessed traders and peasants found powerful common cause against the Government as well as against the wealthy merchant families who, holding the monopoly patents over essential goods such as salt, were able to benefit grossly from the unhappy state of affairs.

It is not certain how many of these early rebellions were in fact led by secret societies, but it is nevertheless highly probable that the leaders of peasant revolts should have at least *begun* their revolts in secret association, however open the rebellions subsequently became. In any case, the similarities between these rebellions and the later ones for which we have clearer evidence of secret society participation and leadership (for example, in the nineteenth century) are enough to justify reference to them, the more so since the myths of the later, better-known societies (the Hung League, for example) them-selves so often hark back to their earlier beginnings in the seventeenth century.[11] Whatever the details of the relationship between secret societies as such and particular peasant revolts, those taking part in them tended to share a common 'heterodox' ideology.

It is well known that the appearance of rebellion and secret societies tended to coincide at the periods of dynastic decline. If we look at the list of rebellions generally associated with secret societies, we will find that nearly all of them occurred at the end of a particular dynasty.[12] The 'first' rebellion occurred at the end of the Ch'in, the Yellow Turban revolt at the end of the Later Han, the Fang La revolt at the end of the Sung, the Red Turbans towards the end of the Yüan. However, the millenarian Buddhist revolts in 515 and at the beginning of the T'ang could not be categorized as 'peasant'. They were largely provoked by the persecution of Buddhists launched by the Northern Wei, Northern Chou and the T'ang emperors in 446, 547, and finally, in 841–5, when the 'Buddhist age' came to an end in the whole of Asia, coinciding in late T'ang China with a rising tide of xenophobia.[13]

In the nineteenth century, the sporadic and regional revolts testified as much to dynastic decline as to the increasing un-popularity of the monarchic principle, and secret societies substantially aided the overthrow of the millennila monarchy and the establishment of a republic for the first time in Chinese history.

This consistent coincidence of secret society activity and peasant revolt throughout the centuries indicates some kind of cooperation, or at least parallel movement, between the two forces, both of which were dedicated to the same aims: the over-throw of corrupt officials and emperors, and the establishment of virtuous government. Both forces were composed (at least during revolt) of desperate individuals driven by circumstances to take the law into their own hands.[14] It should hardly come as a surprise if secret societies, with their skills in organization and warfare, should frequently be found at the head of the more spectacular and organized rebellious peasant movements. These skills, it might be added, could also be used by other forces or individuals rich or powerful enough to exploit them for oppressing the peasantry. However, this Mafia function was functionally less in demand (since there were already the Imperial Army, the personal militia and mercenaries for the use of the wealthy and powerful) *before*, rather than after, political parties came into being in the twentieth century. For the creation of 'modern' political parties, particularly parties of opposition to the Government, deprived the secret societies of their traditional political function as the sole, organized, oppositional force in the orthodox state and society. This left them, in the twentieth century, only the social and economic functions of a surrogate lineage for the protection of the despised, the poor and the criminal members of society. In this confused period (1912–49), secret societies appear to have played an equally confused role, acting both as the oppressive arm of the powerful centrifugal forces (local gentry families, new merchant tycoons, and so on) like the Sicilian Mafia; and as the 'social bandit'[15] protectors of the 'floating population' in the war-torn society.

Prior to the twentieth century, however, the traditional role of Chinese secret societies expanded and narrowed according to the developments in the wider society: in periods of dynastic decline, they led or shared the leadership of regional or national peasant revolts; in periods of relative stability, they confined themselves to protecting the socially and economically deprived and profiting from the endemic administrative contradictions of the Confucian bureaucracy. Secret societies saw their special mission as weeding out curruption from Government, and restoring Chinese rulers to the throne; ostensibly, they harboured no revolutionary ambitions.

Seen from a historical vantage, the political role of secret societies was double-edged. On the one hand, they were organizers and perpetrators of rebellion; on the other, they served as a safety valve for popular dissatisfaction, and so helped to preserve the Confucian *status quo* a little longer. In other words, while they nurtured, so to speak, the 'dangerous classes' of society they also obviously 'contained' their revolutionary power. Their role in Chinese history was that of supporting cast to the official hero: the bureaucrat and/or landowner. Their part was an unequal one partly because they failed to draw up a coherent, viable and detailed political programme. For a similar reason, Taoism and Buddhism failed to compete effectively with Confucianism as a dominant State ideology.

Like these heterodoxies, secret societies formed the 'dark' (*Yin*), though not necessarily quiescent, stream of Chinese life; just as the orthodox institutions, like the Confucian orthodoxy, might be described as its 'bright' (*Yang*) or 'active' expression. It is a truism to reiterate the fact that secret societies were more dependent for their existence on orthodox society than the latter was on them. Materially, too, they were unequal to established power; and were forced to lead a parasitic and restricted existence within the framework of the State, which maintained its political initiative. It was precisely this inability to seize the political initiative that limited secret societies to their ancillary, reformist role, which did not acquire revolutionary overtones until their alliance with the Republican party. Whatever the limitations of the Republican party, it did have some sort of a concerted strategy, a persuasive political and economic programme and, most important, the intention to *seize* national power, not merely to reform it.[16] The fundamental political passivity, relatively speaking, of the secret societies is also reflected in their loose and anarchical methods of alliance, which were not conducive to action on a national scale, especially if such action was already made problematic by regionalist sentiment.[17]

In the role of a reformist and, therefore, non-revolutionary force, secret societies were both inimical and integral to the State, holding the balance between the forces of 'order' and the forces of 'chaos'. For as long as there were no irresistible external or internal pressures on the Government, secret societies were able to continue in this ambiguous but necessary function. As soon as the internal balance of power broke down (see discussion below on the economic aspect of secret societies) and the external pressures became, both independently and as a result of the internal disorder, irresistible (as they were at the end of the nineteenth century), then secret societies were given a clear choice: join the revolution under a different type of leadership and organization, or withdraw from the political stage. Though Chinese secret societies chose both, they were ultimately forced to take the latter course.[18]

In considering this aspect of the secret society role in traditional society, it will be necessary to take into account first the relationship between the bureaucratic institution and the material substructure of a 'subsistence' economy. As David Lockwood[19] points out, structural change arises from within a society not only as a result of the conflicting interests of the groups within the total system, but also as a consequence of a fundamental 'lack of fit' between the 'core institutional order' (in China, the patrimonial bureaucracy) and 'its material base' (the economic system).

Lockwood's convenient simplification of Weber's thesis runs as follows. There are three characteristics of a patrimonial bureaucratic system.[20] First, the pre-condition for the unchanged, continuing existence, if not establishment, of a 'pure' bureaucratic administration requires at least a partial development of a money economy. Second, a large bureaucracy requires a system of taxation, geared to the maintenance of the bureaucratic machinery and its personnel. Third, it follows that the strategic *problem* lies in maintaining a taxation system that can effectively off-set the material needs of a bureaucracy in the context of a 'subsistence' or 'near-subsistence' economy. Thus, 'the focal point of strain is taxation capacity relative to bureaucratic needs'. This point of strain may actuate a process of political decentralization.

In some cases, such political decentralization is the result usually of the disproportionate growth of the bureaucratic body in relation to its material resources, that is, the taxation capacity of the rest of the population. This disproportionate growth (nourished by the sale of offices, ranks, imperial favours, etc.) may create large numbers of officials with sinecures, who, in the absence of work and/or adequate income, appropriate to themselves in compensation the economic, as well as the political resources of the office at the expense of the bureaucratic body itself. (In the Chinese case, this was done both by changing the tax registers, but also by 'customary dues' or squeeze.)

Meanwhile, all large landowners (whether office-holders or not) may seek to gain exemption from taxation by usurping fiscal and political functions on an increasingly large scale, provoking greater resistance from the peasantry.

The evolution of Chinese secret societies is an obvious example of the third stage of development in the decentralization of the state. Decentralization in China normally occurred at the end of about two to three hundred years (or the 'dynastic cycle'), when the 'point of strain' became intolerable. The inevitable outbreak of peasant revolts provoked, in its turn, a chain of other misfortunes: the breakdown of the irrigation system, leading to drought, locusts and epidemics, and so on. Vast sections of the population would be wiped out, sweeping away the old bureaucratic and landowning families. The creation of new officials would initiate a new 'dynastic cycle', the founding emperor of which would be ruling over a reduced population, temporarily solving the land scarcity problem. The inevitable re-distribution of land, relative economic stability and an efficient bureaucracy normally followed, until dynastic decline was set off.

These 'cycles' were, however, not merely repetitive; they were accumulative, both in terms of the old and new political and economic problems, created, for example, by foreign conquest, or invasion. The apparent (and frequently remarked) immutability of Chinese society is therefore deceptive. As the sounding-board, or danger-signal for orthodox misrule, secret societies were also evolving and adding new dimensions to their political role in response to the problems within the larger society.

By the nineteenth century, the effects of the introduction of Buddhism into China, the increasing commercialization of land, and foreign conquest had altered the original aims of the secret societies almost beyond recognition.

Perhaps the most significant single contribution of secret societies to Chinese economic life was their encouragement (albeit unintentional) of the development of a 'petty bourgeoisie' *independent of* official patronage. They did this by organizing resistance against monopoly and commercial taxes. These were the illegal 'businessmen', the salt, tea and liquor, and even horse, smugglers[21] who, ever since the first introduction of Government monopolies on salt and iron in the seventh century B.C., had been evading taxation by defying the law.[22] Legitimate traders, in contrast, were subject, not only to taxation on monopolies, but also to customs duties on the principal trade routes within China, culminating in the notorious nineteenth century *likin* tax, from which foreign traders were exempt.[23] City markets, moreover, were supervised by Government officials,[24] usually merchants with aspirations to gentry status.[25]

The relative independence from Government control of the illegal 'bourgeoisie' enabled it to develop faster, swelling its own ranks and those of the new landlord or official families called *kuan-hu*, and benefiting from the inflated prices produced by Government monopolies. This parvenu 'petty-bourgeoisie' (already conspicuous by the Sung) had few scruples about exploiting the very people who helped to amass their wealth— the peasantry forced to buy their goods, and the rank-and-file of the secret societies. This explains the Triad rules warning against oppression of the poor by the rich, the weak by the strong.[26] Inevitably, as the parvenus became more familiar with officialdom or more 'respectable', their incentive for remaining within the illegal secret societies diminished, and other, hungrier, less successful smugglers took their place.

Economic egalitarianism became prominent in manifestos of revolt around the end of the T'ang dynasty, when the ancient Chinese ideal of the equal distribution of land (the *ching-t'ien* or 'well-field' system) was officially declared irrelevant.[27] After the revolt of A.D. 993, the rebels Hsiao and Li assembled the rich and influential people of the area, registered their grain supplies, confiscated any surplus above their immediate needs and distributed it to the poor.[28] This example was followed by Fang La in 1120, by the White Lotus leader Liu Fu-tung in 1351 and by the Nien and Taiping rebels in the middle of the nineteenth century. The egalitarian strain in secret society thinking is a nostalgic allusion to the ancient Chinese economic concept, finally and officially discarded by the State, but defiantly retained by the heterodox poor as testimony of the extent to which their rulers had strayed from both the principles and practice of the Golden Age.

In the urban areas, the economic role of secret societies took another form: the organization, and management of, and participation in, the entertainments, service, and criminal industries. (See pp. 83–5.) These included the 'services' of prostitution, which was apparently a rich source of municipal income. Brothels were run also by the State in order to sell their monopolized liquor, on which a heavy tax was levied. For example, in the Southern Sung dynasty, in Hangchow the great commercial city, the Government built about twelve brothels near military barracks.[29] However, the formal prohibitions against the use of brothels by Government officials[30] meant that, strictly, prostitution was illegal, whatever may have been the practice. Those most organized and capable of taking over such enterprises were obviously secret societies. While no record of the latter's involvement with prostitution in China exists, overwhelming evidence points to this tie in records of Hong Kong[31] and Malayan police.[32] In an amendment to the report by F. S. Brown to the Penang Commission, it is stated that the secret societies there not only controlled prostitution, but also actually formed 'companies' for the 'importation and hiring out of prostitutes from China', which implied that there were also 'export' companies in China. According to one report, probably exaggerated, Amoy (in Fukien, where the largest number of people emigrate) had a population of 300,000, out of which 25,000 were prostitutes in 1861, while the permanent female population is said to be 'twenty times' the male population.[33] The League of Nations Report of 1933 exposed the sale of female children between the ages of two and three for training in prostitution, in Hong Kong, Dutch East Indies and elsewhere.[34]

The other activities of secret societies in the 'vice' field are gambling, drug contraband, extortion, blackmail and so on, most of which have already been described in Chapter IV. All these parasitic activities did perform one economic function: that of keeping money and goods in circulation, and of subverting the monopolist policies of the Government.

The other function of secret society activities was more general: the protection and encouragement of a developing illegal 'petty-bourgeoisie' which was eventually to overthrow the bureaucratic–merchant class, and with it a foundation-stone of the traditional economy. There was little the Government was able to do against such a development, even if it had been far-sighted enough to identify it. The absence of an effective police force, and the greed of local officials, already dependent on bribes to survive in their office, made any attempt to curb 'crime' and 'vice' a ludicrous proposition.

The contradictions in Government policy itself made it easy to indulge one's weaknesses for slave-trafficking, contraband circulation, or pimping for gentry and officials in the 'flower lanes'.[35]

When such continually subversive activities were finally combined with the problem of industrializing China under foreign imperialism, the situation was ripe for revolution.

SOCIAL

In Chapter V I have argued that most secret society members were deprived of lineage protection; in Chapter IV, I have shown how secret societies acted as surrogate lineages for their members. In this way, Chinese secret societies provided their members with all the political, economic, religious and social benefits which other more fortunate individuals enjoyed by right of birth or wealth.

As a *voluntary* association, however, the secret society directly subverted the lineage organization as an *ascriptive* association. It threatened to replace it and deny it the paramountcy it enjoyed in the heart of the Confucian 'natural' order of things. Indeed, by denying the supreme value of ascription in offering itself as an alternative or substitute form of social organization, the secret society posed a fundamental threat to that very 'natural' order itself.

The religious, craft and trade guilds were, in contrast, much less menacing, because they were more limited in the scope of their activities. They catered only to specialized, and not the totality of the individual's needs. Though religious associations (as corporate bodies) provided their members with more comprehensive services than guilds, they were stunted in their growth by the impossibility of biological continuity (by the segregation of the sexes) and by their size, limited by the law.[36]

It was only when religious associations broke the law, that is, became a secret society, that they realized their potentialities.

Thus, it was by their advocacy and development of voluntary association, and their recognition of moral equality among individuals that secret societies made their most significant inroads into the principles of social organization and relationships in traditional China. They paved the way for the republican and democratic revolution of 1911–12—for the programme of the revolution contained all the traditional aspirations of the secret societies. (Compare secret society aims on p. 73 and the republican revolutionary programme on p. 168.)

Finally, it has to be remembered that secret societies were also a force to be reckoned with in their intermediate position between the State and the powerful local lineages. In the past, secret societies were capable of breaking this balance of power only temporarily—by rebellion. But in the late nineteenth century, by participating in the republican ranks, they helped to break the old symmetry permanently. This 'proto-revolutionary' aspect of secret societies came to its fullness in the republican revolution, then abruptly degenerated into a reactionary social force in face of more radical alternatives such as trade unions and modern political parties.

PRIMITIVE REVOLUTIONARIES

Chinese society had been undergoing continuous and profound changes since the late T'ang and Sung times. Foreign imperialism in the second half of the nineteenth century merely exacerbated the internal conflict and the 'structural misfit' by introducing new needs and pressures, and thus speeding up the process of revolution.

The formalization of land inequalities and its commercialization in the late T'ang was the first visible victory of values of commerce over those of land, and the recognition that peasant impoverishment was inevitable. The unification of the North and South into one common economic area under the Sung altered the pattern of commercial administration and began the shift of the geographical centre of Chinese civilization from the North to Central and South China. This intensified the migration from the North China Plain which had long been set in motion by the 'barbarian' invasions across the northern borders and the lure of fertile land and greater commercial opportunities around the Yangtze River and the South.

The long, relatively peaceful period of Ming rule encouraged a population increase which could only be described as explosive.[37] This factor, combined with the concentration of landownership, more or less completed the process of peasant pauperization. Bureaucratic corruption, long an integral part of government, lost all Confucian restraint, and further aggravated peasant debt and degradation. On top of this was a vacillating Government policy of opportunism, impotent aggression or ignominious capitulation *vis-à-vis* foreign economic or armed threat. The humiliating defeat by Britain in the Opium War of 1840–1 opened up new and bitter rifts within the ruling class, creating factions which were to paralyse the Government altogether.

Meanwhile foreign imperialism, technology, commercial and religious practices continued to change the material base and superstructure of Chinese society. The group affected most immediately by the ideological assault of liberal democracy and technological progress was the disaffected intelligentsia, usually the students returned from abroad. The other groups, the peasants and secret societies, were affected most directly by the Taiping Rebellion (1851–64), which was the most dramatic expression of Christian influence upon a traditional heterodox movement. The Taipings' explicit espousal of certain old egalitarian ideas under Christian guise nearly converted the rebellion into a revolution.[38]

The suppression of the Taiping and Nien rebellions with the aid of foreign troops was not only the most brutal and devastating, but also the most short-sighted political action in modern Chinese history. The human and material destruction was immense and incalculable, sowing profound bitterness and xenophobia in the minds of the survivors. Thousands of these had been driven from their homes and livelihood, while others emigrated abroad, some as indentured labourers in the Americas, and immediately set up secret organizations for the overthrow of the Ch'ing.[39] Those who remained joined in the general mêlée, which was temporarily checked by the last desperate attempt at 'Restoration of the Union for Order' (*T'ung-chih*) in the 1870s.

The officials who carried out the abortive Restoration had learnt the superficial, but not the fundamental, lessons of the Taiping Rebellion. Like all reformists, they sought, classically, to 'repair' the ruling apparatus, refusing to acknowledge that the foundations themselves had decayed beyond repair, for to do so would have meant officially recognizing the need for revolution.

A revolution was certainly the only solution if China was to survive intact in a modern world. The more far-sighted members of the ruling class were beginning to break away, and to advocate a new form of government which would adopt as its programme 'democracy' (through parliament), popular welfare and national independence, eventually known as Sun Yat-sen's *San-min chu-i* or 'Three People's Principles', the chief slogan of the Revolutionary or Republican Party. Sun Yat-sen, a medical doctor with a missionary training was the most enthusiastic and effective advocate of republicanism. One of his first actions was to contact the secret societies abroad, of which he later became a member.[40] On 24 November 1894, Sun formed a republican association in Honolulu called the Revive China Society (*Hsing Chung Hui*), the main purpose of which was national independence.[41] It was organized on the principles of traditional voluntary association, with a president, a vice-president, two secretaries, nine directors and two minor deputies. There were weekly meetings at which either the president or vice-president had to be present. Decisions could only be arrived at by majority vote. The membership fee of five dollars was directed to an 'aid the country' fund. New recruits had to be introduced by a member of the society. In 1895, the operational base of the society shifted to China, more precisely, to Hong Kong, out of reach of Chinese Government interference. There the organization set itself up as the headquarters of a clandestine national society, with the object of forming branches all over China of at least fifteen members each. In these branches, there were to be yearly elections of officers, comprising a chairman, a vice-chairman, a treasurer, one Chinese-language, one English-language secretary, and ten directors. This time decisions could be reached on the basis of agreement between the directors and five members only. New members had to be sponsored by two members, and the membership fee remained at five dollars. The new innovations comprised an educational department, that is, schools for the 'education of the masses' and a revolutionary newspaper.[42]

In the same year, contact was made with the leaders of the Canton Triads who promised to support an uprising with 3,000 men.[43] But this revolt, projected for 26 October 1895, was aborted by leakage of the plans to the Ch'ing authorities. The leaders fled abroad. Sun himself arrived in Japan on 12 November and the Hong Kong Hsing Chung Hui's activities came to an abrupt end. A Yokohama 'branch' of the society was founded, but this too collapsed. Like the Chinese community in Hawaii, the Chinese in Japan had settled into comfortable conservatism, and expressed little enthusiasm, if not outright hostility, for Sun's anti-Ch'ing and anti-monarchical activities.

However, at about this time, Ch'en Shao-pai, one of the founders of the Honolulu and Yokohama Hsing Chung Hui, joined the Hong Kong Triads; while simultaneously a 'Dragon-head' of the Elder Brothers Society, Pi Yung-nien, joined the Hsing Chung Hui in Japan in 1898. Pi kept Sun informed of the state of secret society activity in central China. In 1899, Pi and Hirayama Amane (sometimes called Hirayama Shu), a Japanese adventurer and Sun's friend, were sent to investigate the true strength of the secret societies in Central China. Their report was highly favourable and Pi succeeded in securing the support of the Elder Brothers Society leaders in Hunan and Hupei. In November 1899, Pi brought a group of seven Elder Brothers leaders or 'Dragonheads' to meet Ch'en Shao-pai and the leaders of the Hong Kong Triads. The outcome of this meeting was the formation of a new society called the Hsing Han Hui (Revive Han Society), with Sun as president.[44] In this way, Sun's influence was extended from south to central China. This alliance, however, did not last long, owing to strong competition from a rival pro-Ch'ing (monarchist) society, the Protect the Emperor Society (Pao Huang Hui) which succeeded in drawing away the Hunan and Hupei Elder Brothers Societies.

In 1900, another revolt in Kwangtung (Waichow) collapsed when aid promised by Japanese sympathizers failed to materialize. Returning to Hawaii, Sun found that all the members of the former Hsing Chung Hui had deserted to the pro-Ch'ing group. Sun thereupon joined the local Honolulu branch of the Triads known as the Chih Kung T'ang[45] (which is the name used throughout the Americas for Chinese secret societies) as Red Cudgel or Fighter Official. Sun had, hence, direct access to other Chih Kung T'angs in the Americas, from which he attempted to recruit members for the Hsing Chung Hui. From the American societies he succeeded in getting a hearing but only one recruit, Huang San-te, a leader of the San Francisco society. At this time, the popularity of the Pao Huang Hui, the conservatism, or indifference of the American overseas Chinese to problems of the mother country, and the influence of the American and Hawaiian environment, explained Sun's failure to recruit new members for his society from amongst them.

It was not until 1905 (after Russia's defeat by Japan) that the republican movement got under way. The defeat of a European country by a small oriental country like Japan renewed nationalist and republican hopes in China. Those mandarin republicans who had despised Sun for his low social origins and his associations with 'brigands' of the secret societies, began to think it over. Further, the deepening penetration of China by foreign imperialism and the rapid decay of literati prestige swept away enough of the snobbish objections to rally the revolutionary intelligentsia to Sun's side.

Two years before this, however, Huang Hsing (Sun's rival and deputy) went to Kwangtung and Kwangsi with several others to make contact with leaders of the various 'Black' and 'White gangs' of the Triads, and the result was the formation of the 'Flourish China Society' (*Hua Hsing Hui*), the chief aim of which was to collect money and buy arms. This society, established mainly by returned students from Japan, formed the second most important group, next to the Hsing Chung Hui, in the new 'United League' (*T'ung Meng Hui*) founded by Sun in 1905 in Japan.

Another group, formed in Hangchow, led by T'ao Cheng-chang and Shen Ying called the 'Dragon Flower Society' (*Lung Hua Hui*) and consisting of Triad leaders from Fukien, Chekiang, Anhwei, Kiangsu and Kiangsi, was absorbed into the Ke-ming Tang, at this time.[46] T'ao Cheng-chang's other party, called the 'Restoration Society' (*Kuang Fu Hui*), founded in Shanghai in

1904, also joined the United League. (There is evidence that this society may have been a modified version of the Dragon Flower Society, being composed of both students and secret society members mainly from Anhwei and Chekiang.)[47] Anarchists, educated in Paris, also joined the League.[48]

The United League was thus composed of both the old and the new forces of Chinese rebellion: the secret societies and the foreign-educated students (mainly Japanese) returning to China with ideas of republicanism and revolution current in Japan and the West at the time. It goes without saying there was little love lost between the two forces; but Sun did his best to weld them together and argued that both 'destruction' (represented by secret society activities) and 'construction' (represented by student militancy) were necessary complements of a national revolution. Predictably, the League advocated republicanism, equalization of land rights, and resistance to foreign aggression. The League was the immediate precursor of the Nationalist Party, the Kuomintang.

The role of the Kuomintang in the republican revolution need not detain us here, as a great number of studies of the subject already exists.[49] It has been established that secret societies contributed substantially to the republican nationalist movement headed by Sun Yat-sen, who, in a characteristic tribute to the part played by secret societies in the 1911 revolution, marched in solemn procession to the graves of the Ming emperors and 'informed' them of the success of their victory over the Manchus. As a reward for their support, the secret societies were permitted to operate openly for the first time.[50] This freedom, needless to say, fundamentally changed their functions and nature: they bore, for the remaining decades of the republican period, a close resemblance to the Sicilian Mafia,[51] operating as terrorist syndicates, and shedding what elements of 'social banditry' they once possessed. Their continued and mutually profitable liaison with the Kuomintang during the 1920s and 1930s earned them the reputation of hired assassins of the government (used against unarmed workers in Shanghai, 1927), and agents of the most corrupt and reactionary elements of the Nationalist Party.[52] Their notorious connections with the latter, and with the Shanghai massacre, as well as with the subversion of trade unions[53] won their leaders reputations (in the *Who's Who* of the 1930s) as philanthropists, businessmen and respected 'Government Advisers'.[54] (For example, the Green Gang leader Tu Yuch-sheng was responsible for running arms through the foreign concessions to Chiang's troops, and hunted the workers throughout the city like animals. The working class movement never recovered from this blow.)

Those who remained faithful to their 'social bandit' origins were persuaded to join the Communist Party; the most prominent of these groups was the Hunan Elder Brothers Society (the same group which had played a key role in the Republican Revolution), to whom Mao Tse-tung sent an open letter of appeal.[55] The appeal was not in vain, but Mao's writings reveal that their traditional habits (consorting with prostitutes, opium smoking, etc.) often stood in the way of revolutionary activity.[56] Their role in the Red Army as 'bandit elements' was not an efficacious one, and it was only when they were transformed ideologically that they were useful. Their proportion in the Red Army was probably nearly as large as it had been in the republican armies, whose links with the peasantry had always been, at most, tenuous. The Red Army, however, was mainly composed of peasants who completely outnumbered the representatives of the other classes of Chinese society. The 'popular' character of the Army is generally recognized as the main reason for its eventual success.[57]

From the above discussion it is clear that secret societies contributed as much as the republican revolutionaries to the overthrow of the centuries-old political order, and as such became the direct agents of structural change.

To conclude, it will be necessary to sum up the main features of Chinese secret societies in general terms—combining the findings of the Chinese case with those of Simmel, Wedgwood and others.

Chinese secret societies may be defined as follows. In the nineteenth century they were voluntary associations, possessed of a secret sub-culture, were corporate in that they owned movable and immovable property (meeting hall, common funds, spheres of economic activity) in common, and were dependent for their existence on an oppressive host society. Although they were simultaneously 'conformative' and 'alienative' (see p. 204, n. 4 to Prologue) in their attitude towards the host society, they tended in periods of chaos to be more visibly 'alienative' than in periods of peace when they were more 'conformative'. Similarly, the extent to which they were 'instrumental' or 'expressive'—these are understood as mutually hostile categories—in their mode of adaptation to the orthodox society depended also on the particular conditions of the time. When they became both 'alienative' in attitude and 'instrumental' in expression, it reflected a breakdown in central Government control, and the outbreak of *organized* rebellion (as opposed to spontaneous irruptions of peasant discontent) which usually resulted in dynastic collapse.

This correspondence of secret societies with social disorder may be explained by their connection with the 'dangerous classes'[58] of Chinese society, whose members formed the bulk of the secret societies. For, as long as the social conditions which gave rise to such classes—for example, systematic economic, social and political oppression—continued to exist, secret societies were ineradicable.

The degree of the alienative power of Chinese secret societies was determined by two specific factors: the type of organization; and the degree to which the central bureaucracy was disorganized. If the central administration became too large for its material base (the taxation capacity of the population) the alienative power of the secret societies would express itself in rebellion. If the above dislocation was combined with foreign economic and ideological penetration, then the power of secret societies would become, as it did in 1911, alienative to the point of revolution.

However, such alienative force is revolutionary only if it is combined with an *explicitly* revolutionary party. For two essential features were lacking in secret societies—a coherent, alternative social and political programme upon which to act; and a centralized organization. These two elements tend to be reflections of one another. The dispersed, decentralized character of secret society organizations, their haphazard and impromptu style of federation reflect the limitations and parochialism of their traditional concerns; while their apparent 'nationalism' meant often nothing more than xenophobia.

Their strengths, in contrast, lay in more modest spheres of action: conventional rebellion and mutual protection for their members. For the successful implementation of these aims, the ability to *survive* was most important. Secret societies developed this ability to the utmost. They evolved an adaptable, compact style of organization, which was able to deploy at any one place and time ten men, at the least, or several thousand men, at the most. Leadership was hierarchical, popularly elected, and exercised great authority over the lives and actions of its members.

The necessary physical mobility of secret societies, however, reduced the danger of the bureaucracy becoming overgrown and ineffectual. While internal security was ensured by ritual, sanctions and, most important of all, by the functions of protection for members. It was these functions which distinguished Chinese secret societies from clandestine associations requiring the 'cellular' method of organization. Chinese secret societies replaced the near-total anonymity of members to each other by the near-total identification of members with each other. So much so that the Triads saw themselves as not only members of one 'family' (the Blanquist secret societies in France of 1834 incidentally also called themselves 'Les Familles') but also members of one 'body', and the injury to one 'limb' was seen as affecting all the other 'limbs' equally.[59] The external security of the members was ensured by a deployment of numbers of agents in disguise, creating a favourable climate among the local populace by propaganda and a policy of respect for peasant or poor people's property.

This attitude stood in striking contrast to the policy of the Imperial armies who won the bitter enmity of the population by their scorched-earth policy in the indiscriminate slaughter of rebels and innocents. The protective 'outer wall' of active or passive local support was therefore essential if the secret societies were to survive overwhelming Government repression.

Although Chinese secret societies were not explicitly revolutionary, they nevertheless bridged the gap between a conventional, spontaneous type of rebellion and organized revolution. Further, the Republican revolution might not have 'taken root' in the popular consciousness so early if secret societies had not actively participated in it. Certainly the notion of 'republicanism' was unfamiliar, if not incomprehensible, to any but the most up-to-date Chinese; that is, the revolutionary intelligentsia. The important role played by secret societies in bringing about the military success of the revolution helped to bring it closer to the people by making it *theirs*: the people had participated in the struggle through '*their own*' organizations, familiar and well-tried. The revolution of 1911 (*hsin-hai ke-ming*) was not thus merely the work of the rebellious members of the ruling class.

In more general terms, secret society role and organization are determined by three basic conditions. These are, first, only an oppressive, authoritarian society can produce secret societies which have as their *raison d'être* passive resistance to, or active rebellion against, the State—with its inevitable abuse of power, its internal contradictions expressed in its oppression of the politically weak and the economically impoverished. This may be a development from the second condition which is that a State which pretends to provide orthodox institutional guarantees for protection of its subjects in fact does nothing of the kind, but allows certain small élites to monopolize these guarantees, and manipulate them to their own particular interests against the interest of the majority of the population. In such circumstances, the majority would have no alternative but to erect such guarantees for themselves, independent or defiant of, the wishes of the State and the ruling classes. Such guarantees usually take the form of voluntary associations substituting for orthodox organizations of mutual-aid. Because such voluntary associations question the efficacy of orthodox organization, they are looked upon by the State with suspicion and persecuted. To protect themselves from the destructive attentions of the State, voluntary associations become clandestine. Thus begins the process of the transformation of *social* organizations of mutual-aid into *political* organizations of military self-help. Such clandestine associations (with their *all-round* guarantees of personal protection) necessarily develop the 'familial' or 'communal' type of organization (see p. 125)—with its maximum identification of members with one another—as opposed to the 'cellular' type of organization, where the contact of members is reduced to a minimum, usually three to five members at each level of the hierarchy of command. The differences in organization may be explained in functional terms: the 'familial' type of organization tends to be popular and general in its aims and aspirations, while the 'cellular' type of organization tends to be linked to élitist and specialist undertakings.

Third, secret societies can acquire a revolutionary colouring and even function when the contradictions within a society (e.g. a 'misfit' between the institutional structure and its material base) become irreconcilable. Up until that time, their secrecy helps to protect the young, vulnerable forces of revolution (e.g. a rising social class, a political party) from destruction by the still powerful established order, like the protective shell which surrounds a young fowl before it is hatched. In this way, secret societies are the organized expression, as well as the organizing instrument, of contradictions within a society. That is, their existence is the expression, and their activity, the weapon of the rebellious forces within a given society. So that when the rebellious forces become revolutionary, their activity too, for a time at least, may become revolutionary. Whether this revolutionary activity lasts or not will depend on the *other* components of the revolutionary force. In this sense, then, secret societies are 'primitive' revolutionary arrangements necessary for a transition to more 'developed' or 'advanced' revolutionary organizations, such as trade unions and modern political parties.[60]

However, once such 'familial'-type secret societies are deprived of their political role by new forms of political opposition, then they tend to fall back on either pure ritual, or specific reactionary and/or criminal activities. Not all secret societies, however, begin with social bandit origins—the Mafia is a case in point—and these never acquire a revolutionary character, but rather the opposite.

The Mafia, moreover, unlike most Chinese secret societies, use the structure of the family as a *concrete* basis of recruitment. The Chinese societies of the Triad type did not, even though they evoked the *ideology* of the family generally, and that of the fraternity, specifically. They explicitly denied the supremacy of family and blood ties, and subordinated them to secret society ties, based on voluntary recruitment. In denying the supremacy of the orthodox consanguineal family, secret societies were defying its values, the values of the 'natural order' of things. This 'artificiality' (see p. 140) of secret voluntary association was its progressive force, and reflected the general swing away from ascriptive values in societies in the process of urbanization. In this aspect, secret societies of the Chinese type were socially revolutionary long before they became politically revolutionary. It is in this sense, then, that Chinese secret societies, and those resembling them elsewhere, were not primitive rebels, like those described by Hobsbawm, but primitive revolutionaries.

Appendix A

Rebellions and secret societies

Date	Rebellion	Secret societies
B.C.		
209	'First' rebellion against the Ch'in, the first unified empire, led by Ch'en Sheng and Wu Kuang who believed in 'political' spiritualism	
A.D.		
16–27	Red Eyebrows. Restoration of the Han	Red Eyebrows
184	Yellow Turbans, led by Chang Chüeh, a Taoist faith-healer, and thirty-six generals. Began in eight provinces of the North China Plain, then westwards into the States now known as Szechwan province. Descendants of Chang built up tributary 'church' State in Szechwan	Taiping Tao
		Five Pecks of Rice Sect
515, 713–41 1047	Millenarian revolts led by 'new Buddhas' or Maitreyas	Chai-hui, Pai-yun and other vegetable-eating sects

Date A.D.	*Rebellion*	*Secret societies*
1120–1	Led by Fang-la, Sung-chiang and Lu Ch'un-i in the marshes of Shantung	Hundred-and-Eight Outlaws of Liang Shan Po
1344–82	Red Turbans, led by Han Shan-tung, then Han Lin-erh, finally Chu Yüan-chang, a Buddhist monk who overthrew the Mongol Yüan dynasty and became first Emperor of the Ming dynasty	White Lotus Sect
1761 . . .	Small revolts by millenarian Buddhists; in 1775, a chief of the White Lotus was sent in exile to the province of Kansu	Ming Tsun, Pai-Yun, etc.
1787	Rebellion in Formosa led by Lin Shuang-wan, etc.	Triads
1794–1804	Led by Liu Chi-hsieh in an abortive attempt to restore Ming dynasty	White Lotus
1814	Led by Chung Ti-kang in Kiangsi; Hu Ping-yao and seventeen others from the Triads attempted to set up Mao-li Chu as a pretender to the Ming	Triads, Pure Water Society (a branch of the Triads)
	Led by eunuchs in Peking, a palace coup	White Lotus, Eight Trigrams, Three Incense Sticks, White Feathers
	Revolts in Honan, Shantung and Kiangsi	Rationalists (Tsai-li), Triads
1815	Revolts in Shensi	White Lotus
1817–27	Revolts in Canton	Triads
1832	In Kwangtung, Kwangsi, Hunan with Yao tribes, Fukien	Triads

Date A.D.	Rebellion	Secret societies
1849	Amoy, Shanghai (Shantung)	The Daggers (Ta Tao Hsiao Tao)
1850	Kwangtung, Kwangsi	Triads
1850–64	Taipings, led by Hung Hsiu-ch'üan, began in Kwangsi and ended in Nanking	Christianized Taipings, Triads
1853–68	Nien in Shantung	Nien, White Lotus
1886	Kwangtung, Weichao prefecture, 3,000 men	Triads
1891	Anti-foreign riots in Yangtze basin	Elder Brothers (Kelao)
1892	Riots to free captured leaders	Elder Brothers
	Kwangtung	Triads
1893	Hunan, Hupei, Szechwan	Elder Brothers
1900	At first anti-Manchu, then anti-foreign riots round Peking and in Shantung	The Boxers (I-Ho-t'uan)
1911–12	Republican revolution led by Sun Yat-sen	Elder Brothers, some Triads

Appendix B

Triad vocabulary

This list is from Stanton, *The Triad Society*, 1900 (pp. 93–6) with my revised translations of the Chinese words.

Meaning	*Cant*
a lodge	Red Flower Pavilion
to join society	enter the circle
	respect the orthodox
	be born
to hold a meeting	open the stage
	let loose the horses
a member	fragrance
	Hung hero
	hero
a non-member	wind, or son of a leper
	partridge
a new member	new top
to attend a meeting	see a theatrical performance
secret books of the Society	little jacket
certificate of membership	purse (money-belt)
	eight-cornered sign (plaque)
	eight trigrams

Meaning	Cant
exhibit a sign of membership	hang out a plaque
hair	green silk
hog	hairy melon
pork	smooth melon
toast pork	golden, or red melon
beef	great vegetables
salt beef	one item vegetable
goose	number six
fowl	number seven
duck	number eight
dog	mosquito
fish	wave-plunger, tail-shaker
salt-fish	salt sprout, slave girl
vegetables	girl servants
rice	sand
boil rice	beat sand
boil congee (gruel)	beat waves
eat congee	plough waves
raw tobacco	raw ginger
prepared tobacco	cooked (ripe) ginger
opium	travelling clouds
smoke tobacco	bite ginger
smoke opium	bite clouds
tobacco pipe	Hung bamboo, green dragon
tea	green lotus, red water, green water
wine	family harmony
water	three rivers (*san-ho*)
oil	obedience to Hung
chopsticks	gold bamboo slips
tea-cup	lotus bud
wine-cup	lotus seed
bowl	lotus flower
plate	lotus leaf
incense	cassia twigs
candles	dwarf trees
betel	Honan
betel leaf	fodder
lime	marshall

Meaning	*Cant*
mosquito curtain	lantern
Ming jacket	Buddhist robe
trousers	water chestnut
shoes	iron-soles
cap	cloud-cover
hat	bamboo (coolie) hat
large bamboo hat	cane shield
umbrella	Hung-head, one-leg, black-cloud
handkerchief	white-cloud, twelve-taels
lamp	mosquito curtain
oil lamp	Hung-lamp
road	thread
travel	walk-the-thread
house	beginning of the sixty-year cycle
ancestral hall	privy
market	great peace (*t'ai-p'ing*)
table	square plane
stool	four-legs
sleep (v)	dry
bed	drying booth
sit	drop
junk (boat)	wooden shoe
ship	plane
to board a ship	walk the plane
sword	orange-board, silk crepe
dagger	young lion
cannon	black dog
powder	dog-shit
report of cannon	dog's bark
silver dollars	melon seeds
cash	sesame
a string of 100 cash	blade of grass
a string of 1,000 cash	a rope
hand	five-clawed dragon
ears	follow-the-wind = favourable wind; (in Shanghai) pig's ears
cut off the ears	lower the favourable wind
cut off a head	wash the face
murder by drowning	wash the body

Meaning	*Cant*
sea	great sky
drown in the sea	lower into the great sky
the lodge club	the three-foot-six, dwarf pine
the fan	crescent moon
the bushel (*t'au*), in which the flags and paraphernalia is placed	Willow City
the needle, used for pricking fingers at initiations	iron-headed prince

This list is by Schlegel, *Thien Ti Hwui, The Hung League Secret Society in China and India,* 1866, and consists of words not found in Stanton's list.

Meaning	*Cant*
magistrate	enemy; official bandit
police	wind-draft (breeze)
government troops	wild wind
there are outsiders	there is wind
man	horse
ten men	one ounce
hundred men	one hundred-tael horse
double sword	bridge planks
agent	iron-plank shoe
	night-brother
	grass-slipper
lamp-wick	dragon of the dawning east
lime	marshal
lime spatula (to smear lime on betel leaves)	weapons
eat rice	beat gravel
beef	great multi-red cloth
salt	enter prosperity
rice	heart of a mirror
cooked rice	broken mirror
eye	lantern
wine	family in harmony and prosperity

Triad vocabulary

Meaning	Cant
vinegar	Hung obeys Heaven
oil	hemp water
chopsticks	green twigs
bowl, basin	lotus cup
tea-cup	blue (green) lotus drum
wine-cup	a drum
dog	military post (pissing place)
fish	grass-flower piercing the waves
prepared tobacco	Hung-braves cloud travel
books	clothes
clothes	study (*hsüeh*)
breeches	River Ch'a
a man	one cash
rich	slow-to-take
poor	eager-to-take
highway robbery	shoot partridges
plunder a ship	eat ducks
plunder pawnshops	pull out the ear-pick
plunder a village	make the big cruise, circuit
charge with gun-powder	plant peaches
to go, to do	cold work
kill	wash the body, ears
cut off an ear	off with the fair wind
sleep in an inn	rest in a room
girl or woman	long-grass-leather-seven
open the lodge	make theatricals
enter the society	be born
diploma of membership	purse
the fiscal	red cudgel
laws and statutes	little jacket
lodge	Willow City

This list is by F. V. Faber, colleague of Schlegel.

Meaning	Cant
an elder brother	adopted uncle
a colleague of the same rank	adopted brother
a younger brother	sworn younger brother

silver (money)	white
gold	yellow
cash	pierced-heart
grain	yellow husks
wealthy man	great ginseng
drink tea	swallow green
government troops	cursed-cuckolds
good man	a wasp
attack the provincial capital	beat a big ring
a hundred men	one hundred-tael horse
smoke opium	chew clouds

Appendix C

The Thirty-six Articles of the Oath Hung Chia San-shih-liu Che

Art. 1. From the moment that you have entered the Hung League (Hung Men), you must quietly fulfil your duties, and keep to your own business. It has always been said that filial love is the first of all virtues; therefore you must respect and obey both your parents, and obey and venerate your superiors. Do not resist your father and mother and, so, violate the laws of the Hung-league. He who does not keep this command, most surely, will not be suffered by Heaven and Earth, but he shall be crushed by five thunder-bolts! Each of you ought to obey this.

Art. 2. When you have entered the Hung-league, you ought to keep secret everything from your wife and family, for fear that something might leak out before strangers; even so that, as a father, you don't tell it to your son, as an elder brother, you don't tell it to your younger brother. Do not betray the secrets (*yang-seh*, literally, 'yang colour') of the Hung-league! He who does not keep this command—may Heaven not suffer him; but may he die and become a headless ghost! When it is found out that a brother has betrayed the secrets of strangers, one of his ears will be cut off and he will, besides, be punished with 108 blows.

Art. 3. After having entered the Hung-league, you must consider all the members of the league, the four higher classes, as earls, marquises, generals and ministers, as well as the four middling classes, as scholars, husbandmen, artisans and merchants, and the lower classes, as vagabonds and mendicants, of which rank or station they may be, as brothers. You shall not, trusting to your riches, insult the poor, or, relying upon your power, oppress the good and honest. He who does not keep this command, is a false swearer and a perjurer. May he die in a foreign country! May serpents bite him, and tigers devour him!

Art. 4. After having entered the Hung-league, you shall not insult any more the Buddhist or Taoist priests; for the five founders, originally, were priests, and we venerate them as the founders: are we not, then, disciples of priests? He who does not keep this command—may he die a wretched death! This crime is not easily to be forgiven, and, therefore, the offender will be punished, according to the law, with 72 blows.

Art. 5. After having entered the Hung-league, you ought to be faithful and loyal. You must consider the father of a brother as your own father; his mother as your mother; his sister as your sister; and his wife as your sister-in-law. Do not lie or speak evilly. When you marry the daughter of a brother you ought to employ go-betweens, and marry her with the prescribed ceremonies; and it shall not be allowed to you to come together unlawfully; neither shall you seduce the wife or concubine of a brother. He who does not keep this command— may he perish in a river or lake, may his bones sink to the bottom, and his flesh float on the surface! Besides, if the brethren discover it, one of his ears will be cut off, and he will be punished with 108 blows.

Art. 6. After having entered the Hung-league, you ought to persevere till the end; let not your mouth say Yes and your heart say No. Do not, on account of a small gain, cause discord between brethren; or, on account of a private promise, cause father and son to be at variance. Do not speak slanderously, and disturb the harmony between husband and wife. He who does not keep these commands is an infamous villain; most surely he will die in an unknown land, and be buried in the stomachs of swine or fishes! Besides, he will be punished by the law, according to circumstances.

Art. 7. After having entered the Hung-league, you ought to consider the affairs of the brethren as your own affairs. If one of them has smuggled, or escaped the duties, or has some secret affairs, or trades in smuggled goods, or cheats strangers or the police, you must keep it secret, and not let it leak out. He who does not keep this command, but betrays it, so that the secrets and the affairs of the brethren become known to other people —may he perish under thousands of swords, and may his head be severed from his trunk! The punishment for this crime is not fixed, but it shall be dealt with according to circumstances.

Art. 8. After etc. . . . you ought to consider fidelity and loyalty as the foundation. When brethren travel to and fro they have a badge as a sign of recognition (*kua-p'ai wei hao*). If they have not found, either in the morning or at night, a place to rest or pass the night, you ought to receive them, and not feign not to recognize them. He who etc. . . . is one who has violated his vow in the Red-pavilion. May he never be happy or prosperous, but may he die without posterity.

Art. 9. After etc. . . . you ought to live in peace and harmony with the brethren, and separate yourselves according to the grades. You shall not, relying upon your strength, oppress the poor, or commit manslaughter in drunkenness, or speak wantonly, insulting or vilifying father and mother, or lift up your hands for a scuffle; for that is violating the duties of the brethren and the concord between hands and feet. We who belong to this league, either in the two capitals or the thirteen provinces, are all one body: so we may not make a difference between *mine* and *thine*. We may not ask if we are kindred, but we must act as if we were so. He who does not keep this command shall, surely, die at the wayside. Besides, he will be punished, according to law, with 108 blows.

Art. 10. After etc. . . . you must always remember your oath sworn in the Flower-pavilion, and not forget that bloody oath. You must live and die together, and be attached to each other as if you were born from one womb. Do not give out untruth or truth and deceive the brethren; neither shall you conceal the police and betray the trust of the brethren. You shall not help a stranger who abuses or beats a brother, and, so, violate the concord. He who does not keep this command—may he perish by cannon-shots. Besides, one of his ears will be cut off, according to law.

Art. 11. After etc. . . . you must adopt the name of Hung, and you must then be (attached) like hands and feet; but, as wealth and indigence are unequally divided, and death and life have a fixed time; so, when the parents of a brother have died, or a brother has died himself, and there is no money to bury the corpse properly, we all must come together and deliberate about it: he who has much, may give much, he who has little, may give little; but all of us ought to unite our forces. When other people see this, they will remark the charity of the Hung-league. He who etc. . . . may he perish in the deep mountains, or on wild peaks, and be buried without coffin or shroud. Besides, according to law, he will be punished with 72 blows.

Art. 12. After etc. . . . you having pledged yourself before heaven: so do not say that providence does not avenge, for three feet above our heads are invisible spirits. You must tell your age according to truth, and not give out untruth . . . and so deceive the five founders. When you have returned, you shall not pray before other altars or in other temples for absolution from your present oaths and vows. He who does not keep this command, is a traitor and perjuror; may he be hacked in thousands of pieces and perish. Besides, both his ears will be cut off; he shall be cast out of the brotherhood, and never be allowed to enter it again.

Art. 13. After etc. . . . you are bound by a bloody oath. You have become one gall and one heart. So when you see that a brother quarrels or fights with other people, you ought to advance, and examine fairly. If the other people are in the wrong you must, certainly, help him with all your might and strength; but if the brother is in the wrong, you must exhort him to desist; in this way the equity of the brotherhood will appear. You shall on no account pretend not to have known it. He who etc. . . . beguiles indeed his own heart, and deceives himself. Most surely he shall not be happy or prosperous, and his children will not live in harmony.

Art. 14. After etc. . . . you ought to remember the oath sworn in the Flower-pavilion. Amongst the members of our brotherhood, some are functionaries, others are vagabonds: each of us has some employment, but we are not all of equal rank. So if fire is set to a place, or robbery is perpetrated, or a ship is plundered, or highway-robbery is committed, we ought to look well to the flags or signals before we set to work; for brethren are not allowed to act wantonly, and violate the harmony between hands and feet. He who etc. . . . may he perish under thousands of swords and become a headless ghost.

Art. 15. After etc. . . . though you ought to consider benevolence and justice as the first, and courteousness and faith as the basis, still you are, as brethren, members of one family, and you ought to help each other in disasters and misfortunes. When a brother is summoned before a tribunal, or a price is set upon him, and he cannot remain longer in the place, the powerful must help him to escape, and the less powerful pay his travelling expenses. This is helping him out of danger, like taking a fish out of a dry place, and it is saving him from difficulties, like liberating a bird out of a close net. He who etc. . . . may he perish at the wayside, may the swine devour him, and the gods bite him, and may he never return in this world again.

Art. 16. After etc. . . . you must be faithful and honest; for all things have an owner. Don't take anything without asking, or instigate strangers to steal the property or riches of a brother. If you know that a heavy price is set upon a brother, and you do not think about saving him, but betray him . . . to the troops of the government; or if you give yourself the thread in hands, or lead the way, to make him prisoner, and injure, in this way, a brother—may you be struck by thunder-bolts, or perish in the flames, or come to an end in the ocean, and your corpse remain floating. This is the heaviest crime according to our law; therefore the offender shall be killed, and his head shall be severed from his trunk.

Art. 17. After etc. . . . remember then that since the ancient times happiness and misfortune have no fixed gates, but that man draws them upon himself:

> Heaven has inexhaustible winds and clouds;
> Men have misery and happiness for morning and evening!

So, when a brother has incurred adversities or misfortunes by his own fault, he ought to suffer them himself, and, on no account, shall he be allowed to implicate the other brethren in his misfortune, in order to extricate himself. For such a one, most surely, will become a headless ghost after his death. If it is discovered, both his ears will be cut off, he shall be cast out of the brotherhood, and never be allowed to enter it again.

Art. 18. After etc. . . . and passed the bridge laid before the Hung-gate and the fair has been opened [*k'ai-hsü*], you can be promoted, after a year, to the grade of Introducer. After two years you can become Vanguard. After three years you can become Incense-master, if at least, there is a vacancy. When you wish then to open a fair, you must first send round a circular [see p. 128] to inform the brethren of it. He who etc. . . . but himself opens a market, commits a great sin against the five founders. May his head be severed from his trunk and he perish. May the swine devour him, and the dogs rend him to pieces.

Art. 19. After etc. . . . the members will elect the chiefs by public vote [*kung-chü*]. There will be a President, a Master, a Fiscal, Treasurers, Agents, and those who have flowers on their head. They shall deliberate fairly and act justly; they shall not, trusting to their greatness, oppress the little, or, relying upon their strength, crush the weaker. Those who selfishly take bribes, or make no difference between right and wrong on account of their relations, but are only bent upon violence and tyranny, shall, most surely, perish in an unknown country.

Art. 20. After etc. . . . if a brother gains his livelihood abroad, and he entrusts you with family letters, you must take care of them. But if you think that you cannot take charge of them, you ought first to inform [the head of the lodge] of it, and not neglect it when the time has already come [for delivering them]. Or, if you perceive that there is money in these letters, you shall not pocket that yourself, or remit less money than there is, for such a one is a swindler who shall perish, most surely, by the sword. If it is discovered, he shall . . . be punished with 108 blows, and he shall completely reimburse the goods or money.

Art. 21. After having entered the Hung-league, you shall not secretly show the statutes and diploma of the lodge to strangers, for they are the most important things of the Hung-league. He who covetously sells them secretly to others, is one who has forgotten his duties and perjured his oath. He shall, most surely, perish by the mouth of a tiger in a deep mountain. If it is discovered both his ears will be cut off, he shall be punished with 108 blows, and be cast out of the brotherhood.

Art. 22. After having entered the Hung-league, if one of the brethren has disputed, quarrelled or fought, you shall on no account inform the authorities of the case, whether it be serious or trifling; but a council will be held, which will judge and decide equitably, and give verdict according to the more or less importance of the case. It shall not be allowed to you to act yourself, and to inform the authorities of it. He who does not keep this command, but disobeys the law, most surely shall perish under countless swords according to the laws of the five founders, and his head and trunk shall be severed from the functionaries of the Ch'ing dynasty and of the Hung-league are each their own master.

Art. 23. After etc. . . . you may not remember or cherish old grudges or new enmities. He who does not keep this command —may he perish at the wayside, and may nobody bury him. According to the law, he will be punished besides, with 72 blows.

Art. 24. After etc. . . . if your own brother or a relation of yours, or a friend, and a brother of the Hung-league, quarrel, brawl, or fight together, you may give a signal in order to exhort them to leave off. But if you separate them forcibly, and help them [the strangers], it is a crime of conspiring with the police—may you then perish in a wretched country.

Art. 25. After etc. . . . if one of the brethren has a difference with strangers, and he is perhaps accused before a tribunal, you shall, on no account, give evidence for these strangers in such a case, no matter if you know them or not. For those who do this are guilty of the crime of conspiring with the police—may they perish on the roads and wayfares.

Art. 26. After etc. . . . if you see that a brother possesses lands, you shall not conspire with strangers to rob him; for if you conspire with strangers, it is manifest that you injure him wilfully, and you offend the statutes of the Hung-league. He who etc. . . . may he die unburied. If it is discovered, he shall be punished, besides, according to law, with 108 heavy blows.

Art. 27. After etc. . . . if the master has appointed a meeting, you shall most surely not conceal policemen within the precincts, in order to show them secretly the secrets. To conceal them is to mix serpents amongst dragons. This is a heavy offence against the statutes of the Hung-league—may such people perish by the point of the sword, and may five thunderbolts crush them.

Art. 28. After having entered the Hung-league, you ought to be attached to each other as brethren, and consider each other as kindred. If other people have stolen the money or properties of a brother, you must search for it, that people may see the equity of the Hung-sect. Most surely you shall not pretend not to know anything about it, and not inform him, but, on the contrary, conceal and keep it for these strangers; for, in the first place, you will be rallied by other people for your perjury, and, second, you violate the purity of our harmony and concord. He who does not keep this command, is one who has forgotten his duties. Most surely he will not die a natural death, but shall perish under countless swords.

Art. 29. After etc. . . . if there are great or small cases coming before the society [*kung-ssu*], all the brethren shall range themselves according to the higher and lower grades. The council of the Hung-league then shall decide equitably, and not, trusting to their power, oppress the weak, or, relying upon their majority, oppress the single ones. It, also, shall not be allowed to cry or to be obstinate; neither shall it be allowed to bring along sharp weapons, or carry secretly sticks or clubs. They who do not keep this command—may they perish by a sharp sword.

Art. 30. After having entered the Hung-league, you must observe the etiquette of this society, and keep its regulations. When the wife or concubine of a brother passes you on the road, you shall not address her rudely or dally with her; for this is a heavy offence against propriety. He who etc. . . . may he never be happy or prosperous, but perish in a bare and sterile country.

Art. 31. After having entered the Hung-league, if you have had some words with a brother in a moment of passion, you shall not remember them and think of revenge; neither shall you speak improper words, or insult his parents with low and vile expressions. He who etc. . . . may he perish at the wayside. According to the law he shall be punished besides, with 72 blows.

Art. 32. After etc. . . . if one of the brethren is involved unexpectedly in a lawsuit, or gets implicated with the false authorities [*kuan-fei* = official bandits], and is prevented [from escaping] on account of his wife and children—then he who, being able to do so, receives his wife and children, is a charitable man. But if there is nobody able to do this, the case ought to be reported to the brotherhood, who shall deliberate about it.

Art. 33. After etc. . . . if the brotherhood has elected some-body to the rank of agent [grass-slippers] his name shall be *night-brother.* He shall, also be called *Iron-plank.* These men are destined to go about everywhere, and they live in all places. If there are public affairs, they are sent to transmit the reports. The brethren shall not turn them off; they have free nourish-ment and travelling expenses; but, for private affairs for the brethren, they must be paid, besides, according to the tariff. If a brother refuses to pay him—may he die of sword-wounds, or perish by the mouth of a tiger.

Art. 34. After having entered the Hung-league, you count the years of your age from the moment of your reception. You must celebrate the birthday of the holy Kwan-ti, the Grave-cleansing festival [*ch'ing-ming*] and the All-souls festival [*ch'i-yüeh*]. You must contribute cheerfully to the expenses of these festivals, yes, you must even give money gladly and not, pretending to be poor, refuse to contribute. He who does not keep this command —may he be unfortunate and unprosperous.

Art. 35. After etc. . . . if there are great or small affairs amongst the brethren, either fortunate or unfortunate, you ought to remain in harmony and concord. The joy of the Hung-league will then be seen. He who etc. . . . may he be unfortunate and unprosperous.

Art. 36. After having entered the Hung-league, you must love each other as your own flesh and bones, and be attached to each other as if you were children from the same womb. It has always been said: 'If one enters a house, one must observe its rule.' So you ought to persevere till the end, and be benevolent and just. You must remember and obey the oaths from the first to the thirty-sixth one; then your children will be prosperous, and you will be happy for numberless generations; for in ancient times it was said: 'A family who hoards up virtues, most surely will have abundance of blessings.' You must all obey and observe this.

Appendix D

Chinese associations in Havana, Cuba, 1967-8

These notes are the result of a month's visit to Havana (December 1967 to January 1968), and are therefore highly impressionistic. I visited three out of a purported 'thirty-six' associations in Havana, and attended a Sunday lunch-time meeting of the Dragon Ridge General Association (*Lung-keng Tsung Kung-so*). I also visited the 'china town' in general and the offices of one of the two Chinese language papers in Havana about which I shall write shortly. A young French anthropologist and I were escorted by a teacher of Chinese at the University of Havana called Mr Feng, who kindly explained certain details regarding the Chinese community in Havana.

According to the publisher of the *Kwong Wah Po* (*Enlightened China Daily*), there are at present about 10,000 Chinese in Cuba, of whom 1,500 are in Havana itself. They comprise mostly small traders, herbalists, bar-keepers, restauranteurs, cane-juice store-owners, launderers, and some farmers in Oriente province. The Chinese population outside Havana itself is highly diffused among the Cuban population; but in Havana, they live largely within the area designated as China Town. Those who still spoke and understood Chinese appeared to belong to a generation well above forty years of age, and to know no Spanish, other than the simplest words and phrases. The dialect spoken appears to be the Amoy dialect, for their ties with Amoy began in 1864, when a large number of Chinese were shipped to Cuba as indentured labour. Even today, they read the *Amoy (Hsia Men) Daily*, but no other place in China is as specifically represented. Many immigrants also came from Kwangtung province, Hong Kong and Macao. Between 1847 and 1874, it has been estimated that between a quarter and a half million indentured labourers had been shipped from these regions in China to Cuba, Peru, Chile and the Sandwich Islands. In 1864, 4,479 men were shipped from Macao, in 1865, 5,207; and during the same years, 2,716 labourers were transported by sea from Canton by Cuban agents acting under the French flag.[1] Of the 23,928 men shipped from Hong Kong, 3,342 died on voyage because of the conditions on board.[2]

These indentured labourers were composed of the remnants of the Taiping rebel armies,[3]

> prisoners taken in the clan fights of the province of Kwang-tung, and who are sold by their captors to Chinese or Portuguese man-buyers upon the interior waters; villagers or fishermen forcibly kidnapped along the coast; and individuals who are tempted by prowling agents to gamble [in Macao] and who on losing surrender their persons in payment according to the peculiar Chinese notions of liability in this respect.

MacNair adds,[4]

> The 'crimps', as the collecting agents were called, received from seven to ten dollars a man delivered to the coolie depots, or barraccons in Macao; here the coolie 'signed' a 'contract' for eight years of service; on reaching Cuba the surviving coolies were put up at auction with their contracts and sold for an average of seventy-eight pounds. The legal right of the coolie to appeal to the Spanish courts for enforcement of his rights in case of ill-treatment or lack of payment was assured him but 'no instance is on record of such a proceeding.'

This 'reluctance' or lack of opportunity for the Chinese labourer to appeal to the Spanish courts gave rise to the creation of mutual-aid associations, and, according to a unique local record,[5] these associations were at first 'fraternal associations with religious overtones', and only became illegal 'later'.

But their illegal activities never reached the level of intensity of their counterparts in the United States.

The first societies were founded in Havana itself, comprising the former inhabitants of Kwangtung, Kwangsi, Fukien. They were formed initially to combat the oppressive contract labour system, which has been described by a contemporary observer as follows:[6]

> I believe the coolie slave trade to be as bad as that of the negroes. During the passage, which is always horrible, the latter perhaps suffered rather more; but, once arrived at their destination, the slaves found in the very interest of their proprietor a guarantee of comparative well-being. The coolies have not even this advantage; and they tell me that their fate is the more lamentable because they belong to a race which is more civilized and more intelligent [*sic*] than the negroes.

A report submitted to the Chinese Foreign Office (*Tsungli Yamen*) in 1874 goes into greater detail about the treatment of Chinese labourers on arrival in Cuba:[7]

> On arrival at Havana they were sold into slavery. During the past years a large number have been killed by blows, have died from the effects of wounds, and have hanged themselves, cut their throats, poisoned themselves with opium, and thrown themselves into wells and sugar cauldrons. On the termination of the contracts the employers, in most cases, insist on a renewal of engagements, which may extend to even more than ten years. Almost every Chinese met by us was, or had been, undergoing suffering and suffering was the purport of almost every word we heard.

Later, some of the associations, on the abolition of slavery, became the instruments of the foremen in attacking the liberated slaves. Sometimes, they fell into the hands of the *contratistas* or slave entrepreneurs and aided them in their work. The Cohongs in Canton attempted to protect the coolies against the *contratistas* by giving their considerable support to the other coolie associations.

There had been altogether three 'waves' of Chinese immigration into Cuba: that of 1847 to 1874, that of 1870 to 1900 from the United States as a result of the racial violence; and that after the 1920s from China, consisting of free labourers. The first formed the Chieh I T'ang in 1867, and the Jen I T'ang in 1868, the two oldest associations known, but which no longer exist under the same names. The Hakkas from Amoy formed the I Sheng T'ang. The American Chinese brought their Chih Kung T'ang with them; while the Hung League (which still exists in name, though combined with the 'Democratic Party') had, during the nineteenth century, as many as 2,000 members.

I visited the last association, called in full Hung Men Min-Chih T'ang, once a secret society. It owns a large building in China Town with a high-ceilinged window-less great initiation hall, impressive in its austerity and sombreness. It is entered via a vestibule which is decorated with photographs of past and presumably prestigious members. At the end of the *t'ang* or hall is a raised dais and bare altar, separated from the wall by a space in which the Incense Master formerly stood during ceremonies. On the wall behind the alter are four portraits (framed like the photographs) painted in oil. One is of the Great Ancestor Wan Yun-lung, the second, of the first Master Ch'en Chin-nan, and the third and fourth are obviously portraits of the local founders, one of whom is in European dress, but neither of them is specifically identified. Above the portraits is a striped flag, each stripe representing a colour of each of the Five Triad lodges, and superimposed on the stripes is the masonic sign of an inverted V superimposed on another V. Apparently, there had been some cooperation between the Hung League and the Freemasons in Cuba. Along the walls are placed heavy mahogany chairs. The impression of austere power and wealth is accentuated by the photographs of well-dressed men in European clothes and chorus girls during some Hung celebration. There is no other furniture in the room.

The Dragon Ridge General Association appears to be at the head of a group of five associations, one of which I also visited, called the Lin (or Lam in Cantonese) West River Association, all of the members of which are surnamed Lin. At the New Year Sunday meeting, there were about forty people assembled, mostly men over sixty years of age. There were four women, only one of whom appeared to possess wholly Chinese features, and she had her two young daughters with her. At the head of the cloth-covered table sat the five former and present Presidents of the Association. There were enthroned on elaborately carved, gothic-like chairs of dark wood, curiously ecclesiastical in design, probably reflecting the influence of the Freemasons. All the presidents looked very senior in age, probably in their seventies; the other members were also mostly over their sixties; only a few looked younger. This may mean that only men over a certain age could be elected president. All the presidents made speeches followed by amicable applause. The atmosphere was relaxed and definitely familial. Some other members also spoke from the floor, while others drank tea and nibbled at the snacks (*hsiu-mai*) and highly coloured sponge-cakes laid out at intervals on the long tables. On the walls hung the portraits of José Marti (the hero of the Cuban war of independence against Spain),[8] Sun Yat-sen and Mao Tse-tung. The meeting did not last longer than an hour, after which the members shook hands with each other and the newly arrived visitors from associated *Kungso* and disappeared.

The shrine room, located on the first floor above the meeting hall, was dominated by a large, carved, brightly coloured image of Kwan Kung, the God of War and of Associations. Behind the idol was a glass box containing a piece of silk embroidery depicting the Three Brothers of the Peach Garden accompanied by a fourth called Chao. This art-work had apparently more than a purely ritual significance in that it represented the surnames of the members of the association who are all called after those of the Three Brothers, Liu Pei, Chang Fei and Kwan Yü, as well as Chao. As we were examining the altar, a Chinese woman was telling fortunes to some of the younger members who had come up to the shrine out of curiosity. She very good-humourdley shook the bamboo cylinder with the bamboo slips in it, while an older member read from the *Book of Changes*.

It is very clear after my visit to the other association (Lin Hsi Ho Kung So) that surnames serve as a rallying point for association rather than place of origin. This is confirmed by the long lists of members' names given in the New Year issue of the two Chinese newspapers in which the associations announce their new year 'officers'. Simmel's thesis that secret societies could come to make hierarchies for their own sake seems to be supported by the evidence of the Havana associations, where the lists of functionaries contain sometimes nearly a hundred names. As an example of this development, the Dragon Ridge General excels the others. It boasts 16 Administrative Officers, 1 Chairman, 3 Deputy Chairmen, 8 Expectant Administrators, 8 Examiners, 1 Head Inspector, 1 Private Secretary to the Examiners, 8 Expectant Examiners, 1 Treasurer, 1 Organizer, 1 Propagandist, 1 Auditor, 1 Public Relations or Liaison Officer, 1 Documents Officer, 1 Chief Charity Association Officer, and each of the last six officers have a deputy and two clerks; 13 Councillors or Committee Members, 1 voluntary Doctor of Medicine, 1 voluntary Lawyer, and 1 representative from the Hong Kong Association. This is then followed by a list of representatives in various cities and ports throughout Cuba, numbering 29 altogether.

A General Association recently coordinated all the societies in Havana or Cuba under its aegis. Its origin is shown in the large portraits of Mao Tse-tung and the 'Red Flags festooning one wall of a huge *salle*, in which is installed a large polished wood table on which can be found all the Chinese newspapers available in Cuba. These are the *Jen Min Jih Pao* (*Peoples' Daily*), the *Ta Kung Pao*, the *Amoy Daily* and the local newspapers, the *Kuang Hua Pao* and the *K'ai Ming Kung Pao* of the Hung League and Democratic Party. The former is published by the General Association and is explicitly Maoist in inspiration; it contains news about the cultural revolution in China and its progress in concrete terms. The *K'ai Ming Kung Pao*, however, besides looking decidedly more conservative both in typeface and illustration (the other paper is not illustrated) contains popular fiction serialized from day to day as well as news from Hong Kong, from Prensa Latina and from Canton. In one page of the New Year edition (p. 7) there is even a corner devoted to the Freemasons, announcing its financial takings for the year, for each week and each month, locally and from abroad. The sum recorded was 26 pesos (dollars) 4 cents for the year.

Even in the General Association, there exists a small, albeit rather chaotic, shrine to Kwan Kung, strewn with fortune papers and stale offerings of the local fare—cakes and fried plantain bananas. Scattered on the floor were the usual bamboo slips for fortune-telling, a great many tickets with verses from the *I Ching* (*Book of Changes*) accompanied by *pai-chieh* or 'explanations' printed on them, and a pair of ritual wooden clappers. Along the passage is the General Association library and reading room which the Cuban lawyer attached to the Association has as his office.

The general impression gained from the visits to the associations is that the majority of the members, despite the impressive accommodation and furnishings, have been, and still are, living at a 'subsistence' level. The food served at the Dragon Ridge General and that sold in the shops bear this out. The only recognizably Chinese restaurant is located in the Havana equivalent of London's Mayfair district, and is normally frequented by the white ex-bourgeoisie. However, the standard of living does not appear to be much below that of the average Cuban in Havana who is still suffering from the effects of the massive American blockade.

It is obvious that the associations serve no other purpose than that of friendly societies, providing facilities for recreation outside the home. Moreover, the younger generations have lost most of their original culture, unable either to speak or read Chinese, and having, in most cases, Cuban mothers. The *kung-so* represent all that remains of Chinese institutions and culture in Cuba, and soon they too will lose their function as the younger generation become more and more absorbed into Cuban society. The Chinese community in Cuba is a 'world on the wane', and its isolation is made the more poignant by the fact that no Cuban anthropologist or social scientist has thought it worthwhile to make a study of the Chinese community throughout the hundred years of its existence. It is nevertheless remarkable that so many elements of Chinese culture have survived under slavery, and amid the upheavals of a revolutionary society.

Appendix E

List of other secret societies in the south operative in the late Ch'ing

Szu Hsi T'ang ('The Four Western Halls'), in Szechwan.
Hsi-pei lao-jen t'ang ('West-north old-men hall'), in Kweichow, pro-Manchu society.
Wu Fu T'ang ('Five Happinesses Hall'), in Taiwan, also *Chung I T'ang* ('Loyal Just Hall').
Hung Pang ('Hung Gang'), in Chekiang and Kiangsu.
Ching Pang ('Green Gang'), in Hopei, originally known as the *San Yuan T'ang* ('Society of Three Origins'), included the *Yen Hsiu* ('Salt Owls') and the *Kuang Tan* ('Smooth Eggs'), which attempted to control the Grand Canal and the grain routes; when grain transport was transferred to the sea route and carried by steamers, members of the above societies were left destitute. They then resorted to the smuggling of salt under a man named P'an, and became an associated branch of the Elder Brothers Society.
Other names of the Triad or Hung societies are:
Ch'ing-shui Hui ('Clear Water Society')
Pi Shou Hui ('Dagger Society')
Shuang Tao Hui ('Double Knife Society')
Po-tzu Hui ('(Begging) Bowl Society')
Kao Hua Hui ('Reform Society')
Hsiao Hung Ch'i ('Little Red Flag Society')
Chien-tzu Hui ('Sword Society')
Chih Kung T'ang ('Justice Society').

Notes

PROLOGUE

1 As defined by Maurice Duverger, *The Idea of Politics* (transl. Robert North and Ruth Murphy), London, 1966, pp. 154–5.
2 Used in Tönnies' sense in *Einführung in die Soziologie*, Stuttgart, 1931.
3 As defined by Max Weber in his study of North German fraternities in *The City* (transl. Don Martindale and Gertrud Neuwirth), New York, 1958, 1966, pp. 114–15.
4 See S. M. Lyman, 'Chinese secret societies in the Occident: notes and suggestions for research in the sociology of secrecy', *Canadian Review of Sociology and Anthropology*, 1964, 1, 2, pp. 79–102.

INTRODUCTION

1 The *Mu-yang Ch'eng*, ritual name for the Triad secret society. It is taken directly from the popular Buddhist term for 'paradise'.
2 See John A. Hobson, *Imperialism*, London, 1902, for the earliest known definition of the nineteenth-century phenomenon, and V. I. Lenin, *Imperialism, the Highest Stage of Capitalism*, in Lenin, *Selected Works*, London, 1947, vol. I, pp. 710 ff. for a Marxist elaboration of the above writer's thesis.
3 Date of the republican revolution.
'4 See pp. 64–7 and 141.
5 Georg Simmel, *The Sociology of Georg Simmel* (ed. and transl. by Kurt H. Wolff), New York, 1964.
6 Article in *Oceania*, July 1930, 1, 2.
7 *Primitive Rebels*, Manchester, 1959.

8 *The Secret Societies of the European Revolution: 1776–1876*, 2 vols, London, 1876.

9 Stanford M. Lyman, 'Chinese secret societies in the Occident: notes and suggestions for research in the sociology of secrecy', *Canadian Review of Sociology and Anthropology*, 1964, 1, 2, pp. 79–102. C. N. Reynolds, 'The Chinese Tongs', *American Journal of Sociology*, 1935, XL, 5, pp. 612–23. M. Freedman, 'Immigrants and associations: Chinese in nineteenth century Singapore', *Comparative Studies in Society and History*, 1960, III, 1.

10 *Les Sociétés Secrétes en Chine (19e et 20e siècles)*, Paris, 1965.

11 Père Leboucq, *Associations de la Chine: Lettres*, Paris, *c.* 1880; published also in *Études Religieuses* as 'Lettres', Paris, 1875, VIII, pp. 197–220, 641–64, with some revisions. Gustave Schlegel, *Thien Ti Hwui, The Hung League, Secret Society in China and India*, Batavia, 1866. William Stanton, *The Triad Society*, Hong Kong, 1900. W. P. Morgan, *Triad Societies in Hong Kong*, Hong Kong, 1960. W. L. Wynne, *Triad and Tabut, A Survey of the Origins of Chinese and Mohammedan Secret Societies in the Malay Peninsula A.D. 1800–1935*, Singapore, 1941.

12 Lo Erh-kang, *T'ien-ti-hui wen hsien lu* (Documents on the Heaven and Earth Society), Shanghai, 1948. Hirayama Amane (or Chou P'ing-shan), *Chung-kuo pi-mi she-hui shih* (History of Chinese secret societies), Shanghai, 1935 (reprint).

13 With the exception of the scholarly article by Wang T'ien-chiang, *'Shih-chiu shih-chi hsia-pan-chi chung-kno-ti pi-mi she-hui'* (Chinese secret societies in the second half of the nineteenth century), *Li-shih yen-chiu* (Historical studies), Peking, 1963, 2, pp. 83–100.

14 *Pi-mi she-hui*. See p. 56 for other Chinese terms.

15 See p. 46 for the various terms abusing heterodox religious sects and associations.

I THE IDEOLOGICAL BACKGROUND TO CHINESE SOCIETY, 1840–1912

1 Called the 'Five Classics', comprising the *Classic of Songs*, the *Classic of Documents*, *Classic of Changes*, *Spring and Autumn Annals*, and the *Record of Rites*, sometimes known as the 'thirteen classics' with elaborations. The 'Four Books': *Record of Rites* (divided into Great Learning and Doctrine of the Mean), the *Analects of Confucius*, and *Mencius*.

2 See p. 22 for details of the magistrate's duties.

3 Briefly, the characteristics of a 'Confucianist' society may be summed up as follows: (a) agrarian self-sufficiency; (b) dissipation of commercial capital in the pursuit of status; for example,

in the purchase of land and orthodox education; (c) bureau-cratically controlled commerce—chiefly by means of monopolies on essential goods (salt, tea, liquor, silver, etc.); of maritime and internal customs duties, the new *likin* tax on goods in transit instituted in 1853. These taxes brought the government 52 million *taels* out of a total revenue of 89 million *taels* in the early 1890s; (d) absence of a navy, a trained, efficient, modern-equipped army capable of defending China's ports and inland routes against foreign invasion, reflecting an inward-looking, isolationist foreign policy; (e) decentralized control at the village level—no central representative there, only the non-official gentry.

4 The Empress Wu (683–705) introduced the Examination System as the only legitimate channel for civil service recruit-ment in order to cut the old military aristocracy off from the source of power. Initially acting as the Empress's advisers, officials soon developed into a power autonomous from the crown; and in periods of dynastic decline were pitted against the Emperor's personal servants, the powerful eunuchs.

5 Hsiao Kung-chuan, *Rural China: Imperial Control in the Nineteenth Century*, Seattle, 1960, pp. 235ff. See also Chapter II, Section (C), for definition of 'gentry'.

6 See Chapter II, Section (A) on imperial armies.

7 Hsiao, op. cit., pp. 236–7.

8 Ibid., pp. 196–8.

9 Ibid., pp. 187–8, for summary of the Amplified Instructions.

10 See Chapter II, Section (B) on the *pao-chia* system.

11 Hsiao, op. cit., pp. 184–5.

12 See p. 154 for account of the rebellious role of secret religious sects in Chinese history.

13 Three waves of persecutions, directed solely at the organized Church: in 446, 547 under the Northern Wei and Northern Chou, respectively: then the most serious persecutions in 841–5 under 'a half-insane T'ang ruler who had become a fanatic searcher after Taoist immortality', during which time 4,600 monasteries and 40,000 shrines were destroyed, 260,000 monks and nuns defrocked, and, together with their 150,000 slaves, were returned to the tax registers. The third and final persecu-tion crippled Buddhism in China, which had already lost the favour of the upper classes and was fated never to regain it.

14 Reminiscent of the 'Familles' of Blanqui, founded in 1833 in France. See Thomas Frost, *The Secret Societies of the European Revolution: 1776–1876*, London, 1876, vol. 1, pp. 200 ff.

15 The Sung dynasty (960–1126) was a Chinese dynasty, and was overthrown by the Mongols who founded the Yüan dynasty. The Ch'ing too was a foreign dynasty which overthrew a Chinese one, the Ming, though neither the Sung nor the Ming was ever restored.

16 *Ta Ch'ing Leu-Lee* (transl. Sir G. T. Staunton), London, 1810, p. 546.

17 There is a remarkable resemblance to the laws of suppression of secret associations in France under Louis Philippe (1834), and those in England introduced under Charles II and used against the Chartists in 1848, which are still in force. See Frost, op. cit., p. 200.

18 Maxim 7 of the Sacred Edict. (See bibliography for available translation into English.)

19 See Baller's translation of the Sacred Edict, p. 83.

20 Oath 4 of the Thirty-Six Oaths of the Hung League; see Gustave Schlegel, *Thien Ti Hwui, The Hung League, Secret Society in China and India*, Batavia, 1866, p. 136.

21 There is every reason to believe the Triad Legend that the Shaolin was the seat of their founders. The Emperor was only able to persecute the monks after one of them betrayed the monastery's whereabouts to him.

22 See Triad 'Myth of origin' (Chapter III).

23 The secret society best known and most studied by Western scholars. It is believed to be affiliated to the Northern White Lotus Society which brought Chu Yuan-chang to power. See Table III.1, p. 57, for other affiliated societies.

24 See concluding part of Chapter II.

25 Edwin Reischauer, John K. Fairbank and Albert M. Craig, *East Asia: The Modern Transformation*, Boston, 1965, p. 333.

26 Ibid., pp. 333–4.

27 Geomancy. For an anthropological analysis of geomancy see S. D. R. Feuchtwang, 'An anthropological analysis of Chinese geomancy', M.A. thesis, University of London, 1965.

II   THE INSTITUTIONAL BACKGROUND

1 The material for Section (A) is based mainly on the study by W. F. Mayers, *The Chinese Government*, Shanghai, written in 1877, 1896 3rd edn.

2 See below, pp. 19 ff.

3 By contrast, such 'quislings' were originally excluded from membership of the Elder Brothers Society, the central and western confederates of the Hung League.

4 Edwin O. Reischauer and John K. Fairbank, *East Asia: The Great Tradition*, Boston, 1960, p. 352. The book will, for the sake of convenience, be referred to subsequently as *EAGT*.

5 Ralph Powell, *The Rise of Chinese Military Power, 1895–1912*, Princeton, 1955, p. 11.

6 Mayers, op. cit., p. 64.

7 Lo Erh-kang, *Hsiang-chun hsin-chih* (New History of the Hsiang Army), Shanghai, 1938, p. 1.

8 Powell, op. cit., p. 13.

9 Ibid.

10 Père Leboucq's contemporary eyewitness reports have some relevance here: 'In 1861 and 1862 [towards the end of the Taiping Rebellion and during a White Lotus Society Rebellion], having had the opportunity to live for several months among the imperial troops who were ordered to put down the Nenuphar insurrection, it was easy for me to see the sympathy of the population for the rebels. Nearly everywhere, when we were not sufficiently numerous to intimidate the villages which we passed through, we were even refused water for the horses. All around us was deserted, whereas at the approach of the rebels the whole population, men, women and children, ran out to meet them, welcoming them as old acquaintances and friends . . .' *Associations de la Chine: lettres*, 27 February 1875, p. 29. This account reveals that the 'social bandit' aspect of the rebels must have had some basis in practice, and their membership grown from a popular base.

11 See Chapter V.

12 The material for this section is based chiefly on the work of Ch'ü T'ung-tsu, *Local Government in China under the Ch'ing*, Cambridge, Mass., 1962, and Hsiao Kung-chuan's massive documentation, *Rural China: Imperial Control in the Nineteenth Century*, Seattle, 1960.

13 The Chinese titles for each of these departments are: *Fu-cheng-shih-ssŭ, An-ch'a-shih-ssŭ, Yen-yun-shih-ssŭ*, and *Liang Tao*, respectively. The term for provincial government is *Tu-fu-ssŭ-tao*.

14 Ch'ü, op. cit., p. 194.

15 See p. 25 for definition of 'gentry' and p. 29 for the position of the gentry in the social structure.

16 *Ch'ing T'ung-K'ao: Ch'ing-ch'ao wen-hsien t'ung-k'ao* 300 *chüan*, Shanghai, 1936, reprint.

17 These are those men who have acquired an ability to read and write but have not passed the requisite number of examinations, or reached the level required for obtaining official jobs. See

p. xiii in *The Chinese Civil Service, Career Open to Talent?* (ed. J. M. Menzel), Boston, 1963, for a summary of the examinations and degrees available to candidates for office or gentry status (those who, among the latter, had no official appointment were called 'commoners').

18 Ch'ü, op. cit., p. 130.

19 *Ch'ing t'ung-k'ao*, 19/5024.

20 See p. 26 for a brief account of militia recruitment and organization.

21 See p. 29 for the position of gentry in the social hierarchy, and p. 23 for their role in local government.

22 See Ch'ü, op. cit., pp. 173–5, for a more detailed account of official and gentry privileges.

23 Ibid.

24 Hsiao, op. cit., p. 305.

25 See Frederick Wakeman, Jr, *Strangers at the Gate, Social Disorder in South China, 1839–1861*, Berkeley, 1966, pp. 22–8.

26 Powell, op. cit., pp. 22–3; and John Scarth, *Twelve Years in China*, Edinburgh, 1860, pp. 155–6: 'During the progress of the Rebellion, we have seen that the Government soldiers have been of little use, and that the chief checks sustained by the rebels have been from bands of *volunteers*, induced, by the high pay of wealthy men, to engage themselves against the enemies of the Emperor. At Tient-tsin it was the volunteers who saved Pekin, when it was almost in the grasp of the insurgents. It was these "braves" who routed the Canton rebels, and inflicted their chief disasters.'

27 Hsiao, op. cit., pp. 301–2, reports a contemporary writer's description of peasant reluctance to join the militia as follows: 'villagers were secretly concerned with their own safety, and were unwilling [to join *t'uan-lien*] when the danger was not yet personally experienced. Thus, while *t'uan-lien* [units were organized] to defend against the bandits and prepare for their coming, the units fell apart before the bandits had actually arrived.'

28 Ibid., p. 295.

29 Chiang Siang-tseh, *The Nien Rebellion*, Seattle, 1954, p. 32.

30 Chang Shou-yung (1876–1945), *Hui-pien: Huang-ch'ao chang-ku hui-pien: nei-pien* (Collection of Imperial Historical Records), 60 *chüan*, 1902, 53/25 a–b.

31 Letter quoted in Chang Ch'in, *Chung-hua t'ung-shih* (History of China), 5 vols, Shanghai, 1934, V, 1391.

32 In the *Tso Chuan Chu-su*, a Confucian classic, ch. 30, p. 16a,

transl. James Legge as *The Chinese Classics*, London, 1861–72, 5 vols, p. 440, vol. V, part II, it is said (and repeated in different forms) that 'It is a rule of the former kings that superior men should labour with their minds and inferior men labour with their strength'.

33 Farmers were the 'root' (*ken*) of society, while the merchants were merely the 'branch' (*chih*).

34 Ch'ü T'ung-tsu, *Law and Society in Traditional China*, Paris and The Hague, 1961, pp. 129–30.

35 Ibid., pp. 135 ff.

36 Ibid., p. 129, note 2.

37 Ho P'ing-ti, 'Aspects of social mobility in China 1368–1911', *Comparative Studies in Society and History*, June 1959, I, p. 333.

38 Powell, op. cit., p. 33.

39 T. W. Kingsmill, 'Retrospect of events in China and Japan during the year 1865', *Journal of the North China Branch of the Royal Asiatic Society*, 1865, II, p. 143.

40 Fei Hsiao-t'ung, 'Peasantry and gentry: an interpretation of Chinese social structure and its changes', *American Journal of Sociology*, July 1946, 52, p. 10.

41 Chow Yung-teh, *Social Mobility in China*, New York, 1966, p. 239.

42 Ibid., pp. 235–7. The novel *Spring Silkworms* by Mao Tun, a 'naturalist' writer of the May 4th Movement of 1919, gives a stark picture of the life of the rural artisanate as it degenerated from a subsistence existence to desperate penury.

43 Professionals in the sense of 'specialists' in any field whatever. As we have already seen, professionals have unequivocally been put in the underclass of traditional Chinese society; only craftsmen connected with a secondary form of agricultural production, manufacture of silk, production of tea, cotton yarn and textiles, etc., were considered to have any respectability at all. Thus the rise of the professional class, particularly doctors and technicians (shortly to become engineers, scientists, etc.), was a revolutionary phenomenon in Confucian society whose ideal had always been the universal *amateur* and man of intellect.

44 See Jean Chesneaux, *Le Mouvement Ouvrier Chinois de 1919–1927*, Paris, 1962, pp. 28–30.

45 Originally meaning 'servants' in foreign firms; the word is, of course, Portuguese. See also Fei, op. cit., p. 14.

46 See p. 37 for further discussion of the entrepreneurial association.

47 Wakeman, op. cit., pp. 48 ff., has a detailed account of the

massacres of the *Han-chien* and *chien-sang*, 'traitorous merchants', in Canton during the Opium War of 1840–1.

48 See pp. 64–7 for Triad political aims; pp. 162–4 on the identity of economic interests among secret societies, illegal petty bourgeoisie and hard-pressed and dispossessed peasantry.

49 This figure was given by Chesneaux, op. cit., p. 83, varying from a half to three quarters of a million. In Edwin O. Reischauer, J. K. Fairbank and A. M. Craig, *East Asia: The Modern Transformation*, London, 1965 (known subsequently as *EAMT*), the figure was given as over a million. See p. 660.

50 John Meskill, editing *The Pattern of Chinese History, Cycles, Development, or Stagnation?*, Boston, 1965, 1966. 'During the Han dynasty [202 B.C.–A.D. 220], a theory of a cyclical process in all events in nature (and the world altogether) became influential in Chinese thinking. Beginning with the elemental forces of nature—the Five Agents—and extending to colors, directions, animals, planets, and other things mutual correspondence and sequences came to be used in explanation of events, even of the succession of dynasties and dominant virtues that came to be associated with them. An abridged chart of one arrangement of correspondences (not necessarily the same as those expressed in the selection below) might look like this:

AGENT	Fire	Earth	Metal	Water	Wood
VIRTUE	Wisdom	Faith	Righteousness	Decorum	Benevolence
COLOUR	Red	Yellow	White	Black	Green
DYNASTY	Emperor	Emperor	Emperor	Shang	Chou
or RULER	Yao	Shun	Yü Hsia dynasty	dynasty	dynasty'

Each cycle can be seen in these 'five' phases or in 'three' phases, and there are other variations. It is interesting to note that the secret societies (Triads) also have such symbols attached to each of the 'Five Lodges': see p. 65 for Chart of Lodges and Symbols.

51 Based mainly on M. Freedman's *Lineage Organization in South-Eastern China*, London, 1958; C. K. Yang, *Chinese Communist Society: The Family and the Village*, Cambridge, Mass., 1965, especially the second volume dealing with the transitional period; S. Gamble and Ting Hsien, *A North China Rural Community*, New York, 1954; Hu Hsien-chin, *The Common Descent Group in China and Its Functions*, New York, 1948.

52 The literati gentry formed 1½ to 2 per cent of the Chinese

population and received 23 per cent of the national income. See Franz Michael, 'State and society in nineteenth-century China', *Modern China* (ed. Albert Feuerworker), New Jersey, 1964, p. 63.

53 See the discussion in *EAGT*, pp. 224–5, on foot-binding and the declining position of women in the late T'ang.

54 See Chapter V for role of female and juvenile members in secret societies.

55 Compare the image of the lineage with the Triad 'City of Willows'.

56 Outside the lineage jurisdiction were cases dealing with land disputes, inheritance, marriage and divorce, inter-lineage conflicts, village defence, welfare, etc. For a comprehensive and lucid discussion of lineage functions and juridical scope see S. van der Sprenkel, *Legal Institutions in Manchu China*, London, 1962, 1966, Chapter 7, pp. 80–9, Chapter 8, pp. 97–8.

57 P. B. Maybon, *Essai sur les associations en Chine*, Paris, 1925, p. 174; M. L. Wynne, *Triad and Tabut, A Survey of the Origins of Chinese and Mohammedan Secret Societies in the Malay Peninsula A.D. 1800–1935*, Singapore, 1941, p. 2.

58 See Chapter IV on Purposes and Activities for comparison.

59 Wou Monpeng, *L'Evolution des corporations ouvrières et commerciales dans la Chine contemporaine*, Paris, 1931.

60 Ibid., pp. 37–8.

61 Ibid., p. 36.

62 Ibid., p. 32.

63 Taken from the *Romance of the Three Kingdoms* (*San Kuo Shih Yen-i*) revised and edited by Lo Kuan-chung of the late Sung, a famous picaresque 'novel' about the period of the Three Kingdoms following the break-up of the Han.

64 See Chapter III.

65 Images of the God Kwan can be found as far afield as Havana in Cuba to this day! See Appendix for 'Notes on Chinese Associations in Havana, Cuba'.

66 Wou, op. cit., p. 34.

67 H. B. Morse, *The Gilds of China, with an Account of the Gild Merchant or Cohong of Canton*, London, 1909, p. 31.

68 J. S. Burgess, *The Guilds of Peking*, New York and London, 1928, pp. 133–4.

69 Morse, op. cit., p. 12.

70 Ibid., pp. 53–4.

71 Burgess, op. cit., p. 137.

72 See Chapter VIII.

73 Morse, op. cit., pp. 10–11.
74 Ibid., p. 27.
75 Ibid., p. 56.
76 Burgess, op. cit., p. 142.
77 Ibid., p. 135.
78 Ibid., pp. 135–6.
79 Ibid., p. 136.
80 The word usually used to translate 'doctrine' or 'religion' is *chiao*, or 'teaching', which can have no transcendental religious overtones at all. *Hsieh hsin*, 'depraved beliefs', or similarly value-loaded terms were the only ones officially applied to heterodox religions.
81 Not only did secret societies come under the contempt of the literati, but all 'private institutions', as possible subjects of research. Etienne Balazs remarks in preface to a very interesting article on 'Fairs in China', *Chinese Civilization and Bureaucracy* (transl. H. M. Wright and ed. Arthur P. Wright), New Haven and London, 1964, p. 56: 'Chinese historical writings scarcely mention the ruled over classes—the peasants, the artisans, and the merchants—except insofar as their relations with the state were concerned, and even then no more than the bare minimum deemed worthy of note by the literati in their capacity as officials of the fiscal administration.'
82 See C. K. Yang, *Religion in Chinese Society*, Berkeley, 1961, pp. 192 ff.
83 J. Chesneaux, *Les Sociétés secrètes en Chine (19e et 20e siècles)*, Paris, 1965, p. 83.
84 Quoted in Wynne, op. cit., p. 2.
85 See Chapter III.
86 See 'myth of origin' in Chapter III.
87 Rev. D. H. Porter, 'Secret societies in Shantung', *Chinese Recorder*, January/February 1886, p. 65.
88 Ibid.; see Chapter VI, section (c).
89 Yang, op. cit., p. 34.
90 *EAGT*, p. 126; Max Weber, *The Religion of China*, New York and London, 1951 and 1964, pp. 193 ff. See also Chapter IX for discussion of history of heterodox rebellion.
91 *EAGT*, p. 146.
92 Ibid., p. 141.
93 Ibid.
94 Weber, op. cit., pp. 194–5.
95 Père Leboucq, *Associations de la Chine: lettres*, Paris, *c.* 1880, p. 180.
96 Porter, op. cit., p. 7.

97 *I-ho-t'uan yun-tung shih-lun-ts'ung* (Articles on the History of the Boxer Movement), Peking, 1956, pp. 60–1.

98 Tao Ch'en-chang, article '*Chiao-hui yüan-liu k'ao* (Origins of the sects and Societies), reprinted in *Chung-kuo shih-hsüch hui* (ed. Hsin-hai Ke-ming), to be referred to subsequently as *HHKM*, 1957, vol. 3, p. 109.

99 Porter, op. cit., p. 6; Leboucq, op. cit., p. 15.

100 Tai Hsüan-chih, *I-ho-t'uan yen-chiu* (Studies on the Boxer Rising), Taiwan, 1963, p. 23.

101 The 'Five Directions' were North, South, East, West and Centre; the 'Four Sides' were of course as above without the centre; and the 'Five Elements', as have already been described in n. 50, p. 211, were fire, earth, metal, water and wood, the five 'basic' elements of Nature.

102 Porter, op. cit., p. 65.

103 Jerome Ch'en, 'The nature and characteristics of the Boxer Movement', *Bulletin of the School of Oriental and African Studies*, 1960, XXIII, part 2, p. 297.

104 Leboucq, op. cit., p. 36.

105 In a collection of his own essays, *Studies in Chinese Institutional History*, Harvard–Yenching Institute Studies, XX, Cambridge, Mass., 1961, pp. 204–6.

106 Maybon, op. cit., pp. 170 ff.

107 Morse, op. cit., pp. 7–8.

108 Temples were also erected by the superstitious rich with the hope of winning themselves a privileged place in the next world.

109 Also the generic name for overseas Chinese secret societies, usually pronounced 't'ong' in the Cantonese dialect.

110 Morse, op. cit., p. 9.

111 Marjorie Topley discusses in some detail the specific appeal of heterodox and salvationist sects to the female population in Singapore in her Ph.D. thesis: 'The Organisation and Social Function of Chinese Women's Chai T'ang in Singapore', London, 1958.

112 Women were prohibited from ancestor worship in the lineage hall, and by this token excluded from the process of decision-making undertaken by the lineage leaders. Women were *never* (unlike even the *chien-min*) permitted to take the Civil Service Examinations.

113 By the late nineteenth century, one-third of the 1,450,000 gentry qualified only by purchase; while the kind of education which it tested was increasingly irrelevant with modern industrialization, etc. See *EAMT*, p. 330.

114 Or 'benevolence', *jen*, normally to be meted out by superiors to inferiors for the prevention and pacification of seditious sentiments among the discontented.

115 B. Favre, 'Les sociétés de "Frères Jurés" en Chine', *T'oung Pao*, 1920, xix, p. 4.

116 The socially despised, the heterodox, the poor were *de facto* and sometimes *de jure* excluded from the protection of the State and lineage laws.

117 The distinction here between 'organization' and 'structure' follows that of Raymond Firth's in *Elements of Social Organization*, London, 1951, reprinted 1961, pp. 28 ff.

118 *EAMT*, p. 89.

119 Ibid.; see also Kuo P'ing-chia, *China, New Age and New Outlook*, London, 1956 and 1960, p. 2.

120 Hsiao, *Rural China*, pp. 382–3.

121 Ibid., pp. 396 ff.

122 See *EAMT*, p. 339, for map of foreign incursion in China.

III ORIGINS AND FORMATION OF CHINESE SECRET SOCIETIES

1 Chiang Siang-tseh, *The Nien Rebellion*, Seattle, 1954, p. 15.

2 See Chapter VII.

3 The popular name for the Hung League; see pp. 61–2.

4 See Chapter VI.

5 See p. 49.

6 The number of officers and grades might also have depended on the variety of purposes and activities a certain society took over for itself.

7 See Chapter VI.

8 See list of rebellions associated with secret societies in Appendix A.

9 The first of their kind, opened in 1842 by the Treaty of Nanking concluded between China and the victorious British after the Opium War.

10 List based on that of Tao Ch'eng-chang, vol. 3 of *Chung-kuo shih-hsüch hui* (ed. Hsin-hai Ke-ming), pp. 99–111.

11 William Stanton, *The Triad Society*, Hong Kong, 1900, p. 8; G. Schlegel, *Thien Ti Hwiu, The Hung League, Secret Society in China and India*, Batavia, 1866, p. 4.

12 See Chapter V.

13 Hsiao I-shan, *Chin-tai pi-mi she-hui shih-liao*, Peking, 1935, vol. 1, p. 4a.

14 This paraphrase attempts to incorporate the elements of the legend common to all of the different versions given by Hirayama

Shu, Stanton, Schlegel, Morgan, Tao Ch'eng-chang. See Chapter VII (Ritual).

15 Sometimes referred to in the singular, this name usually covered a number of occasionally federating societies; see Chapter VI.

16 Especially their skill in weaponless self-defence, such as boxing. Indeed, there still exists today a school of boxing called the Shaolin school, details of which can be obtained in a work called *The Secrets of Shaolin Temple Boxing*, Robert W. Smith, Formosa, 1964, based on material found in Formosa.

17 Probably a smoke-screen of sulphur already in use during the Three Kingdoms period (A.D. 222–80).

18 See n. 14, p. 215.

19 Eunuchs had always been a prominent feature of decaying dynasties, but none so much as during the end of the Ming, when the eunuch Wei Chung-hsien, backed by a small eunuch army and a network of spies and informers throughout the empire, ruled the country by terror. The Emperor was a half-wit who was only interested in carpentry.

20 Article I of the Fundamental Laws or *Lü* of the Ch'ing Code.

21 In George Staunton's translation *Ta Ch'ing Leu-lee*, London, 1810, p. 175.

22 A nationalism intensified by the Manchu monopoly of high offices, and their discrimination against the Chinese in dress and marriage laws, etc.

23 In an article on 'Secret religious societies in north China in the Ming dynasty', *Folklore Studies*, 1948, 7, p. 102, Chao Wei-pang describes a religious society called the Gathering Sources Society, *Shou-yüan chiao*, which mentions this deity in a myth of the origin of the world: 'at first there were no heaven and earth, no sun and moon. From the void emerged an old Buddha, by the name of Wu-chi t'ien-chen ku-fo, who arranged heaven and earth; and a goddess called Eternal Mother [*wu-shong-lao-mu*], who then took charge of heaven. There is no mention of where Eternal Mother came from and what relation she bore to Old Buddha. Mankind is said to have originated from Eternal Mother, who gave birth to the twins, Fu Hsi and Nu Wa; though brother and sister, they married and became the first parents of mankind, begetting sixty-nine thousand children, who were sent to the East Land, i.e. China.'

24 See Chapter VI.

25 Oath 4, Schlegel, op. cit., p. 136.

26 See p. 38.

27 That is, the basic or pivotal relationship; term coined by Firth.

28 Female children were also frequently adopted, but for different purposes—such as that of serving as cheap domestic servants, or as future brides for male children.

29 See p. 137 for description and Figure 7, p. 138, for the 'written contract' of membership among the Triad.

30 B. Favre, 'Les sociétés de "Frères Jurés" en Chine', *T'oung Pao*, 1920, xix, pp. 1–40; quotation on pp. 140–1 in the text taken from pp. 6–7 of Favre's article; information on splintering process on p. 14.

31 Ibid.

32 Ibid.

33 Frederick Wakeman, Jr, *Strangers at the Gate, Social Disorder in South China, 1839–1861*, Berkeley, 1966, p. 122.

34 Ibid., and Hsiao Kung-ch'uan, *Rural China: Imperial Control in the Nineteenth Century*, Seattle, 1960, p. 462, makes a useful distinction between 'professional' and 'occasional' bandits: 'The distinction between them is (a) that occasional bandits were often rural inhabitants compelled to join bandit groups for one reason or another, whereas professional bandits came from habitually predacious, unruly elements of local communities: and (b) that occasional bandits were usually ready to return to peaceful occupations as soon as the compulsion which made them bandits was removed, whereas professional bandits engaged in robbery and pillage regularly and perhaps permanently.'

35 See Chapter V.

36 Hsia Hsieh, *Yueh-fen chi-shih* (A Record of the Noxious Influences in Kwangtung), chüan 13, 1869, ch. 1, 2a.

37 Quoted in *Chih-hsin pao* (The Reformer China), Macao, 1897–9, ch. 82, 2b.

38 Quoted in Hsiao, op. cit., p. 460—a memorial submitted to the Emperor by the Governor of Kwantung in 1899.

IV   PURPOSES AND ACTIVITIES

1 Max Weber, *The City* (transl. and ed. Don Martindale and Gertrud Neuwirth), New York and London, 1958, p. 14.

2 Gustave Schlegel, *Thien Ti Hwui, The Hung League, Secret Society in China and India*, Batavia, 1866, p. 133 (Art. 5): see also p. 136 (Art. 9) and p. 137.

3 Maurice Freedman, *Lineage Organization in South-Eastern China*, London, 1958, p. 17: see also note on Gamble.

4 Schlegel, op. cit., p. 159; William Stanton, *The Triad Society*, Hong Kong, 1900, p. 64 (Art. 27).

5 Schlegel, op. cit., p. 155 (Art. 27).
6 Ibid., p. 160 (Art. 67).
7 Stanton, op. cit., Appendix, p. 119 (Oath 7).
8 Schlegel, op. cit., p. 119 (Art. 7).
9 Ibid., p. 164 (Art. 19); p. 157 (Art. 45); p. 138 (Art. 11).
10 Ibid., p. 163 (Art. 14).
11 Stanton, op. cit., p. 64 (Oath 33); also Oath 34.
12 Schlegel, op. cit., p. 154 (Art. 20).
13 Ibid., p. 140 (Art. 22); p. 161 (Art. 3) concerns disputes with outsiders.
14 See p. 51.
15 Schlegel, op. cit., p. 153 (Art. 6).
16 Ibid., p. 154 (Art. 15).
17 Ibid. (Art. 17).
18 Ibid., p. 158.
19 Stanton, op. cit., p. 62 (Oath 15).
20 See Chapter VII (Ritual).
21 W. P. Morgan, *Triad Societies in Hong Kong*, Hong Kong, 1960, p. 273.
22 See p. 63.
23 Schlegel, op. cit., p. 157 (Art. 44).
24 See quotation from Skinner, p. 79; see also an observer's account in Han Suyin, *The Crippled Tree*, London, 1965, p. 95, of China in the 1890s. See also p. 250 on use of fairs as meeting places for planning insurrection; p. 251 on temples as another favoured meeting place.
25 Père Leboucq, *Associations de la Chine: lettres*, Paris, *c.* 1880, p. 15: 'The Nenuphar Society (White Lotus) has its royal house in each province; one might say that it follows the ancient division of China and regards as null and void the union of the principalities and the conquests of the emperors who, for the Nenuphar, are nothing but tyrants.

I know the little White Lotus king of Tcheli province. I visited his dwelling and his village a long time ago and received a friendly welcome there. The prince of Tcheli is to-day an old man of sixty-eight, of remarkable corpulence. His revenue has been increasing considerably for some years. When he was installed "Grand Orient" some twenty years ago he had only a few acres of poor uncultivated soil; to-day he owns more than twelve hundred acres of arable land, which brings him an annual revenue of eight or ten thousand francs. It is said that his real estate is immense, but he is prudent enough not to draw public attention to this. Moreover, he has to keep deposits of large sums of money against the day when his subjects are bound to arm themselves afresh and try their hand at revolt.'

26 Han, op. cit., p. 249 (Li Chieh-jen was known as the Chinese Maupassant).

27 Jean Chesneaux, *Les Sociétés secrètes en Chine*, Paris, 1965, p. 109 (1965).

28 For an account of feuds among Chinese secret societies in Malaya see M. L. Wynne, *Triad and Tabut*, Singapore, 1941, Chapter VII, p. 245.

29 G. W. Skinner, 'Marketing and social structure in rural China', *Journal of Asian Studies*, xxiv, p. 37.

30 Ibid.

31 Freedman, op. cit., pp. 124–5.

32 See discussion of Nien and clan alliance in Chiang Siang-tseh, *The Nien Rebellion*, Seattle, 1954, pp. 45–8: 'What surprises us is that the big clans provided the Nien with a tremendous number of leaders. Analogies cannot be found in other contemporary rebellious groups.' Chiang goes on to analyse types of gentry leaders of the Nien, most of whom belonged to the lower degree holder group, if they had degrees at all; while most of the Nien leaders held no degrees at all (p. 50). There appear to be two main reasons for the Nien association with lineages in the north, and these are, first, that the Nien societies had been hereditary bandit groups, and appear to have been unique in this practice in China; second, that the northern lineages were, unlike the southern ones, neither strong nor rich and were therefore unequal to the power of the central Government (which was besides too close for comfort, being situated in the north in the province of Chihli now called Hopei). Their relative weakness in comparison with their southern counterparts, as well as their closeness to the capital (Peking) could have been a strong factor in deciding them to join with the Nien rebels.

33 This is not as remarkable as it might first appear, since the most widespread type of kinship organization in China was not the lineage (in the sense of a corporate group) but the family.

34 See Chapter V, p. 87, second Triad rule quoted.

35 See Chapter IX for further discussion. There appears to be little evidence regarding the role of secret societies in *male* slavery; there is no evidence that they dealt in it commercially. In fact, slaves (for example, in Cuba) formed secret societies among themselves along the lines of the Triads in China, taking even the name (Hung Men) as well as its rituals. See attached report in Appendix D on Chinese associations in Havana.

36 Morgan, op. cit., pp. 73–5.

37 For a contemporary account of the work of secret societies in trade unions see Harold R. Isaacs, 'Gang rule in Shanghai', *Five Years of Kuomintang Reaction*, reprinted from *China Forum*, Shanghai, May 1932.

38 See Chapter IX, p. 171.

V RECRUITMENT AND SOCIAL COMPOSITION

1 Lo Erh-kang, *T'ien-ti-hui wen-hsien lu* (Documents on the Heaven and Earth Society), Shanghai, 1948, p. 34.

2 W. P. Morgan, *Triad Societies in Hong Kong*, Hong Kong, 1960, p. 273.

3 Lo, op. cit., p. 34.

4 Lieut. T. J. Newbold and Maj. Gen. F. W. Wilson, 'The Chinese secret Triad society of the T'ien-ti-hui', *Journal of the Royal Asiatic Society*, 1841, VI, p. 136. See also the Hikayat Abdullah, pp. 184–5.

5 See Chapter VIII.

6 William Stanton, *The Triad Society*, Hong Kong, 1900, p. 119 (Oath 5).

7 Hirayama Amane (Shu), *Chung-kuo pi-mi she-hui shih* (History of Chinese secret societies), Shanghai, 1935, p. 86.

8 Capt. Frank Brinkley, *China, Its History, Arts and Literature*, Boston and Tokyo, 1902, p. 228.

9 See Table v.1, p. 93.

10 T'ang Leang-li, *The Inner History of the Chinese Revolution*, London, 1930, pp. 5–6; Gustave Schlegel, *Thien Ti Hwui, The Hung League, Secret Society in China and India*, Batavia, 1866, pp. vi–vii.

11 Arthur H. Smith, *Chinese Characteristics*, London, 1892, p. 257.

12 That is, that the members are drawn from the highly respectable members of society, and the orientation of the society has become mainly expressive and conformative.

13 Morgan, op. cit., p. 263: 'This question [of the possibility of the revocation of membership] was discussed with leading Triad officials in Hong Kong and all stated categorically that once a person has been initiated into the Hung Mun only death can release him from his membership. At the initiation ceremony the member mixes his blood with those of other initiates and once they have sipped of the mixture they all become blood brothers, a fact which no power can alter. What can happen is that a member may be expelled from his particular branch society but such expulsion applies only to that branch and not to the Hung

Mun itself. The situation may be likened to the "black sheep" cast out of a family. He is still a member of the family but no longer recognized by it. Unlike some "black sheep" however, he cannot withdraw from the family of his own volition. Once he has accepted membership he is bound to obey the instructions of the society leaders and failure to do so renders him liable to whatever punishment the leaders consider appropriate.'

14 See the Hikayat Abdullah, pp. 184–5, for description of the punishments meted out to the recalcitrant recruits.

15 Leboucq, 'Lettres', *Études Religieuses*, Paris, 1875, V, VIII, p. 203.

16 Sun Yat-sen, *Memoirs of a Chinese Revolutionary*, London, 1927, p. 191.

17 See Frederick Wakemann, Jr, *Strangers at the Gate*, Berkeley, 1966, p. 122, for further discussion of the role of officials in secret society membership.

18 Bernard Martin, *Strange Vigour, A Biography of Sun Yat-sen*, London, 1944, p. 47.

19 Wang T'ien-chiang, '*Shih-chiu shih-chi hsia-pan-chi Shung-kuo-ti pi-mi she-hui*' (Chinese Secret Societies in the second half of the nineteenth century), *Li-shih Yen-chiu* (Historical Studies), Peking, 1963, no. 2, pp. 83 ff.

20 Jean Chesneaux, *Les Sociétés Secrètes en Chine*, Paris, 1965, p. 105.

21 *Tan Ssu-t'ung ch'uan chi* (The Collected Works of Tan Ssu-t'ung), Peking, 1954, pp. 63–4. This treatment of vagabonds in China was motivated by the same kind of fear which all governments have faced with a vast and growing mass of the unemployed: during the fifteenth and sixteenth centuries in Europe, vagabonds created by the land 'enclosure' acts were treated as 'voluntary' criminals. An Act in 1530 in England gave licences to beggars too old to work, but sturdy vagabonds were to be tied to the cart-tail, whipped until the blood streamed from their bodies, then forced to swear an oath to go back to their birth-place or to where they had lived the last three years and 'to put themselves to labour'. In 1537, the amendments to this statute stipulated that for the second arrest for vagabondage the whipping was to be repeated and half the ear sliced off; but for the third relapse the offender was to be executed as a hardened criminal and enemy of the common weal. These Acts, with additions in 1547 of branding vagabonds with a 'V' if found wandering about for more than three days, continued to be enforced throughout Western Europe despite protests from Thomas More and others. In France, for example, the Ordinance of 13 July 1777 ruled that

every man in good health from 16 to 60 years of age, if without means of subsistence and not practising a trade, was to be sent to the galleys.

22 Wang, op. cit., pp. 84–5.

23 Ibid., pp. 85–6.

24 Hirayama, op. cit., p. 12. The political aims of the Kelao Hui were identical with those of the Triads.

25 Wang, op. cit., p. 88.

26 Han Suyin, *The Crippled Tree*, London, 1965, p. 249.

27 Wang, op. cit., pp. 85–6.

28 Ralph Powell, *The Rise of Chinese Military Power, 1895–1912*, Princeton, 1955, pp. 13 and 24 respectively.

29 Han, op. cit., p. 255.

30 List provided by C. A. Curwen of London University and cited by Chesneaux, op. cit., p. 101.

31 J. Chesneaux, *Le Mouvement Ouvrier Chinois de 1919–1927*, Paris, 1962, p. 83.

32 Ibid., p. 78.

33 Ibid., p. 81.

34 Wakeman, op. cit., p. 14.

35 Chesneaux, *Le Mouvement Ouvrier Chinois*, p. 83.

36 Even as late as 1926–35, 52 to 79 per cent of urban workers were of peasant origin. See Chesneaux's article in *The Economic Development of China and Japan* (ed. C. D. Cowan), Studies on Modern Asia and Africa, Series 4, London, 1964, pp. 111–13, on social origins of the workers.

37 See Hsiao Kung-chuan, *Rural China: Imperial Control in the Nineteenth Century*, Seattle, 1960, pp. 383–4. In a table drawn up by Western writers in 1888, it is revealed that in nineteenth-century China tenants formed up to approximately 50, 70, 75 and 80 per cent of the populations of Fukien, Chekiang, Kwangtung and Kiangsu respectively; while it was not uncommon for tenants to pay their landlords (*ti-chu*) 50 to 70 per cent of their produce for renting buffaloes, carts, seeds and fodder.

38 See Georges Coulet, *Les Sociétés Secrètes en terre d'Annam*, Saigon, 1926, pp. 197–292.

39 Leboucq, op. cit., p. 203.

40 Ibid.

41 Père Leboucq, *Associations de la Chine: lettres*, Paris, c. 1880, p. 19.

42 Rev. D. H. Porter, 'Secret societies in Shantung', *Chinese Recorder*, 1886, XVII, p. 8.

43 Ibid., p. 65.

44 Rev. J. Hutson, *Chinese Life on the Tibetan Foothills*, Shanghai, 1921, p. 87.

45 Jerome Ch'en, 'The nature and characteristics of the Boxer Movement', *Bulletin of the School of Oriental and African Studies*, 1960, vol. XXIII, part 2, p. 298.

46 Ch'en Chieh, *I-ho-t'uan yun-tung shih* (History of the Boxer Movement), Shanghai, 1931, p. 27.

47 Hutson, op. cit., p. 87.

48 M. L. Wynne, *Triad and Tabut*, Singapore, 1941, p. 35.

49 Leboucq, *Associations de la Chine: lettres*, p. 15.

50 During periods of dynastic decline, China traditionally collapsed into a feuding agglomeration of independent States led by a prince or general. It was only when an effective hegemony emerged that China was re-united into one State. The disintegration of Chinese society in the late nineteenth century once more re-created, rather revived, the old regional divisions, and gave free rein to the centrifugal forces. It is not surprising that secret societies in the north associated themselves with feudal anarchy and the Three Kingdoms period. See n. 25, p. 218, and Chapter III.

51 I am referring, of course, to Isabel and David Crook's book, *Revolution in a Chinese Village, Ten Mile Inn*, London, 1959, p. 16, as well as to Skinner's article which I have already discussed in Chapter IV. The secret society described by the Crooks in Ten Mile Inn village was, during the twenties, completely taken over by the Nationalist Party (Kuomintang) and made its village branch! Incidentally, it was this secret society, the Green Circle Gang, which became notorious in the late twenties for its brutal participation in the massacre of unarmed workers in Shanghai (1927) under the leadership of Tu Yuch-sheng, one of the 'Advisers' to the Nationalist Government. (See Chapter IX for further discussion of the Secret Society–Kuomintang (the ruling party of republican China) alliance.) The Government patronage of secret societies in the republican period naturally gave impetus to other powerful groups and individuals to follow their example.

52 Schlegel, op. cit., pp. 57–8.

53 Leboucq, *Associations de la Chine: lettres*, p. 14.

54 *Journal of the Malaysian Branch of the Royal Asiatic Society*, 1955, 28, p. 180.

55 See Hsiao, op. cit., pp. 475–7; see also quotation on p. 71.

56 Overseas Chinese secret societies tended to recruit members from all classes of Chinese population and served frequently as convenient administrative units for colonial governments; for

example, in Malaya, Singapore and Thailand. There the heads of secret societies were nearly always wealthy and respected leaders of the community, or were the 'captains' to the colonial administration, exchanging relative order among the Chinese community for non-interference by the colonial government in Chinese affairs. The separation of Chinese and colonial communities reduced the traditional anti-official sentiments of the secret society members, while the truly mixed class origins of the membership made any conflict between different classes within the Chinese community less relevant than it was in nineteenth-century China.

VI STRUCTURE AND ORGANIZATION

1 'Structure' is used here in Raymond Firth's definition of the word: 'principles of organization', as distinguished from the actual operation of this structure in time and space which he termed 'organization'. See *Elements of Social Organization*, London, 1961 (3rd edition), pp. 28–40.

2 *Canton Journal* (*Kwantung Hsüeh-pao*), 1 January 1937, no pagination.

3 Wang Yu-chuan, 'The organization of a typical guerilla area in south Shantung', in E. F. Carlson, *The Chinese Army: Its Organization and Military Efficiency*, New York, 1940, p. 105.

4 Hsiao I-shan, *Chin-tai pi-mi sheh-hui shih-liao* (History of modern secret societies), Peking, 1935, vol. 2, p. 9b.

5 Georg Simmel, *The Sociology of Georg Simmel* (transl. and ed. K. Wolff), New York and London, 1964, p. 367, writes *à propos* this kind of membership: 'The contrast between exoteric and esoteric members, such as is attributed to the Pythagorean order, is the most poignant form of this protective measure. The circle composed of those only partially initiated formed a sort of buffer region against the non-initiates. It is everywhere the dual function of the "middler" to connect and to separate, or, actually, rather to play only one role which, according to our perceptual categories and our viewpoint, we designate as connecting or as separating. In the same way, the real unity of superficially contradictory activities is here seen in its clearest light: *precisely because the lower grades of the order mediate the transition to the center of the secret, they create a gradual densification of the sphere of repulsion which surrounds this center and which protects it more securely than could any abrupt and radical alternative between total inclusion and total exclusion.*'

6 *The Idea of Politics* (translated from *Introduction à la Politique*, Paris, 1964), London, 1966, pp. 154–5.

7 Gustave Schlegel, *Thien Ti Hwui, The Hung League, Secret Society in China and India*, Batavia, 1866, p. 55.

8 See Figure 3 (p. 112) for facsimiles of notice of election of officers.

9 The only two units mentioned in the Triad vocabulary. See Appendix B.

10 William Stanton, *The Triad Society*, Hong Kong, 1900, pp. 8–24, for history of Triads' role in rebellions.

11 T'ao Ch'eng-chang, *Chung-kuo shih-hsuch hui* (ed. Hsin-hai Keming), n. 3, p. 110.

12 Stanton, op. cit., p. 42.

13 W. P. Morgan, *Triad Societies in Hong Kong*, Hong Kong, 1960, p. 96.

14 Hirayama Amane (Shu), *Chung-kuo pi-mi she-hui shih* (History of Chinese secret societies), Shanghai, 1935, p. 82; these terms were normally used by the Elder Brothers Society.

15 Jerome Ch'en, 'The nature and characteristics of the Boxer Movement', *Bulletin of the School of Oriental and African Studies*, 1960, xxiii, part 2, p. 297.

16 Georges Coulet, *Les Sociétés Secrètes en terre d'Annam*, Saigon, 1926, p. 279.

17 T'ao, op. cit., p. 110.

18 Ibid.

19 Seminar paper given at University College, London, 1966, in the Department of Political Economy.

20 Stanton, op. cit., p. 42; indeed, as we shall see in the chapter on ritual, the whole initiation ceremony was a symbol of rebirth.

21 Morgan, op. cit., p. 100.

22 Ibid.

23 T'ao, op. cit., p. 110.

24 Morgan, op. cit., p. 97.

25 Père Leboucq, *Associations de la Chine: lettres*, Paris, c. 1880, p. 190.

26 T'ao, op. cit., p. 110. The word for 'four' (*ssŭ*) is pronounced the same as 'to die' (also *ssŭ*).

27 Ibid.

28 Hutson explains the taboo among the Elder Brothers in terms of the sound similarity between the Chinese words for 'seven' and 'to slice' (*ch'i*). A more logical explanation is provided by that of the Triad legend, which makes 'Number Seven' stand for the traitor monk who was seventh in the boxing hierarchy: and the cock decapitated at the ceremony of initiation as a warning to

potential traitors is known in Triad slang, in fact, as Number Seven (*Ah-ch'i*).

29 Morgan, op. cit., p. 100.

30 Schlegel, op. cit., p. 62.

31 Frederick Boyle, article in *Harper's Magazine*, September 1891, pp. 601–2.

32 D. H. Porter, 'Secret societies in Shantung', *Chinese Recorder*, 1886, XVII, p. 6.

33 Schlegel, op. cit., p. 164 (Art. 21).

34 Ibid., p. 140 (Oath 22), p. 142 (Oath 29), p. 163 (Art. 14) (Art. 15). These articles of the Twenty-one Regulations state categorically: 'When brothers of the Hung-league have serious or trifling dissensions, the council is there to decide upon them according to justice, but it shall not be allowed to bring the case before the magistrates. If anybody should not observe this law, the council will decide the case effectually, and, besides, will punish the plaintiff with 108 blows.

'When there are public affairs, and the brotherhood is invited to deliberate upon them, and if they are intrusted to the council, it shall not be allowed to injure the equity by boisterous speeches. Neither shall it be permitted to carry sharp weapons, or to have sticks or cudgels in one's hands.

'The offender shall be punished, according to law with 72 blows.'

35 Stanton, op. cit., p. 64 (Art. 33).

36 T'ao, op. cit., p. 110.

37 Schlegel, op. cit., p. 143 (Oath 33).

38 Stanton, op. cit., p. 118 (Oath 3).

39 By which officials were known to each other by a symbolic number. Only L. Comber, *Chinese Secret Societies in Malaya, A Survey of the Triad Society From 1800 to 1900*, New York, 1959, p. 17, and Morgan, op. cit., p. 101, mention this system of ranking. Comber's report gives the following:

1 Incense Master	989 or 489
2 White Fan	983 or 415
3 Vanguard	992
4 Red Staff	426
5 Glass Slipper	415 or 432

Simplified further, we get:

1 President	108
2 Officer	72
3 Recruit	36

Morgan's report is more detailed in the explanation of the

numerical symbols (pp. 101–4), and his table is set out as follows:

1	Shan Chu (President)	489
2	Fu Shan Chu (vice-President)	438
3	Heung Chu (Incense Master)	438
4	Sin Fung (Vanguard)	438
5	Sheung Fa Officials (Flower)	438
6	Hung Kwan (Red Cudgel)	426
7	Pak Tsz Sin (White Fan)	415
8	Cho Hai (Grass Sandals)	432
9	Ordinary Member	49

The ritual repetition of the simplified table by Comber in the number of strokes to be applied to society miscreants, adding only 21, says something interesting about the application of the punishments.

40 Morgan, op. cit., p. 101.
41 See Hutson's selected translation in 'The Heaven and Earth Society', *China Journal*, November 1928, p. 219.
42 B. Favre, 'Les sociétés de "Frères Jurés" en Chine', *T'oung Pao*, 1920, XIX, p. 14.
43 Stanton, op. cit., p. 63 (Oath 26).
44 Ibid., p. 122 (Art. 21).
45 Morgan, op. cit., p. 266.
46 Translated and edited by S. Tretiakov, *Tan Shih-hua: A Chinese Testament*, London, 1934, p. 55.
47 Leboucq, op. cit., p. 37.
48 Porter, op. cit., p. 65.
49 Hutson, op. cit.
50 Schlegel, op. cit., p. 165 (Art. 2).
51 Ibid., p. 153 (Art. 12), p. 162 (Art. 9); Stanton, op. cit., p. 67 (Art. 5).
52 Simmel, op. cit., p. 360. See also, pp. 140, 143.
53 Maurice Freedman, *Lineage Organization in South-Eastern China*, London, 1958, p. 84.
54 Although the Examination System came in more recent centuries to symbolize the triumph of merit over birth and wealth in deciding the redistribution of power, its formal institution in the seventh century by the Empress Wu had no such 'democratizing' motive behind it. The incorporation of the system into bureaucratic selection accorded with the Empress's own political ambitions: she brought in the lesser known literate nobility, from the outlying areas to counter the influence of the Imperial princes in the capital. Her success in installing the Examination

System was as much the symbol of the final surrender of the old aristocracy (with its military bias) as of the rise of the lesser nobility and its literate members to power. Moreover it represented a new alliance between the throne and the bureaucracy, which was to bring them both overwhelming power over the other political forces in the country, the commercial classes, for example.

55 Mencius, IIb. 8. VIIb. 144.

56 The extent to which this electoral democracy was put into practice is of course open to question; but if hierarchization is incompatible with democratic elections, then the Western democracies must also be condemned as unworkable, since they, too, combine to a high degree these two principles.

57 See Chapter VIII.

58 See pp. 103–4.

59 For a thorough examination of this problem see *The Chinese Civil Service: Career Open to Talent?* (ed. and introd. Johanna M. Menzel), Boston, 1963.

60 See Chapter VIII: also Freedman, op. cit., pp. 45, 123.

61 Ibid.

62 Hutson, op. cit., p. 88, writes of the Elder Brothers Society members when caught: 'If any of the gang should be caught, there is danger that secrets may be let out; but some of Lan Ta-shun's bands will defy torture and scorn death. No officials can get their secrets either by torture or cajolery; and no severities used on them seem to have any moral effect on the rest of the gang; indeed it sometimes seems as though the more are killed the more the membership grows.' C. W. Heckethorn, *Secret Societies of All Ages and Countries*, London, 1897, vol. II, p. 136, supports this picture of Triad *omerta*: 'In November, 1891, a famous Ko Lao Hui leader named Chen-kin-lung fell into the hands of the Chinese government. . . . His examination was conducted with the greatest secrecy by the magistrate and deputies of the Viceroy and the Governor. . . . Three examinations were held, but Chen preserved the strictest silence. Torture was employed but in vain; the only words that could be extracted from him were "Spare yourselves the trouble and me the pain; be convinced that there are men ready to sacrifice their lives for the good of a cause which will bring happiness to this country for thousands of generations to come". Then more gentle words were used, but, with what result is not known.'

63 See p. 119 and Chiang Siang-tseh, *The Nien Rebellion*, Seattle, 1954, p. 18.

64 Ibid., pp. 18–20.

65 Ibid., p. 20.

66 Ibid., p. 21; see also Hutson's selected translations of Hirayama Amane in *China Journal*, November 1928, p. 219.

67 Chiang, op. cit., p. 21.

68 Ibid.

69 Chiang, op. cit., p. 6.

The 'Ten Heavenly Stems':	'The Five Elements':
(*Shih t'ien-keng*)	(*Wu Hang*)
chia, i	*mu* (wood)
ping, ting	*huo* (fire)
ching, hsing	*chin* (metal)
yin, kuei	*shui* (water)
wu, chi	*t'u* (earth)

70 Porter, op. cit., p. 6, reports that the Eight Trigrams were divided into eight sections according to the eight positions of the tongue in the mouth, which contains eight apertures for the egress or ingress of the soul.

71 Chiang, op. cit., p. 30.

72 Ibid., p. 31.

73 Ibid., p. 32.

74 Ch'en, op. cit., p. 297.

75 E. F. Carlson, *The Chinese Army*, New York, 1940, p. 105.

76 See p. 19.

77 In the Triad cant, 10 men were called *i-liang* (one ounce) and 100 men were called *i-p'ing-ma* (one standard weight horse).

78 See Figure 6 in Chapter VII, p. 130.

79 Stanton, op. cit., p. 68 (Art. 5); but this is exceptionally severe; Schlegel's documents, op. cit., p. 163 (Arts 11, 12), stipulate the loss of both ears or 72 blows.

80 Ibid., pp. 155–6 (Art. 31).

81 Ibid., p. 163 (Art. 10).

82 Wynne, op. cit., p. 30.

83 See p. 108.

84 Stanton, op. cit. (Oath 34): 'If a brother offends, let all the brethren discuss his case and punish him, and if he harbours resentment or disobeys this injunction, may the gods look down and punish him.'

85 See Morgan, op. cit., pp. 74–5, for illustrations of weapons manufactured by the Triads themselves in Hong Kong.

VII RITUAL

1 W. P. Morgan, *Triad Societies in Hong Kong*, Hong Kong, 1960, p. 266.

2 Gustave Schlegel, *Thien Ti Hwui, The Hung League, Secret Society in China and India*, Batavia, 1866, p. 52, writes: 'The meetings are generally held on the 25th of the month, in commemoration of the day of the foundation of the league; besides the common Chinese festivals are celebrated by the brotherhood as:

'The lantern festival (*k'an hua-teng*) on the 15th of the first month, when each member contributes 360 cash.

'The Grave-cleansing festival (*ch'ing-ming*) and the festival of the Gods of the land (*t'u-ti t'an*), when each member contributes 108 cash.

'The Dragon-boat-festival (*P'a-lung-ch'uan*) in the fifth month, to which each member contributes 36 cash.

'The Birthday of the God Kwan (*Kuan-ti t'an*), to which each member contributes 72 cash.

'On the 15th of the 7th month each member contributes 72 cash.

'On the 25th of the 7th month, the anniversary of the society, each member contributes 36 cash.

'On the 15th of the 8th month each member contributes 21 cash for fruits, and sun and moon-cakes (*rih-yueh ping*) for the autumnal festival (*ch'iu chi*).' The amounts (360, 108, 72, 36 and 21) correspond to the number of blows to be inflicted on miscreant members of the society, and may not have more than a ritual or symbolical significance for the real sums paid. Poorer members could not be charged the same amount as the more wealthy ones, and the amounts had to be changed accordingly.

3 The use of restaurants (which contained private rooms), brothels, teahouses, etc., in the market places was normal, for 'business' deals of every kind.

4 See illustration in Morgan, op. cit.

5 Ibid., p. 194, verse and note.

6 For example, if the horoscope indicates that one of the five elements was missing on the birthday of the child, it was usual for the parents to insert that missing element (fire, water, earth, metal or wood) in his name.

7 E. O. Reischauer and J. K. Fairbank, *East Asia: The Great Tradition*, Boston, 1958 and 1960, p. 27.

8 William Stanton, *The Triad Society*, Hong Kong, 1900, p. 42.

9 Hirayama Amane (Shu), *Chung-kuo pi-mi she-hui shih* (History of Chinese secret societies), Shanghai, 1935, p. 86.

10 Ibid.

11 Stanton, op. cit., p. 40.

12 M. L. Wynne, *Triad and Tabut*, Singapore, 1941, p. 118; Stanton, op. cit., p. 43.

13 Couched thus:

'Where do you come from?'
'I come from the East.'
'How can you prove it?'
'I can prove it by a verse.'

The verse which is the password, follows every answer of the candidate as represented by the Vanguard.

14 John Scarth, writing about Triads he had observed in Shanghai, described their hairstyle as follows: 'The hair was long, and gathered up into a knot on the crown, in a similar way to the ancient style in China, before the Tartar conquerors forced the Chinese to adopt the tail. It is said that the Tartars took this extraordinary mode of showing their power over the Chinese from policy, that the Chinese might not be able to see how few Tartars were among them, and be led to attempt revolt, both people being made to dress alike.' *Twelve Years in China*, Edinburgh, 1860, p. 194. John Davis gives another explanation for the Manchu imposition: 'Many are the changes which may be made in despotic countries, without the notice of or even the knowledge of the lower portion of the community; but an entire alteration in the national costume affects every individual equally, from the highest to the lowest, and is, perhaps, of all others, the most open and degrading mark of conquest.'

15 Georg Simmel, *The Sociology of Georg Simmel* (transl. and ed. K. Wolff), New York and London, 1964, pp. 358–60.

16 For example, among the Carbonari of the early nineteenth century the counter image of the official religious views was expressed in the ritual of Pontius Pilate and his two assistants Caiaphas and Herod 'pardoning' Christ. See Thomas Frost, *Secret Societies of the European Revolution: 1776–1876*, London, 1876, pp. 213 ff., for a comparison of the Carbonari ritual with Triad ritual.

17 Schlegel, op. cit., p. 159.

18 See Chapter VIII.

19 According to Morgan's account, op. cit., p. 46, members were given a Triad surname on admission to the society which indicated the position of their 'generation' beginning from that of the Five Ancestors.

VIII SANCTIONS

1 See Sybil van der Sprenkel's chapter on codified law (pp. 56–65) in her sociological analysis of the *Legal Institutions in Manchu China*, London, 1966, especially pp. 64–5 for a summary of the peculiar features of Chinese law.

2 G. W. F. Head, *The Philosophy of History* (lectures delivered during 1830–1) (trans. J. Sibree), New York, 1956, p. 113, 'The Oriental World'.

3 See G. T. Staunton, *Ta Ch'ing Leu-lee being the Fundamental Laws and a selection from the Supplementary Statutes of the Penal Code of China*, London, 1810, and quoted in van der Sprenkel, op. cit., p. 59: 'The *Leu*, or Fundamental Laws, are those of which the Penal Code upon its formation soon after the accession of the present dynasty appears originally to have consisted, and which, being, at least nominally, permanent, are reprinted in each successive edition, without either alteration or amendment.

'The *Lee*, or Supplementary Laws, are the modifications, extensions and restrictions of the Fundamental Laws, which after undergoing a deliberate examination in the Supreme Councils, and receiving the sanction of the Sovereign, are inserted in the form of clauses at the end of each article or section of the Code, in order that they might, together with the Fundamental Laws, be equally known and observed. They are generally revised every fifth year, and subjected to such alterations as the wisdom of the government determines to be expedient.'

4 See p. 11.

5 J. S. M. Ward and W. G. Stirling, *The Hung Society*, London, 1925–6, vol. 1, p. 65.

6 Stanton, *The Triad Society*, Hong Kong, 1900, p. 118, Appendix.

7 Hirayama Amane (Shu), *Chung-kuo pi-mi she-hui shih* (History of Chinese secret societies), Shanghai, 1935, p. 106, which gives the following rules (my translation):
> One, do not cheat elder brothers, oppress younger brothers
> Two, do not bully your father and mother
> Three, do not raise the wick of the lamp and seize the fire
> Four, do not permit the great to oppress the small
> Five, do not deceive Heaven and blame the sea
> Six, do not stir oil into other [people's] soup
> Seven, do not be unjust and unkind
> Eight, do not levy taxes [?] and dabble in business [?].

8 Respectively, Gustave Schlegel, *Thien Ti Hwui, The Hung League, Secret Society in China and India*, Batavia, 1866, pp. 161 ff., pp. 165 ff. and pp. 152 ff.; Stanton, op. cit., pp. 67, 68.

9 W. P. Morgan, *Triad Societies in Hong Kong*, Hong Kong, 1960, p. 263, states that expulsion was only possible from the branch societies, not from the Hung Men itself, for, once a person was initiated into the society, he was a member for life and only death could release him from his membership. The use of boycott was, however, spare, and the Hong Kong police had only found one document specifically dealing with the expulsion. In M. L. Wynne, *Triad and Tabut*, Singapore, 1941, p. 257, is a verbatim report of the proceedings of the Penang Riot Commission of 1868 (p. 4), where a Triad member answers the Question: What is the punishment for disobedience?

A. The member is excommunicated.

Q. What is done to him on excommunication?

A. If the order is of importance he is flogged, if of no importance, he is beheaded. But this is never done in this country.

Murder as a punishment is, as we know, of commonplace occurrence amongst secret society members in Malaya. It is also likely that murder was the preferred method of punishment and solution of the problem posed by life membership in Hong Kong.

10 See J. Hutson, *Chinese Life in the Tibetan Foothills*, Shanghai, 1921, p. 92.

11 Stanton, op. cit., p. 67 (Art. 2), p. 68 (Art. 1); Schlegel, op. cit., p. 158 (Art. 53), p. 161 (Art. 71) and below.

12 Ibid., p. 154 (Art. 21).

13 Ibid., p. 161 (Art. 70).

14 Ibid., p. 158 (Art. 53), p. 161 (Art. 71).

15 Ibid., p. 152 (Art. 2).

16 Ibid., p. 159 (Art. 54).

17 Ibid., p. 155 (Art. 29).

18 Ibid., p. 153 (Art. 5): Stanton, op. cit., p. 67 (Art. 4).

19 Schlegel, op. cit., p. 154 (Art. 18), p. 159 (Art. 61).

20 Ibid., p. 158 (Art. 50).

21 Ibid., p. 158 (Arts 52, 55, 57).

22 Ibid., p. 159 (Art. 58), Stanton, op. cit., p. 68 (Art. 18).

23 Ibid., p. 68 (Art. 20).

24 Ibid., p. 121 (Art. 22).

25 Schlegel, op. cit., p. 153 (Art. 12), p. 160 (Art. 68); Stanton, op. cit., p. 122 (Oath 24).

26 Schlegel, op. cit., p. 163 (Arts 10, 11), p. 166 (Art. 5).

27 Ibid., p. 154 (Art. 13).

28 Ibid. (Art. 14); Stanton, op. cit., p. 121 (Art. 21).

29 Schlegel, op. cit., p. 155 (Art. 31).

30 Ibid., p. 158 (Art. 49), p. 162 (Art. 8).

31 Ibid., p. 159 (Art. 59).

32 See p. 104.

33 Van der Sprenkel, op. cit., pp. 61 ff. It is interesting to note here that 'cutting off the ears' does not form part of the 'Five Punishments (*wu-hsing*) of the State.

34 See p. 146.

35 Sometimes called the 'Ten Articles' (*Shih-t'iao shih kuan*). For example, in Hsiao I-shan, *Chin-tai pi-mi she-hui shih-liao* (History of modern secret societies), Peking, 1935, p. 9b, though not specified, probably refers to those crimes I have mentioned of incest, economic exploitation and betrayal.

36 Mentioned by G. Schlegel and F. Boyle.

37 Stanton, op. cit., p. 64 (Oath 33).

38 Ibid., Oath 34.

39 Schlegel, op. cit., p. 163 (Art. 14).

40 Ibid., p. 139 (Oath 15): 'when a brother is summoned before a tribunal, or a price is set upon him, and he cannot remain longer in the place, the powerful must help him to escape, and the less powerful pay his travelling expenses. This is helping him out of danger, like taking a fish out of a dry place, and it is saving him from difficulties, like liberating a bird out of a closed net.'

41 S. Tretiakov, *Tan Shih-hua: A Chinese Testament*, London, 1934, p. 52.

42 Schlegel, op. cit., pp. 164–5 (Art. 21).

43 See p. 37.

44 S. Gamble, *Peking: A Social Survey*, London, 1921, pp. 194–5.

45 Tretiakov, op. cit., p. 49.

IX CONCLUSIONS

1 Yuji Muramatsu, 'Some themes in Chinese rebel ideologies', in *Confucian Persuasion* (ed. A. F. Wright), Stanford, 1960, p. 243.

2 Ibid., pp. 244–5: 'Chang Lu's power was based on the political and religious system he built up in his territory, in which he was spiritual "master" (*shih-chün*) of the "Rice" sect as well as secular ruler. The newly converted commoners were supervised by priests and grand priests, who served also as local officials in the civil administrative system. The people were taught to believe in the Way of the Spirit (*kuei-tao*) and to worship the Spirit. The population was controlled through a well-organized penal system. Persons guilty of misdeeds were punished by being assigned to road-building and similar tasks. "Public cottages" (*i-she*) were established along the highways, and free food was supplied to

travelers. The five pecks of rice, which under Chang Ling and Chang Heng had been occasional payments for cures, presumably later became regular taxes collected on fixed dates.'

3 See p. 34.

4 See pp. 62 ff. for summary of the myth of origin.

5 The Double Tax system was instituted in 780, and was levied in the sixth and eleventh months of each year on land areas, regardless of ownership, rather than on the peasants as individuals, replacing the ancient 'Equal Field' (*chün t'ien*) system, which assumed that land had been divided equally among the farmers. The new tax system recognized for the first time the inequality of land-holdings. The abuses arising from the Double Tax systems are obvious: powerful landlords altered the registers to make their land appear small and poor, or omitted to declare landownership altogether. Poorer farmers, without this power, were forced to pay all the taxes on their produce and land as they were registered by the local gentry landlords. The new system also saved the administration a great deal of paperwork, as there was no longer the need to register each household working on the land. The development of tenantry allowed landlords further opportunities for evading the burden of the taxation by shifting it to the shoulders of their tenants in the form of exorbitant rents and squeeze. Moreover, 'Because local officials were responsible for collecting a fixed amount of tax from a certain area, the expansion of such privileged land-holdings inevitably increased the burden on the common farmer. Many hard-pressed farmers sold their land at a nominal price to the *kuan-hu* and became tenants; some registered their land under the *kuan-hu*'s name, after paying a fee for the privilege; *t'ou k'ao*, "seeking protection", became more and more popular, and many farmers fled from their homes to become tenants or hired hands on the large estates. Still others joined outlaw bands'. Muramatsu, op. cit., p. 259; see also pp. 81–2 for a brief summary of the Double Tax system and p. 186 in *Chinese Thought and Institutions*, ed. J. K. Fairbank, Chicago, 1957, for a summary of the Equal Field System.

6 *Chung-kuo nung-min ch'i-i lun-chi* (A Collection of essays on Chinese peasant rebellions), Peking, 1954, pp. 76–84.

7 Muramatsu, op. cit., p. 257.

8 During the southern Sung, taxes on salt (50 per cent), alcohol (36 per cent), tea (7 per cent), tolls, customs, commercial tax (7 per cent), gave the Government 90 per cent of its total revenue from taxation.

9 Muramatsu, op. cit., p. 259.

10 Ibid.

11 See p. 62.

12 See list of rebellions associated with secret societies in Appendix A.

13 E. O. Reischauer and J. K. Fairbank, *East Asia: The Great Tradition* (hereafter *EAGT*), Boston, 1960, pp. 174–5.

14 See Chapter V.

15 See E. J. Hobsbawm, *Primitive Rebels*, Manchester, 1959, Chapter II, pp. 13–29, for an elaboration of the concept of 'social banditry'.

16 For a detailed discussion of the methods of revolutionary organization by a successful revolutionary, see V. I. Lenin, *What Is to be Done?*, Chapter 4, beginning with the section on 'Workers' organization and revolutionary organization'.

17 Franz Michael's study of the Taiping Rebellion, 'Military organization and power structure of China during the Taiping Rebellion', *Pacific Historical Review*, 1949, 18, pp. 469–83, notes the conflict between the Punti and Hakka societies. A more systematic study of the content of regionalist sentiments in action may reveal, however, that their strength could be reduced by the appeal to class sentiment, or, indeed, their strength, in some cases, was created by local class resentments.

18 See pp. 168–71.

19 In 'Social Integration and System Integration', in *Exploration in Social Change*, Boston, 1964 (ed. G. K. Zollschan and W. Hirsch).

20 See Max Weber, *The Theory of Social and Economic Organization* (ed. with an introduction by Talcott Parsons), New York and London, 1964, 1966, pp. 346 ff. for an exposition of the concept of patrimonialism.

21 According to the *Sung Shih* (Official Sung History), 198, 2b–4a, the State had pre-emptive rights over the purchase of horses. The appearance of 'horse-leaders' and 'horse-dealers' in Triad ritual and myth may not be totally eccentric.

22 It is no surprise to find in the Triad slang that the term for 'salt' is *chin-hsing*, 'enter prosperity', and that for 'wine' is 'the family in harmony and prosperity' (*chia-ho-hsing*).

It is probable that smuggling also extended to exports of textiles (silk), porcelain, silver, gold, lead, tin as well as imports of incense, all of which formed the basis of a very profitable overseas trade. Certainly references to the above are very frequent in Triad ritual and slang.

23 E. O. Reischauer, J. K. Fairbank and A. M. Craig, *East Asia:*

The Modern Transportation (hereafter *EAMT*), Boston, 1965, pp. 326–7. In the early 1890s *likin* (including native opium *likin*) brought in 15 million *taels* out of 89 million *taels* of silver in tax, in the early 1900s *likin* brought in 14 million out of 103 million *taels*.

24 Etienne Balazs, *Chinese Civilization and Bureaucracy*, New Haven and London, 1964–7, p. 58, p. 61.

25 *EAGT*, p. 222.

26 Gustave Schlegel, *Thien Ti Hwui, The Hung League, Secret Society in China and India*, Batavia, 1866, p. 136 (Oath 3), p. 161 (Art. 2), pp. 164–5 (Art. 21).

27 See p. 235, n. 5.

28 Muramatsu, op. cit., p. 257.

29 Balazs, op. cit., p. 97.

30 Officials were punishable by 60 bamboo strokes if they were caught in a house of prostitution according to law; but this was obviously a dead letter. See G. Schlegel, *Histoire de la prostitution en Chine*, 1880, pp. 6–7.

31 W. P. Morgan, *Triad Societies in Hong Kong*, Hong Kong, 1960, p. 74.

32 M. L. Wynne, *Triad and Tabut*, Singapore, 1941.

33 Schlegel, *Histoire de la prostitution*, p. 37.

34 G. R. Scott, *Far Eastern Sex Life*, London, 1943, Chapter V.

35 Schlegel, *Histoire de la prostitution*, p. 6.

36 See pp. 14 ff.

37 See p. 55.

38 Eugene P. Boardman, *Christian Influences Upon the Ideology of the Taiping Rebellion, 1851–1864*, Madison, Wisconsin, 1952.

39 The associations in Havana, Cuba, for example, even joined in the movements for independence against Spain. See the appendices for further discussion.

40 See p. 170.

41 G. T. Yu, *Party Politics in Republican China—The Kuomintang, 1912–1924*, Berkeley and Los Angeles, 1966, p. 16; the oath aimed at driving out 'the Manchu Barbarians, restore China to the Chinese, and create a republic'.

42 Ibid.

43 Ibid., p. 17.

44 Ibid., p. 27; Hirayama Adame, *China Journal*, January 1929, p. 14.

45 Yu, op. cit., p. 28.

46 *China Journal*, January 1929, p. 16.

47 Yu, op. cit., p. 48.

48 R. A. Scalapino and G. T. Yu, *The Chinese Anarchist Movement*, Berkeley, 1961.

49 Yu, op. cit.

50 While some, like the Ch'ing Pang, were taken over lock, stock and barrel by the Kuomintang as their local branches, the elimination of the KMT's most dangerous enemy, the revolutionary working class of Shanghai, by the Ch'ing Pang effectively cast the secret societies in the role of a fascist-type paramilitary force.

51 For an historical account of the Mafia in Sicilian political life, see M. Pantaleone, *The Mafia and Politics*, London, 1966.

52 Han Suyin, *A Mortal Flower*, London, 1966, pp. 70 ff.

53 H. R. Isaacs, 'Gang rule in Shanghai', *Five Years of Kuomintang Reaction*, reprinted from the special May edition of the *China Forum*, Shanghai, 1932.

54 Han, op. cit., p. 70.

55 S. R. Schram, *The Political Thought of Mao-Tse-tung*, New York and London, 1963, p. 189.

56 Ibid., p. 201, where Mao describes the military limitations of the 'roving insurgent' mentality as well as its traditional love of city life and 'eating and drinking'.

57 'Popular' in the sense that it was dominated by the peasantry after the second half of the thirties period; the peasantry of course formed something like 80 per cent of the population. See Chalmers A. Johnson's study, *Peasant Nationalism and Communist Power; The Emergence of Revolutionary China, 1937–45*, Stanford, 1962, 1966, for a lucid and informative account of the development of the Red Army. The *you-min* or *éléments déclassés* did, according to Mao, dominate the Red Army in the late 1920s; but not all these elements need have been secret society members. For a fuller discussion of the social composition of the Red Army, see Schram, op. cit., p. 196; and for an account of the relationship between Mao and the secret societies in the revolution, see Schram's article, 'Mao and the secret society', *China Quarterly*, 27, pp. 1–13.

58 Lucien Bianco's category in his review article of Hsiao Kung-chuan's book cited 'Classes laborieuses et classes dangereuses dans la Chine Imperiale aux XIXe Siècle', *Annales, Economies, Sociétés et Civilisation*, December 1962, pp. 1175–82.

59 See p. 150; Morgan, op. cit., p. 157 (Oath 1); William Stanton, *The Triad Society*, Hong Kong, 1900, p. 124 (Oath 36).

60 See, for example, Thomas Frost, *The Secret Societies of the European Revolution: 1776–1876*, London, 1876, and the bibliography given in Hobsbawm, op. cit.

APPENDIX D   CHINESE ASSOCIATIONS IN HAVANA, CUBA, 1967–8

1 H. F. MacNair, *The Chinese Abroad*, Shanghai, 1924, p. 210.
2 Consular letter cited by H. B. Morse in *The International Relations of the Chinese Empire*, London, New York and Shanghai, 1910, 1918, vol. II, p. 171.
3 MacNair, op. cit., p. 211.
4 Ibid.
5 Juan Luis Martin, *The Chinese in Cuba*, Havana, 1939.
6 Baron von Hubner quoted in Morse, op. cit., p. 176.
7 Ibid., pp. 179–80.
8 The Taiping exiles were involved in the war of independence against Spain in 1895–8, in which their participation was far from negligible.

Select bibliography

A GENERAL

Aron, Raymond, *German Sociology* (transl. Mary and Thomas Bottomore), New York and London, 1964.

Boas, F., 'Secret societies and social organization of the Kwakiutl Indians', *Report of the American Museum of National History*, 1895.

Boissevain, J., 'The Sicilian Mafia: A Sociological Interpretation', unpublished article, 1966.

Duverger, Maurice, *The Idea of Politics* (*Introduction à la politique*, Paris, 1964), London, 1966.

Feinstein, Otto (ed.), *Two Worlds of Change, Readings in Economic Development*, New York, 1964.

Firth, R. W., *Elements of Social Organization*, London, 1951, 1961.

Frost, Thomas, *The Secret Societies of the European Revolution: 1776–1876*, 2 vols, London, 1876.

Heckethorn, C. W., *Secret Societies of All Ages and Countries*, 2 vols, London, 1897.

Hegel, Georg W. F., *The Philosophy of History* (transl. J. Sibree, with a new introduction by Professor C. J. Friedrich), Harvard University, New York, 1956.

Hobsbawm, Eric, *Primitive Rebels—Studies in Archaic Forms of Social Movement in the 19th and 20th Centuries*, Manchester, 1959.

La Hodde, Lucien de, *Histoire des sociétés secrètes et du parti républicain de 1830 à 1848*, Paris, 1850.

Hutin, Serge, *Les Sociétés Secrètes* (Que Sais-je? series), Paris.

Lockwood, David, 'Systems integration and social integration', in *Explorations in Social Change* (ed. G. K. Zollschan and W. Hirsch), Boston, 1964.

MacKenzie, Norman, *Secret Societies*, London, 1967.

Pantaleone, Michele, *The Mafia and Politics*, London, 1966.

Perreux, G., *Au Temps des sociétés secrètes*, Paris, 1931.

Simmel, Georg, *The Sociology of Georg Simmel* (transl. and ed. K. H. Wolff), New York and London, 1964.

Weber, Max, *The Theory of Social and Economic Organization* (transl. A. M. Henderson and Talcott Parsons; ed. and with an introduction by Talcott Parsons), New York and London, 1947, 1964, 1966.

Weber, Max, *The City* (transl. and ed. Don Martindale and Gertrud Neuwirth), New York and London, 1958, 1966.

Wedgwood, C. H., 'The nature and function of secret societies', *Oceania*, July 1930, vol. 1, no. 2.

B   BOOKS ON THE CHINESE BACKGROUND

Balazs, Etienne, *Chinese Civilization and Bureaucracy*, New Haven and London, 1964–7.

Ball, Dyer, *Things Chinese*, Shanghai, 1903.

Baller, F. W., *The Sacred Edict* (translation from the Chinese), Shanghai, 1892.

Burgess, J. S., *The Guilds of Peking*, New York and London, 1928.

Chang Chung-li, *The Chinese Gentry: Studies on their Role in Nineteenth-Century Chinese Society*, Washington, 1955.

Chi Ch'ao-ting, *Key Economic Areas in Chinese History*, London, 1936.

Chesneaux, Jean, *Le Mouvement Ouvrier Chinois de 1919–1927*, Paris, 1962.

Chow Yung-teh, *Social Mobility in China*, New York, 1966.

Ch'ü T'ung-tsu, 'Chinese class structure and its ideology', in *Chinese Thought and Institutions* (ed. J. K. Fairbank), Chicago, 1957, pp. 235–50.

Ch'ü T'ung-tsu, *Law and Society in Traditional China*, Paris and The Hague, 1961.

Ch'ü T'ung-tsu, *Local Government in China under the Ch'ing*, Cambridge, Mass., 1962.

Elliott, A. I. A., *Chinese Spirit-medium Cults in Singapore*, London, 1955.

Fairbank, J. K. (ed.), *Chinese Thought and Institutions*, Chicago, 1957.

Fei Hsiao-t'ung, *China's Gentry: Essays in Rural–Urban Relations* (rev. and ed. Margaret P. Redfield), Chicago, 1953.

Fei Hsiao-t'ung, 'Peasantry and gentry: an interpretation of Chinese social structure and its changes', *American Journal of Sociology*, July 1946, 52, pp. 1–17, and in *Class, Status and Power: Reader in Social Stratification*, London, 1954, pp. 631–50.

Feng Yu-lan, *A Short History of Chinese Philosophy* (ed. Derk Bodde), New York and Toronto, 1948.

Feuerwerker, Albert, *China's Early Industrialization*, Cambridge, Mass., 1958.

Feuerwerker, Albert (ed.), *Modern China*, New Jersey, 1964.

Freedman, Maurice, *Lineage Organization in South-Eastern China*, London, 1958.

Freedman, Maurice, 'Immigrants and associations: Chinese in nineteenth-century Singapore', *Comparative Studies in Society and History*, 1960, III, 1.

Fried, M. H., *Fabric of Chinese Society: a study of Social Life in a Chinese County Seat*, New York, 1953.

Gamble, S., *Peking: A Social Survey*, London, 1921.

Gardner, C. T. 'Amoy emigration to the Straits', *The China Review*, 1897, vol. xxii, no. 4.

Granet, Marcel, *Civilisation Chinoise: la vie publique et privée*, Paris, 1946.

De Groot, J. J. M., 'Militant spirit of the Buddhist clergy in China', *T'oung Pao*, June 1891, pp. 127–39.

De Groot, J. J. M., *The Religious System of China, its Ancient Forms, Evolution, History and Present Aspect*, Leyden, 1892–1910, 6 vols.

De Groot, J. J. M., *Sectarianism and Religious Persecution in China*, Amsterdam, 1903.

Ho P'ing-ti, 'Aspects of social mobility in China 1368–1911', *Comparative Studies in Society and History*, June 1959, I, pp. 330–59.

Ho P'ing-ti, *The Ladder of Success in Imperial China*, New York, 1962.

Ho P'ing-ti, 'The salt merchants of Yang-chou: a study of commercial capitalism in eighteenth-century China', *Harvard Journal of Asiatic Studies*, 1962, vol. xvii, pp. 130–68.

Hsiao Kung-chuan, *Rural China: Imperial Control in the Nineteenth Century*, Seattle, 1960.

Hsieh Pao-chao, *The Government of China (1644–1911)*, Baltimore, 1925.

Hsu, F. L. K., 'Social mobility in China', *American Sociological Review*, December 1949, 14, pp. 764–61.

Hu Hsien-chin, *The Common Descent Group in China and Its Functions*, New York, 1948.

Jamieson, G. (ed.), 'The tenure of land in China and the condition of the rural population', *Journal of the North China Branch, Royal Asiatic Society*, vol. xxiii, pp. 59–174.

Johnson, Chalmers A., *Peasant Nationalism and Communist Power, The Emergence of Revolutionary China 1937–45*, Stanford, 1962, 1966.

Kato, Shigeshi, 'On the Hang or Association of Merchants in China', in *Memoirs of Toyo Bunko* (in English), 1936, pp. 45–83.

Kuhn, P., 'The T'uan-lien, local defense system at the time of the Taiping Rebellion', *Harvard Journal of Asiatic Studies*, 1967, v, 27.

Lang, Olga, *Chinese Family and Society*, Yale, 1946.

Levenson, Joseph R., *Confucian China and its Modern Fate*, London, 1958.

Levy, Marion, *The Family Revolution in Modern China*, Cambridge, Mass., 1949.

Li Ch'en-nung, *The Political History of China, 1800–1928*, Princeton, 1956.

Liu, H-C. W., *The Traditional Chinese Clan Rules*, New York, 1959.

Lynn, J. Chi-hung, *Political Parties in China*, Peking, 1930.

MacGowan, D. G., 'Chinese guilds or chambers of commerce and trades unions', *Journal of the North China Branch of the Royal Asiatic Society*, 1886, pp. 133–92.

MacNair, H. F., *The Chinese Abroad*, Shanghai, 1924.

Martin, Bernard, *Strange Vigour, A Biography of Sun Yat-sen*, London, 1944.

Maspero, Henri and Escarra, Jean, *Les Institutions de la Chine: essai historique* (with preface by Paul Demieville), Paris, 1952.

Maybon, Pierre B., *Essai sur les associations en Chine*, Paris, 1925.

Mayers, W. F., *The Chinese Government, 1877* (ed. and rev. G. M. H. Playfair), Shanghai, 1896, 3rd edn.

Meadows, T. T., *The Chinese and their Rebellions*, London, 1856.

Menzel, J. M. (ed.), *The Chinese Civil Service, Career Open to Talent?*, Boston, 1963.

Meskill, John (ed.), *The Pattern of Chinese History, Cycles, Development, or Stagnation?*, Boston, 1965, 1966.

Michael, Franz, 'Military organization and power structure of China during the Taiping Rebellion', *Pacific Historical Review*, November 1949, 18, pp. 469–83.

Michael, Franz, *The Taiping Rebellion, I. History*, Washington, 1966.

Morse, H. B., *The Gilds of China, with an Account of the Gild Merchant or Cohong of Canton*, London, 1909.

Muramatsu, Yuji, 'Some themes in Chinese rebel ideologies', in *Confucian Persuasion* (ed. A. F. Wright), Stanford, 1960.

Powell, Ralph, *The Rise of Chinese Military Power, 1895–1912*, Princeton, 1955.

Reischauer, Edwin and Fairbank, John K., *East Asia: The Great Tradition*, Boston, 1960.

Reischauer, Edwin, Fairbank, John K., and Craig, Albert M., *East Asia: The Modern Transformation*, Boston, 1965.

San Kuo Chih Yen-i (Romance of the Three Kingdoms) (transl. C. H. Brewitt-Taylor), 2 vols, 1925.

Scalpine, R. A. and Yu, G. T., *The Chinese Anarchist Movement*, Berkeley, 1961.

Scarth, John, *Twelve Years in China*, Edinburgh, 1860.

Schlegel, G., *Histoire de la prostitution en Chine*, Rouen, 1880.

Schurmann, H. F., 'Traditional property concepts in China', *Far Eastern Quarterly*, 1956, vol. 15, pp. 507–16.

Scott, G. R., *Far Eastern Sex Life*, London, 1943.

Shih, Vincent Yu-chung, 'Some Chinese rebel ideologies', *T'oung Pao*, 1956, 44, 1–3, pp. 150–226.

Skinner, G. W., *Leadership and Power in the Chinese Community of Thailand*, New York, 1958.

Skinner, G. W., 'Marketing and social structure in rural China. Part I', *Journal of Asian Studies*, 1964–5, 24, 1, pp. 3–42; Part II, *Journal of Asian Studies*, 24, 2, pp. 195–228; Part III, *Journal of Asian Studies*, pp. 363–99.

Smedley, Agnes, *Chinese Destinies*, New York, 1933.

Smith, Arthur H., *Chinese Characteristics*, London, 1892.

van der Sprenkel, Sybille, *Legal Institutions in Manchu China*, London, 1962, 1966.

Staunton, Sir G. T., *Ta Ch'ing Leu-lee, being the Fundamental Laws and a selection from the Supplementary Statutes of the Penal Code of China*, London, 1810.

Sun Yat-sen, *Memoirs of a Chinese Revolutionary*, London, 1927.

T'ang Leang-li, *The Inner History of the Chinese Revolution*, London, 1930.

Tawney, Richard Henry, *Land and Labour in China*, London, 1932, 1964.

Teng Ssu-yu and Fairbank, John K., *China's Response to the West, a Documentary Survey, 1839–1923*, New York, 1963.

Thery, François S. J., *Les Sociétés de commerce en Chine*, Tientsin, 1929.

Topley, Marjorie D., *The Organization and Social Function of Chinese Women's Chai T'ang in Singapore*, unpublished Ph.D. Thesis, London, 1958.

Vaughan, J. D., *Manners and Customs of the Chinese*, 1879.

Wang Yi-chu, 'The intelligentsia in changing China', *Foreign Affairs*, January 1958, 36, 2, pp. 315–29.

Wang Yi-chu, 'Western impact and social mobility in China', *American Sociological Review*, 1960, 25.

Waley, Arthur, *The Analects of Confucius*, London, 1938.

Weber, Max, *The Religion of China* (introduced by C. K. Yang, and transl. H. H. Gerth), New York and London, 1951 and 1964.

Wen Chün-t'ien, *Chung-kuo Pao-chia Chih-tu* (The Pao-chia System in China), Shanghai, 1935.

Wou Monpeng, *L'Evolution des corporations ouvrières et commerciales dans la Chine contemporaine*, Paris, 1931.

Wright, Arthur F., *Buddhism in Chinese History*, Stanford, 1959.

Yang, C. K., 'The functional relationship between Confucian thought and Chinese religion', in *Chinese Thought and Institutions* (ed. Fairbank, John K.), pp. 269 ff.

Yang, C. K., *Chinese Communist Society: The Family and the Village*, Cambridge, Mass., 1959, 1965.

Yang, C. K., *Religion in Chinese Society*, Berkeley, 1961.

Yang Lien-sheng, *Studies in Chinese Institutional History*, Cambridge, Mass., 1961.

C   WORKS ON CHINESE SECRET SOCIETIES (CHINESE)

Ch'en Chieh, *I-ho-t'uan yun-tung shih* (History of the Boxer Movement), Shanghai, 1931.

Chu Lin, *Hung Men Pang Hui Chih* (Records of the Hung League), Shanghai, 1947.

Fan Wen-lan, *Chung-kuo chin-tai shih* (Chinese Modern History), Peking, 1949, 1953.

Hirayama Amane (Shu), *Chung-kuo pi-mi she-hui shih* (History of Chinese secret societies), Shanghai, 1935.

Hsiao I-shan, *Chin-tai pi-mi sheh-hui shih-liao* (History of modern secret societies), Peking, 1935.

Li Chu-jan, *Hsin-hai ke-ming ch'ien-ti ch'ün-chung tou-cheng* (Popular movements before the revolution of 1911–12), Peking, 1957.

Liu Ju-lin (on Boxer internal organization), *I-ho-t'uan yun-tung shih-lun ts'ung* (Collection of articles on the Boxer movement), Peking, 1956, pp. 60–1.

Liu Lien-k'o, *Pang-hui san-pai-nien ke-ming shih* (Three hundred years of revolutionary history), Macao, 1940, 1942.

Lo Erh-kang, *T'ien-ti-hui wen-hsien lu* (Documents on the Heaven and Earth Society), Shanghai, 1948.

Lo Han, '*T'ien-ti-hui wen-chien*' (Documents of the Heaven and Earth Society), *Kwangtung Hsüeh-pao* (Canton Journal), in English and Chinese, Canton, 1 January 1937, 1, 1, pp. 1–16.

Ma Ch'ao-chün, 'Pang-hui chih', *Chung-kuo lao-kung yun-tung shih* (Record of the secret societies in History of the Chinese Labour Movement), Chungking, 1942, pp. 73–7.

Peking, *Chung-kuo nung-min ch'i-i lun-chi* (Collection of essays on Chinese peasant rebellions), 1954.

Peking, *Chung-kuo nung-min chang-cheng shih-lun wen-chi* (A collection of essays on the history of the Chinese peasant wars), 1935.

Tai Hsüan-chih, *I-ho-t'uan yen-chiu* (Studies on the Boxer Rising), Taiwan, 1963.

T'ao Ch'eng-cheng, '*Chiao-hai yuan-lin k'ao*' (Origins of the sects and societies), *Chung-kuo shih-hsüch hui* (ed. Hsin-hai Ke-ming) (Collection of Materials in the 1911 Revolution), 8 vols, Peking, 1957, vol. 3, pp. 99–111.

T'ien-ti-hui wen-chien sha-pen (Documents in Manuscript of the Heaven and Earth Society), British Museum MSS, OR.8207, and 2239.

Wang T'ien-chiang, '*Shih-chiu shih-chi hsia-pan-chi Chung-kuo-ti pi-mi she-hui*' (Chinese secret societies in the second half of the nineteenth century), *Li-shih Yen-chiu* (Historical Studies), Peking, 1963, 2, pp. 83-100.

Wei Chu-hsien, *Chung-kuo Pang-hui* (Chinese political societies), Chungking, 1949.

Wu Yü-chang, *Hsin-hai Ke-ming* (the 1911 Revolution), Peking, 1961, 1963.

D   WORKS ON CHINESE SECRET SOCIETIES (ENGLISH AND FRENCH)

Blythe, W. L., 'The interplay of Chinese secret and political societies in Malaya', *Eastern World*, March/April 1950.

Boyle, Frederick, *Harper's Magazine*, September 1891, pp. 601–2.

Brace, A. J., 'Some secret societies in Szechwan', *Journal of the West China Border Research Society*, 1936, 8, pp. 177–80.

Chao Wei-pang, 'A Chinese secret society: the rise and growth of the Ch'ing Pang', *China Review*, 1934, 3, iv, pp. 35–7.

Chao Wei-pang, 'Secret religious societies in north China in the Ming dynasty', *Folklore Studies*, 1948, 7, pp. 95–115.

Ch'en, Jerome, 'The nature and characteristics of the Boxer Movement', *Bulletin of the School of Oriental and African Studies*, 1960, XXIII, part 2, pp. 289–308.

Chesneaux, Jean, *Les Sociétés Secrètes en Chine* (19e et 20e siècles), Paris, 1965.

Chiang Siang-tseh, *The Nien Rebellion*, Seattle, 1954.

Chinese Repository, 'Oath taken by Triad Society, and notices of its origin', vol. XVIII, pp. 281–95, Canton, 1849.

Comber, Leon F., *An Introduction to Chinese Secret Societies in Malaya*, Singapore, 1957.

Comber, Leon F., *Chinese Secret Societies in Malaya, A Survey of the Triad Society From 1800–1900*, New York, 1959.

Cordier, Henri, 'Les sociétés secrètes chinoises', *Revue d'Ethnographie*, 1888, VII, no. 1–2.

Coulet, Georges, *Les Sociétés Secrètes en terre d'Annam*, Saigon, 1926.

Dunstheimer, G. G. H., 'Le Mouvement des Boxeurs: documents et études publiés depuis la deuxième guerre mondiale', *Revue Historique*, April 1964, no. 470, pp. 387–416.

Favre, B., 'Les sociétés de "Frères Jurés" en Chine', *T'oung Pao*, 1920, xix, pp. 1–40.

Favre, B., *Les Sociétés secrètes en Chine: Origines, role historique, situation actuelle*, Paris, 1933.

Glick, C. and Hong Sheng-hwa, *Swords of Silence, Chinese Secret Societies—Past and Present*, New York, 1947.

Gutzlaff, Rev. Charles, 'On the secret Triad Society of China chiefly from papers belonging to the Society at Hong Kong', *Journal of the Royal Asiatic Society of Great Britain and Ireland*, 1846, VIII, pp. 363 ff.

Hake, A. E., *Events in the Taiping Rebellion*, London, 1891.

Hill, A. H. 'The Hikayat Abdullah, annotated translation', *Journal of the Malayan Branch of the Royal Asiatic Society* 1955, 28, part 3.

Hughes, G., 'The Small Knife Rebels' (An Unpublished Chapter of Amoy History), *China Review*, 1872–3, vol. 1, no. 4.

Hutson, Rev. James, *Chinese Life on the Tibetan Foothills*, Shanghai, 1921.

Hutson, Rev. James, 'Chinese secret societies', *China Journal*, Shanghai, 1928, vol. ix, nos 4, 5 and 6, pp. 164–170, 215–20, 276–82.

Isaacs, Harold R., 'Gang rule in Shanghai', *Five Years of Kuomintang Reaction*, reprinted from special May edition of the *China Forum*, Shanghai, 1932.

Leboucq, Père, 'Lettres', *Etudes Religieuses*, Paris, 1875, V, VIII, pp. 197–220, 641–64.

Leboucq, Père, *Associations de la Chine: lettres*, Paris, c. 1880.

Lyman, Stanford M., 'Chinese secret societies in the Occident: notes and suggestions for research in the sociology of secrecy', *Canadian Review of Sociology and Anthropology*, 1964, 1, 2, pp. 79–102.

Lyman, S. M. and Willmot, W. E. and Ho, B., 'Rules of a Chinese secret society in British Columbia', *Bulletin of the School of Oriental and African Studies*, 1964, 27, 3, pp. 530–9.

Melve, W., *Some Account of a Secret Association entitled 'The Triad Society'* by R. Morrison, 1825.

Morgan, W. P., *Triad Societies in Hong Kong*, Hong Kong, 1960.

Morrison, Rev. R., 'A transcript in Roman characters, with a translation, of a manifesto in the Chinese language, issued by the Triad Society', *Journal of the Royal Asiatic Society of Great Britain and Ireland*, 1834, vol. I, pp. 93–5.

Newbold, Lieut. T. J. and Wilson, Major Gen. F. W., 'The Chinese secret Triad society of the Tien-t'i-hui', *Journal of the Royal Asiatic Society*, 1841, VI, pp. 120–58.

Pickering, W. A., 'Chinese secret societies and their origin', *Journal of the Straits Branch of the Royal Asiatic Society*, 1878, vol. I, pp. 63–84; 1879; vol. III, pp. 1–18.

Porter, Rev. D. H., 'Secret societies in Shantung', *Chinese Recorder*, January/February 1886, pp. 1–16, 64–73.

Purcell, Victor, *The Boxer Uprising, A Background Study*, Cambridge, 1963.

Reynolds, C. N., 'The Chinese Tongs', *American Journal of Sociology*, 1935, XL, 5, pp. 612–23.

Schlegel, G., *Thien Ti Hwui, The Hung League, Secret Society in China and India*, Batavia, 1866.

Schram, S. R., 'Mao and the secret societies', *China Quarterly*, 27, pp. 1–13.

Skinner, G. W., 'Marketing and social structure in rural China', *Journal of Asian Studies*, xxiv, pp. 3–43, 195–228, 363–99.

Stanton, William, *The Triad Society*, Hong Kong, 1900.

Teng Ssu-yu, *New Light on the History of the Taiping Rebellion*, Cambridge, Mass., 1950.

Teng Ssu-yu, 'Dr. Sun Yat-sen and Chinese secret societies', *Studies on Asia*, Lincoln, 1963, pp. 81–99.

Teng Ssu-yu, *The Nien Army and their Guerilla Warfare*, Paris, 1964.

Tretiakov, S., *Tan Shih-hua: A Chinese Testament*, London, 1934.

Vaughan, J. D., *Manners and Customs of the Chinese of the Straits Settlement*, Singapore, 1879.

Wakeman, Frederick, Jr, *Strangers at the Gate, Social Disorder in South China, 1839–1861*, Berkeley, 1966.

Wang Yu-chuan, 'The organization of a typical guerilla area in south Shantung', *The Chinese Army: Its Organization and Military Efficiency*, New York, 1940, pp. 104–5.

Ward, B. E., 'Chinese secret societies', in *Secret Societies* (ed. Norman McKenzie), London, 1967.

Ward, J. S. M. and Stirling, W. G., *The Hung Society*, London, 1925–6, 3 vols.

Wylie, A., 'Secret societies in China', *Shanghae Almanac for 1850*, Shanghai, 1853.

Wynne, M. L., *Triad and Tabut, A Survey of the Origins of Chinese and Mohammedan Secret Societies in the Malay Peninsula A.D. 1800–1935*, Singapore, 1941.

Index